James Whidden is Associate Professor of History at Acadia University, Canada. He holds a PhD in History from the School of Oriental and African Studies (SOAS), University of London, and has taught at Dalhousie and Concordia Universities in Canada and Murray State University in the US.

MONARCHY AND MODERNITY IN EGYPT

Politics, Islam and Neo-Colonialism
between the Wars

JAMES WHIDDEN

I.B. TAURIS
LONDON • NEW YORK • OXFORD • NEW DELHI • SYDNEY

I.B. TAURIS
Bloomsbury Publishing Plc
50 Bedford Square, London, WC1B 3DP, UK
1385 Broadway, New York, NY 10018, USA
29 Earlsfort Terrace, Dublin 2, Ireland

BLOOMSBURY, I.B. TAURIS and the I.B. Tauris logo
are trademarks of Bloomsbury Publishing Plc

First published in Great Britain 2013
This paperback edition published 2022

Copyright © James Whidden, 2013

James Whidden has asserted his right under the Copyright,
Designs and Patents Act, 1988, to be identified as Author of this work.

For legal purposes the Acknowledgements on p. vi constitute
an extension of this copyright page.

All rights reserved. No part of this publication may be reproduced or
transmitted in any form or by any means, electronic or mechanical,
including photocopying, recording, or any information storage or retrieval
system, without prior permission in writing from the publishers.

Bloomsbury Publishing Plc does not have any control over, or responsibility for,
any third-party websites referred to or in this book. All internet addresses given
in this book were correct at the time of going to press. The author and publisher
regret any inconvenience caused if addresses have changed or sites have
ceased to exist, but can accept no responsibility for any such changes.

A catalogue record for this book is available from the British Library.

A catalog record for this book is available from the Library of Congress.

ISBN: HB: 978-1-8488-5706-3
PB: 978-0-7556-5024-8
ePDF: 978-0-8577-2285-0
eBook: 978-0-8577-3428-0

Library of Middle Eastern History 29

Typeset by Newgen Publishers, Chennai

To find out more about our authors and books visit
www.bloomsbury.com and sign up for our newsletters.

CONTENTS

Acknowledgements	vi
List of Illustrations	vii
1. Introduction	1
2. Historical Context	13
3. Democracy, Aristocracy, Autocracy	33
4. Effendis and Notables: The Elections	65
5. Radicals and Conservatives: The Parliament	101
6. Traditionalism	133
7. Neo-Colonialism	165
8. Conclusion	183
Notes	193
Select Bibliography	219
Index	227

ACKNOWLEDGEMENTS

Photographs were reproduced from a reprint of a 1926 publication: Zaki Fahmi, *Safwat al-'Asr* (Cairo: Madbouli's Bookstore, 1995). The cartoons originally appeared in 1923 and 1924 in the periodical *Kashkul*; copies were provided by the Image Library, National Archives, UK. Funding for the collection of these images and research in archives and libraries in the UK was provided by the Acadia University Research Fund. Research in Egypt was made possible by institutional support from the School of Oriental and African Studies, University of London, and the University of Alexandria. Some of the material in chapters 5 & 6 previously appeared in Goldschmidt, Johnson, and Salmoni, eds., *Re-envisioning Egypt 1919-1952* (Cairo: American University in Cairo Press, 2005) and *The Journal of North African Studies*, Vol. 2, No. 2, 1997.

LIST OF ILLUSTRATIONS

1. King Ahmad Fu'ad.
2. From the popular journal *Kashkul*, the cartoon represents the uneasy alliance between effendi politicians and the notables during the election campaign of 1923.
3. Sa'd Pasha Zaghlul reading the speech from the throne before the king and the national deputies, 1924.
4. This cartoon from *Kashkul* depicted the cultural and political schisms in the parliament, exploited by the Watani Party deputy, Amin al-Rafi'i, during the first sitting of parliament in 1924.
5. As Egyptian Prime Minister in 1924 Zaghlul was also attacked by Huda Sha'rawi, who was frustrated that the Wafd Party failed to revise constitutional and electoral laws to meet feminist demands.
6. After the fall of the Wafd government in late 1924, Muhammad Pasha al-Shawarbi was one of the first of the great landed notables to support the monarchist Ittihad Party: his interest in politics was largely to gain access to state patronage.
7. The Imam Shaykh Muhammad Bakhit abandoned the Liberal-Constitutional Party for the Ittihad Party in September 1925 because of the controversy occasioned by 'Ali 'Abd al-Raziq's *Islam and the Bases of Government*. Bakhit's opinion was that Islamic law had to be the fundamental basis of any constitutional law in Egypt.

8. Sa'd Pasha Zaghlul (centre) and his rivals, 'Abd al-Khaliq Tharwat (left) and 'Adli Yakan Pasha (right). The photograph was taken in 1926 when the Liberal Constitutional Party and the Wafd Party formed a coalition to defeat the monarchists.

CHAPTER 1

INTRODUCTION

The Egyptian Sources

Documents on the monarchical period in the Egyptian National Archives (*dar al-watha'iq*) are mostly found in the files of the Council of Ministers (*majlis al-wuzara'*) and those marked Abdin, the name of the royal palace. The Ministry and Abdin constituted the two poles of political power in Egypt during the period between the world wars, with the British High-Commission (Embassy after 1936) throwing its support behind one or the other as conditions warranted. The Egyptian National Archives contain ministerial correspondence, parliamentary speeches, lists of political party memberships, electoral rolls by district, reports from the Egyptian intelligence service, letters and other documents addressed to the president of the royal cabinet (*diwan*), as well as selections of newspapers. Most of the sources available to researchers in the 1990s dealt with the events of the 1920s, although there was a scattering of records for the 1930s. The content of the archive has shaped this book, focussed mostly on the pivotal period between 1919 and 1927.

The sources illuminate a political society composed of elected politicians alongside a bureaucratic and landholding aristocracy. The British were integral but marginal players. This viewpoint is also reflected in political treatises focusing on the monarchy, such as Zaki Fahmi's *Safwat al-'Asr* (*The Elite of the Age*) published in Cairo in 1926 and Diaeddine Saleh's *Les Pouvoirs du roi dans la constitution Egyptienne* (The Powers of the King in the Egyptian Constitution), which appeared in 1939.[1] While not unheard of, these books have certainly not been very well read. Partly this is the result of their content and style; panegyrics to aristocracy and monarchy would hardly have found favour among Egyptian intellectuals in either the liberal (1922–1952) or republican (1952 to the present) periods.[2] Zaki Fahmi's book was written in a form resembling the *tabaqat* or biographical dictionary. A copy of it could not easily be purchased in Cairo in the mid-1990s. The Madbouli bookshop in Talat Harb Square had not heard of it, although Madbouli subsequently produced a softbound reprint. References to it could be found in a few dissertations and a copy was uncovered at the Sainte Famille Seminary in Cairo. Upon delivery the custodian of the library, Père Martin, blew dust from its sheaves to graphically demonstrate its obscurity. Nevertheless, the content of Fahmi's book underscored the impression that the monarchy was not simply manufactured by colonial agents, collaborators, or big money interests. The tactics of the monarchists were not controlled by the British or even entirely by the king, but rather represented an autonomous political and cultural force committed to crushing the democratic nationalists at any cost. While the monarchy was not credited with meaningful politics in the works of the most renowned of the Egyptian historians working on this period, 'Abd al-Rahman al-Rafi'i, nevertheless the republican language and concepts used in Rafi'i's works are suggestive of the deep ideological and cultural divisions within Egyptian political society. Rafi'i offered a counterpoint to the historical works produced by historians working under royal patronage.[3] Similarly, political analysis produced in this period pointed to the centrality of the ideological conflict between autocratic monarchists and democrats. The contrary constitutional viewpoints of White Ibrahim's *La Nouvelle constitution de l'Egypte* (The New Egyptian Constitution) and Diaeddine Saleh's *Les Pouvoirs du roi dans la constitution Egyptienne* demonstrated that republican nationalists and monarchists formulated quite distinct views on Egypt's political community and identity.[4]

The diverging cultural or ideological orientations manifested themselves in political party contests. The democratic nationalists preferred to speak of modernity, represented by terms such as nationalism, liberalism, citizenship, secularism and republicanism, whereas the monarchists articulated the disquietude that accompanied modern change. For them, the monarchy was understood as a 'traditional' solution to very modern problems.

The period was defined by the 'revolution' (*thawra*) of 1919 and the constitutional and electoral processes that followed. The monarchy was created with the British government's unilateral declaration of Egyptian independence in 1922, but the declaration only changed the formal title of a ruler belonging to a dynasty that had governed Egypt for over a century. The monarchy represented continuity and order. Although a 'liberal constitution' was written by an appointed constitutional commission in 1923, the disagreements it occasioned suggest that politics in the interwar period was very much an attempt to redefine or rewrite that constitution according to the differing assumptions of liberals, nationalists and monarchists. These contests can be interpreted as a struggle over the culture of modernity in Egypt, which was on the one hand influenced by French republicanism and on the other by strains of British liberalism and conservatism. Those Egyptians trained in French private schools or the largely British-staffed state 'higher' schools came under the impact of all these ideas, most obviously the French. But it would be incorrect to underestimate the impact of British culture upon the Egyptians. The irony of an Egyptian with the forename of 'White' writing in French in defense of French constitutional thinking, which was indebted to a large degree to Montesquieu who of course regarded the English parliamentary system as exemplary, should not be lost on us. But it would be equally wrong to imagine that Egyptian culture in this period was remade in the image of the West. The first Egyptian to translate and interpret European political and social thought, Rifa'a al-Tahtawi, compared Montesquieu to Ibn Khaldun. 'Montesquieu est un Ibn Khaldun occidental dont la pensée constitue un équilibre entre les doctrines religieuses et politique' (Montesquieu is a Western Ibn Khaldun whose thought constitutes a balance between religious and political doctrines).⁵ Pointing to the importance of Islamic ideology in a similar melding of cultural strands, Saleh argued in French for a postcolonial state that figured into the medieval pattern of rule by the Islamic prince with arguments that owed something to Edmund Burke and Herbert Spencer. It is significant that the monarchists wanted to make Islam the symbol, if not the substance, of political authority in the 'new Egypt' emerging after the revolution of 1919. Their appeal to Islam was almost certainly instrumental, as a tool to mobilize support from certain social sectors, but a specific type of Islamic political ideology was also the prime source of the monarchist riposte to democracy and liberal constitutionalism. Thus, rather than Egyptians mimicking European political or social theory, the point was that Egyptian political society was undergoing the same sort of strains characteristic of Europe in the early modern and modern periods.

Whether in the French revolutions of 1789 or 1848, or the Egyptian revolutions of 1919 or 2011, a similar course of events can be discerned: firstly, a popular outburst that destabilized autocratic rule, followed by an attempt to assert popular sovereignty through elections, a national convention and the writing of a new political constitution. In 1919, the Egyptian nationalist delegation or *Wafd* was frustrated in its attempt to represent the Egyptian nation at the international conference at Versailles. Massive popular protests in the spring of 1919 compelled the British government to recognize the Wafd as representative of the Egyptian nation in treaty negotiations in 1920 and 1921. Perhaps more importantly, ordinary Egyptians invested their hopes and aspirations for social and political justice in the Wafd Party as it emerged as a distinct political organization between 1921 and 1923. The Wafd continued to stand as a symbol of those aspirations throughout the interwar period, although the party fragmented into ideological 'units'.⁶ It is more instructive of the political process to study the fragments, rather than to follow the long saga of the Wafd's dramatic confrontation with the British. Some of the ideological fragments that emerged after the revolutionary enthusiasm of 1919 continued to agitate for the formation a 'new Egypt', as represented by a more egalitarian political system. Other fragments envisioned Egypt's political future as dependent upon some sort of compromise on, or diversion from, the revolutionary aspirations of 1919. The post-revolutionary constitutional process was fraught by ideological contests between radicals and conservatives, with the latter rallying around the monarchy and Islam as symbols of political and cultural continuity. Liberalism also served as a counterpoint to revolutionary radicalism and monarchism because of its distrust of demagogic politics, whether of the radical or conservative varieties. The interwar period is thus rich in ideological controversy and is best understood when the various ideological positions and political fragments are shown to have equally shaped Egyptian political modernity. The revolutionary forces should not be underestimated, nor the conservative and liberal ripostes.

The British Sources

Other important sources for this study are the files, letters, memoirs and books produced by British officials employed by the British Foreign Office or the Egyptian administration. British diplomatic staff, as well as advisers or inspectors in the Egyptian service, documented Egyptian events because of the country's status as an autonomous state under British military 'protection' and administrative supervision. Therefore the National Archives in London, England, hold material relevant to modern Egyptian history. Postcolonial theory has cautioned us that literature from the 'colonial library' should be read with an eye to the negation of the colonized and thus distortion.[7] The writings of Lord Cromer, the preeminent British pro-consul in Egypt (1883–1907) certainly confirm the view that colonial knowledge was an arm of imperial power.[8] For one thing, Cromer cemented the idea that Egyptians were not yet ready to adopt elements of modernity: they did not constitute a nation, did not have effective civil or political institutions, and therefore were incapable of administering a bureaucratic state. Cromer's influence ensured that it was a doctrine of British colonial thinking that the British safeguarded the welfare of the Egyptian peasantry (*fallahin* or 'fellahin') against the tyranny of the Egyptian ruler (*khadiwi* or khedive), as well as the self-interested character of the Egyptian upper classes, notables (*a'yan* and *dhawat*, literally 'the ones').[9] Thus, the British consul-general took responsibility for Egypt's finances, bureaucratic oversight and hydraulic works while devising a political constitution that, in a colonial bargain with the elites, sustained the authority of khedive and notables. This type of mutually beneficial relationship meant that any reading of colonial records required sensitivity to the interdependence of British colonial theories and Egyptian political thought, not to mention the interests and objectives of British agents and Egyptian elites. The sustaining of this political bargain after the revolution of 1919 has, in this study, been termed neo-colonialism.

In the pre-war period, Cromer developed a type of indirect colonial rule that required the collaboration of the Egyptian elites in a 'traditional' form of authoritarian government by means of summary justice, while refusing to recognize the nationalism of the official and professional classes (*afandiyya* or effendiyya) as legitimate. However, with the national revolt of the spring of 1919, British policy confronted a critical decision on whether to make concessions or to suppress the nationalist opposition. The most influential British officials employed in the day-to-day activities of the Egyptian administration pushed for concessions by offering a nuanced appreciation of Egyptian political society that overturned the principles of 'Cromerism'.[10] The British adviser to the Egyptian Ministry of Justice, Maurice Amos, and the acting adviser to the Ministry of Interior, Reginald Patterson, explicitly denied the idea that the nationalistic effendis were unrepresentative of Egyptian society. Thus, neo-colonial theory converged with nationalism on the principle that Egypt was a constitutionally autonomous nation-state. In particular, Amos diagnosed the underlying republican strain in the culture of Egyptian nationalism. To avoid revolutionary change, he recommended a policy of conciliation to nationalist demands while nurturing a moderate or liberal Egyptian nationalism as a counter to the republican nationalists.[11]

Imperial policy in Egypt during the interwar period might be understood as a neo-colonial settlement that involved the invention of an Egyptian monarchy so as to create the conditions for collaboration while weakening Egyptian revolutionary fervor. The major compromise for the imperialists was the recognition of Egyptian national self-government. The phrase the 'Egyptian model' was used by Churchill to describe the decision of the British government to recognize Egypt as an autonomous nation-state in 1922, free of any formal incorporation into the British Empire but bound by an international treaty that safeguarded Britain's imperial interests.[12] For him, this arrangement spelt disaster for the future of the British Empire. It was a prescription for perpetual conflict with nationalists. It 'abandoned the pass' (the Suez Canal) to the nationalists, who were motivated only by the desire to dismantle British interests in the region.[13] For critics like Churchill, the 'Egyptian model' was the misguided policy of colonial officials in Cairo, such as Amos and Patterson, who won the ear of statesmen like Lord Milner and Viscount Field Marshall Edmund Allenby. Churchill therefore tried to block the policy of conciliation. As recourse, he and other imperialists did all in their power to twist a policy of conciliation into a new system of colonial control.[14] To a large extent they succeeded, although Churchill's policy was resisted by some Foreign Office staff, some British officials in Egypt, and of course by Egyptian nationalists. A principal agent of Churchill's policy was High-Commissioner Lord George Ambrose Lloyd (1925–1929), who successfully blocked treaty negotiations until 1929.[15] Nor would the British government negotiate a treaty with the Wafd until Antony Eden, another ally of Churchill's, spearheaded the negotiations that led to the treaty of 1936. But this treaty was acceptable because in the short term it transformed the Wafd from an uncompromising opponent into a collaborating instrument, while the British government concentrated on suppressing the Palestinian revolt and preparing defenses against a likely Italian invasion of Egypt or war with Germany. The treaty of 1936 secured Egypt as a military base and the administrative centre of the British Empire in the Eastern Mediterranean, which had been Britain's primary concerns in Egypt from the First World War.

While the objectives of the British Empire and the Egyptian monarchy sometimes aligned, to view the monarchy only as a vehicle of British imperial interests is to adopt the political and ideological vision of the more radical nationalists and obscure ideological conflicts within Egyptian political society. Having said that, it is also important to understand the way British colonial doctrines influenced the ideological content of Egyptian liberalism and conservatism. Churchill attempted to influence the shape of the new political 'model' in Egypt by favoring what he referred to as 'Cromerism', by which he meant 'traditional' authority under the guidance of a British agent backed up by the British army.[16] These ideas were underpinned by a belief commonly held in British colonial circles that Egypt was not yet prepared for democratic elections or parliamentary politics. That belief was shared by the Egyptian monarch and conservative Egyptian patricians with a strong allegiance to the throne, as well as Egyptian liberals motivated in equal measures by fear of mob rule and religious or autocratic threats to responsible government.[17] In his analysis of the monarchic regime, Diaeddine Saleh defended the king by claiming, as many British officials since Cromer had done, that democratic elections in a society where the majority of the population was illiterate could only result in the election of an unrepresentative, oligarchic political society. Pashas and notables dominated the Egyptian peasantry; thus, said Saleh, the claims of the democrats were false. Their bid for power was selfish or founded on their obsession with the question of liberation from colonial influence. Only a paternalistic type of government guaranteed the welfare of the masses. Saleh was one example of a conservative ideologue upholding 'tradition' as a symbol of social cohesion and cultural continuity against the threat posed by democracy. In this way, Saleh's thought resembled colonial theory. Also, the conservative critique of democracy appealed to some liberals.[18] On the other hand, conservatives showed themselves quite capable of ideological and sometimes violent disputes with the ideologues of both the liberal and democratic parties of Egypt.

The conflicts involved basic questions on the culture of modernity in Egypt. This domestic struggle shaped modern Egyptian politics. A history of this process of cultural and political conflict necessarily investigates certain conventional interpretations of the political history of the era: 1) that Egyptian politics in the interwar period was in essence an elite type of politics; 2) that the Egyptian monarchy was the invention of colonialism and its prime instrument; 3) that Egypt's political community after the First World War was defined by liberal, territorial nationalism, not religious or ethnic nationalism.[19]

Secondary Sources

Sources for this study also include secondary material relevant to the above discussion of what political 'model' should be applied to Egyptian political modernity. Western social scientists discussed the same sort of problems entertained by colonial officials and the monarchists. Robert Springborg's thesis on types of political association in Egypt cautioned that 'a model of politics should not impose a logic external to the system and its participants'.[20] Rather, it must operate within the assumptions of the polity it is analyzing. Patronage, according to Springborg, was the most important factor motivating Egyptian political life – access to rewards and control over people. Categories such as class, political party and ideology were thus inappropriate in any analysis of Egyptian politics. In a related study, Leonard Binder used the term *class* only as a 'bit of ordinary language'. In his analysis of political society, Binder concentrated on the social 'origin' of political actors and identified the provincial notability, or as Springborg said 'gentry', as the origin of the actors. Like Springborg, Binder claimed that politics depended upon primordial groupings, based on family or regional base, rather than occupational groupings.[21] Another important study was that of Louis Joseph Cantori, who said that rather than horizontal cleavages of class, social relations in Egypt were founded on sectarian, family, clan, or patron-client types of relationships. Accordingly, ideology, such as it existed, had to be related to these types of social relations.[22] This line of analysis was pursued by Nathan Brown, who spoke of the 'cooperation' between notables and peasants in the 1919 revolution and the elections that followed in the 1920s.[23] There was a kind of community of interest between notables and the mass of the cultivators. Social relations between notables and peasants could enable cooperative political action inducing state control, or opposition to autocratic or colonial rule in revolutionary 'moments'.

The 'moment' is a reference to Karl Marx's distinction in *The Eighteenth Brumaire of Louis Bonaparte* between political revolution and radical revolution for universal emancipation. Political revolution involved a sector of civil society emancipating itself and attaining domination:

'No civil society can play this part unless it can arouse, in itself and in the masses, a moment of enthusiasm, in which it associates and mingles with society.'[24] In 1919 there was just such a political revolution in Egypt dominated by the rural notable and effendi sectors of civil society, each group having similar 'origins'. While some members of the *effendiyya* or bureaucratic cadre imagined a radical revolution, this was unacceptable to more conservative effendis, incomprehensible to the *dhawat*, and beyond the imaginings of most rural notables. It might have had meaning to the rural peasantry, but, if so, took millenarian forms. At least this was Reinhard Schulze's analysis of the situation in 1919.[25]

The events of 1919 amounted to a political revolution. The sectors of civil society involved were the effendiyya and notables. As in the examples from modern French history, the political revolution was ultimately dominated by a Bonapartist type of monarch. Thus, an important topic investigated in this study is how these notables mobilized the people in revolutionary activity, electoral contests and the formation of political party organizations. The changing role of the notables in national politics was first analysed by Albert Hourani.[26] Philip Khoury's study of national politics in Syria showed how the patricians of Damascus pledged themselves to a national movement because it met national and particular, local interests.[27] In Egypt, a similar process was evident after the First World War. Ideological differences appeared however among the leading notables of Egypt, mostly resident in Cairo, because the nationalist policy of the Wafd Party challenged the existing norms of elite political society. The history of these disputes is told in Chapter 2, which recounts the political history of the era and provides the necessary historical context for the study of specific texts in liberal-nationalist and conservative-monarchist ideological formats in Chapter 3. That chapter is an examination of the type of political language current in the so-called 'liberal era' when religious ideology had not been muted, nor historical literary forms superseded. Nevertheless, each ideological tendency was very much influenced by European modernity. An examination of these diverse tendencies provides a clearer picture of the ideological positions involved in political contests. Chapter 4 investigates the politics of the notables in the elections, at the local level and national party contests in Cairo. Many notables were interested firstly in maintaining or establishing power bases in their local communities. The bureaucratic cadre, or effendiyya, was however intent on imposing a centralized party organization upon these diverse communities. The tension between the particular interest and the national became problematic after the election of the first Wafd government. The formation of parliamentary blocs laid bare some of the divisions between notables and the effendis, conservatives and radicals. Monarchists were able to exploit these divisions and build up a body of support in opposition to the Wafd Party, breaking the informal alliance between the king and the Wafd Party that existed between 1922 and 1924. These events are the subject of Chapters 5 and 6. Chapter 6 also returns to the topic of monarchist political theory, pointing to fundamental differences of political identity across Egyptian society. The book concludes with a chapter discussing the way the British were able to position themselves on the margins of this fragmented political landscape.

CHAPTER 2

HISTORICAL CONTEXT

The formation of a modern political society in Egypt took place over a long period; however, the period following the First World War was a transitional period. The British proclaimed a Protectorate at the outbreak of the war in 1914, ending thirty-two years of indirect British rule, known as the 'Veiled Protectorate' and four hundred years of Ottoman over-lordship. During the period before 1914, the British consul-generals in Egypt ruled through the khedive, technically a viceroy of the Ottoman Sultan, and the khedive's ministers. Prominent premiers or prime ministers who led governments during the period of British indirect rule were Boghos Nubar Pasha, Mustafa Riyad Pasha, Mustafa Fahmi Pasha and Butrus Ghali Pasha. These statesmen were mostly of Ottoman or Turkish political culture; however Egyptian political society expanded with the inclusion of new men of Egyptian, Arabic culture, like Sa'd Zaghlul, with the expansion of the bureaucratic state from the mid-nineteenth century.[1] During the period of British political domination there were tensions between liberal reformers, like Zaghlul, and the ruling dynasty. Power tended to shift from the reformers to the dynast after Lord Cromer's resignation in 1907 when Sir Eldon Gorst and Lord Kitchener sought to neutralize nationalist agitators by appeasing the power ambitions of

Khedive 'Abbas II. Liberal reformers were, however, determined to limit the khedive's powers, particularly over religious institutions. As a consequence, Zaghlul resigned from the ministry in 1914 and led an opposition block in the legislative assembly where 'Adli Yakan Pasha was the president of the assembly and the official representative of a government led by Muhammad Sa'id Pasha. With the declaration of the Protectorate in 1914, Muhammad Sa'id resigned and was replaced with Husayn Rushdi Pasha. The Rushdi ministry also included 'Adli Yakan, 'Abd al-Khaliq Tharwat and Isma'il Sidqi. These men represented a clique tied together by bureaucratic service to the khedival regime during the period of indirect British rule. Rushdi's government supported the British war effort against the Ottoman Empire, whereas 'Abbas II was dethroned and resided in Istanbul, the Ottoman capital. At the same time, the British consul-general was replaced with a high-commissioner, a post held by Sir Arthur Henry MacMahon between 1915 and 1917. Also, a new Egyptian sultanate was set up by Rushdi's government under British supervision. Initially the sultanate was occupied by 'Abbas' uncle, Prince Husayn Kamil; however, upon his death in 1917, Kamil's brother Ahmad Fu'ad acceded to the throne. In that year Sir Reginald Wingate was appointed high-commissioner.

The decree of accession of 10 October 1917 proclaimed that the sultan would collaborate with the representatives of the 'people' to assure the 'material and moral' progress of the country.[2] Tharwat commented in a confidential report that such provisions would curtail the powers of patronage held by the sultan over the ministries and the royal household. The political concept thus expressed was liberal, a constitutional monarchy with royal powers limited by a responsible ministry. Tharwat said that the sultan would only exercise influence if he accepted 'our officials', which was to say those recommended by the ministers.[3] At the end of the war in November 1918, Rushdi's government supported the formation of an Egyptian delegation (*al-wafd al-misri*), led by Sa'd Zaghlul, to demand the termination of the Protectorate and Egyptian representation at the Versailles Peace Conference. Wingate agreed to entertain the demands of the delegation in Cairo; however, the British government in London refused to allow the delegation to travel to Paris. At this juncture, the delegation or Wafd chose not to call for a restoration of the khedive and the Ottoman connection, but rather proclaimed a popular movement for national independence against the British Protectorate. In solidarity with these demands, Rushdi's government resigned on 1 March 1919. At the same time the Wafd delivered a letter, also distributed as a handbill, to Sultan Ahmad Fu'ad warning him against forming a new ministry. By making a bid for leadership of the nation with an appeal to ideals of political liberty and universal rights, the Wafd adopted a new political style that challenged the old guard of Egyptian statesmen and the princes of the ruling dynasty. Zaghlul thus checked the leadership claims of a prince of the royal house, 'Umar Tusun, and a leading *dhawat*, Muhammad Sa'id Pasha, with the claim that 'a movement of the people is not one of princes or a caliphate'.[4] Indeed, histories of the 'revolution of 1919' point to the republican political language used by Zaghlul and those 'Wafdists' loyal to him.[5]

The Wafd campaign in 1919 had the benefit of support from officials in the bureaucracy, students and professionals. All of these groups had their contacts in other sectors of society, business people, shopkeepers and rural families. So when on the tenth day of March the leaders of the Wafd (Zaghlul, 'Ali Sha'rawi, Isma'il Sidqi and Muhammad Mahmud) were exiled from Egpyt, there were demonstrations, pickets, strikes and boycotts. A massive rally occurred in Sayyida Zaynab Square, nearby Zaghlul's residence, on that first day of the 'revolution'. The crowd, mostly young men, confronted a mounted troop of Egyptian police led by a British officer. On the second day of the revolution, 11 March, there was a strike of government workers. Also, on that day the students and clerics (*'ulama'*) of the Islamic university and mosque, al-Azhar, joined the protests. Thousands marched from al-Azhar on the city's eastern perimeter toward the government institutions in Ministries Street adjacent to the Sayyida Zaynab quarter. Whereas during the first day of the revolt students from the government schools initiated the protests, on the second day there were larger numbers of common workers alongside the middle class students and professionals. There was also violence, with gangs of young men (*futuwwa*) from lower class (*baladi*) residential quarters invading the European quarters and destroying property symbolic of colonial Egypt, including trams and shops.[6] The British army was deployed to assist the police. As a consequence there were pitched battles, particularly in the residential quarters nearby al-Azhar. Indeed, by the second and third days of the revolt, all social classes, men and women, were in the streets.[7] The first female casualty or 'martyrdom' occurred on 14 March when Shafiqa bint Muhammad, from a *baladi* neighborhood, died before al-Husayn mosque adjacent to al-Azhar. On 16 March, veiled upper class women joined the protests; they were led by Huda Sha'rawi, wife of one of the arrested and exiled delegates.[8] These events were considered evidence that the demonstrations were a manifestation of modern changes in Egyptian society and political culture. Labour groups were also involved, including the labour union (*niqaba*) organizations from modern sectors of the economy like the railway and tramway industries, some influenced by socialist ideology.[9] Once set in motion, the demonstrations and clashes spread throughout Cairo and Alexandria, lower and middle class quarters, and to provincial towns and villages. Indicating an underlying class or economic motive, there were attacks on the estates of prominent landholders in the provinces.[10] Unrest lasted for a month, with as many as 800 Egyptians dying in confrontations with Egyptian police and British troops. The demonstrations were remarkable for crossing social boundaries of class, gender and sect. Groups involved included youth (*shubban*), '*ulama*', veiled women (*muhajjibat*), educated people (*muta'allimin*), cultured people (*muthaqqafin*) and uncultured (*ghayr muthaqqafin*).[11] The spring of 1919 was a remarkable moment of political engagement and national unity; it also appeared to signal significant cultural transformations.

The British army, numbering 30,000, effectively suppressed the revolt by 26 March. However, the army was unable to contain or control political events. With bureaucrats on strike and state infrastructure held up by workers across the country, the British government released the leaders of the Wafd from captivity on 8 April. The delegation travelled freely to Paris. In the course of these events, Zaghlul emerged as the leader of the nation (*za'im al-umma*), the man of the people (*rajul al-sha'b*), gaining legendary stature in the popular imagination. Meanwhile, Rushdi formed a government. In Britain the government of Lloyd George, with Lord Curzon as Foreign Secretary responsible for Egypt, appointed Field Marshall Edmund Allenby as the new High-Commissioner. Also Lord Alfred Milner, the Colonial Secretary, was tasked with organizing a special 'mission' of experts to draw up a report on the situation. By the following year, Milner was recommending the abolition of the Protectorate and a negotiated treaty between Britain and Egypt. The report nevertheless delineated Britain's vital security interests in Egypt, essential for imperial communications by sea and air.[12] Guidelines for negotiations with the Wafd were based on Milner's recommendations, with the security concerns given prominence by making certain stipulations a prerequisite for talks: that Egypt would be ruled by a constitutional monarch, that Britain was responsible for the security and defence of Egypt, that British troops would be stationed in strategic locations and that British personnel would remain as advisers to the ministries of Interior and Justice, which were responsible for domestic security.[13] Therefore, when Zaghlul travelled to London for talks with Curzon in July of 1920, it was obvious that the British government was unwilling to concede as much ground in negotiations as envisaged by the Wafd. Talks broke down on the unwillingness of the British government to agree to recognize Egypt's complete independence (*istiqlal tamm*) as a precondition for negotiations. Also, Zaghlul and the Wafd were well aware of the variety of 'reservations' entertained by the British government regarding Egyptian independence, given that Milner's Report was made available to members of the British and Egyptian publics through a government leak in August 1920.[14]

Initially a national revolt against the British Protectorate, the 'revolution of 1919' transmuted into a domestic, Egyptian political struggle also. It began with attempts to create a 'moderate, liberal party' to counter Zaghlul's leadership of the Wafd.[15] The liberal party was led by Husayn Rushdi, 'Adli Yakan, and 'Abd al-Khaliq Tharwat. While Rushdi had resigned on 1 March 1919 in solidarity with the Zaghlul-led delegation, he formed a new government on 26 March 1919 with the purpose of restoring public order. Zaghlul referred to the ministers in this administration as 'traitors' because they countenanced the Protectorate, martial law, and repression of the press, individual liberties and freedom of association. Similar accusations were thrown at Rushdi's successors, particularly Tawfiq Nasim Pasha, who served as premier from May 1920 until March 1921. After Zaghlul failed to reach an agreement with Lord Curzon in 1920, a group within the Wafd favourable to the Milner treaty proposals threw their support behind 'Adli Yakan.[16] The contest between Zaghlul and his Egyptian opponents escalated with the formation of a government by Yakan in March 1921, with terms such as 'infidel' and 'heretic' applied by the 'Wafdists' to Yakan and his 'party' of followers.[17] When Yakan led an 'official delegation' in treaty negotiations with Curzon, Zaghlul refused to join with the claim that only the Wafd represented the 'people'. Support for Yakan had nevertheless increased over the previous year among elite statesmen and the higher level bureaucrats; however, Zaghlul's steadfast dedication to 'our sacred cause' (*qadiyatuna al-muqaddasa*) of complete independence meant there was also significant opposition to Yakan.[18] As it turned out, Curzon's bargaining position in the negotiations fell short of the concessions already recommended in the Milner Report, which weakened Yakan's position. The talks broke down on 29 April 1921. In May of that year, protests against Yakan's government were accompanied by violent attacks upon foreigners in Alexandria. Winston Churchill, the Colonial Secretary, took this opportunity to claim that Egypt would descend into anarchy if the British army was withdrawn, as demanded by the Wafd.[19]

The British government's position hardened after the Imperial Conference of July 1921. Curzon's explanatory note of 10 November 1921 on Britain's 'reserved points' (the Canal, the Sudan, foreign communities and the defence of Egypt during war) tended to bring the Egyptian factions back together.[20] Yakan resigned. Muhammad Sa'id formed a ministry. There were attempts by the 'dissentients', those who had chosen to part with Zaghlul in 1920, to develop more orderly forms of political resistance to the British, as well as the formation of a broad-based alliance that included some members of the Wafd. Street demonstrations were sustained in Cairo and Alexandria through December. There were attacks on British troops and civilians. The British high-commission in Cairo was thus confronted by a crisis similar to that of 1919. Zaghlul was arrested on 21 December 1921 and deported two days later. This led to even more massive demonstrations, violent confrontations, and assassinations of British soldiers, civilians, and Egyptian 'collaborators'.[21] The spectre of disorder or revolution drove the British into secret talks with the 'dissentients', led by 'Abd al-Khaliq Tharwat, who agreed to form a government in exchange for the British recognition of Egyptian independence. Allenby was only able to secure the agreement of the British government to this policy by threat of his resignation and that of other top British officials in Cairo; however the 'reserved points' already outlined by Curzon were written into the unilateral declaration of Egyptian independence when it was proclaimed as law in February 1922.

After the unilateral declaration the 'dissentients' founded a new political organization, the Liberal-Constitutional Party (*hizb al-ahrar al-dusturiyyin*).[22] The new party was committed to a negotiated settlement with the British and the suppression of political disorder, with considerable support among the more conservative elements in Egyptian political society because of the fear and unease occasioned by the Wafd's tactics. Of concern was the radicalism of manifestos published by Wafd supporters: anti-European, anti-Turk, and anti-landed classes. British observers regarded such language as a sign of 'rule by a mob committee'. Likewise, among Egyptian statesmen the Wafd's demand for democratic elections and universal suffrage was described as likely to 'put power into the hands of the mob leaders'.[23] Clearly anxious at the threat of social anarchy or political revolution, the old political elite, organized as a liberal party, relied on the support of the British high-commission to counter the Wafd. After the 1922 unilateral declaration 'Abd al-Khaliq Tharwat was appointed premier by the king with British advice. Tharwat set out to draft a constitution that would define the powers of an elected assembly, ministers, and the king. From this point until the emergence of a royalist party, the Wafd regarded the liberals as their main adversaries on the nationalist principle that the liberals had collaborated with the British, as well as the fact that the liberals represented leading professional and bureaucratic groups and some of the most rich and influential landholding families in Egypt.[24] Virulent language directed at the liberal leadership in the Wafd press preceded the assassination attempt against the most prominent liberals, Yakan and Rushdi, in 1922. The attempt failed; however it did result in the death of two members of the Liberal-Constitutional Party, one of whom was a patriarch of the 'Abd al-Raziq family, one of the richest and most powerful families in Egypt. The political arena was thus increasingly factionalized, with personal and ideological differences driving the discord.

At this juncture, King Ahmad Fu'ad entered into the political contest between liberal and more radical nationalists. He trusted neither. In 1920 Fu'ad had described the Wafd as having 'fomented a revolution against himself'.[25] Whilst serving as premier in 1920 and afterwards as president of the royal cabinet, Tawfiq Nasim used his influence to enhance the profile of the monarch through public engagements. For his efforts, he was the target of a bombing attack in 1920, most likely the work of the Wafd's 'secret apparatus' or militant wing.[26] The king also attributed anti-royalist plots to prominent liberal statesmen like Tharwat, Isma'il Sidqi and Muhammad Mahmud.[27] Likewise the liberals were distrusted by Fu'ad for their commitment to the principle of a constitutional monarchy limited in power by a responsible ministry. Ideologically committed liberals like 'Abd al-'Aziz Fahmi only agreed to formally split from the Wafd and support the 1922 unilateral declaration on assurances from Tharwat that a constitution would be written with such provisions. The liberals were as much motivated by the threat of absolutist rule as they were of a Wafd-led revolution. Likewise, for observers in the Residence of the High-Commissioner the political arena was, by 1922, divided between the extremes of democratic anarchy (Wafd) and autocratic tyranny (the king).[28]

With the 1922 declaration and the creation of an Egyptian monarchy, the newly anointed king quickly moved to assert royal authority. The Wafd and the monarchy, seemingly at opposite ends of the political spectrum, allied against the British-supported government of Tharwat. Whereas in the early stages of the revolution the Wafd appeared republican in temper and thus hostile to the ruler, after the 'dissentient' split, Yakan and Tharwat were the main rivals to Zaghlul.[29] Therefore, from 1921 there was an effective alliance of radicals and monarchists or, as the latter were described by the British in 1922, 'conservatives'.[30] The convergence of radicals and monarchists was tactical. The Wafd opposed Yakan and Tharwat's policy of compromise in treaty negotiations to secure recognition of Egyptian self-government, rather than complete independence and the withdrawal of British forces. The king regarded the political prestige carried by Rushdi, Yakan, and Tharwat inside and outside Egypt as a threat to his own dynastic ambitions. There were also differences on political principle. Relations between Tharwat's ministry and the king broke down because of provisions drafted by the constitutional committee restricting the king's powers to grant orders and decorations, which reduced his powers of patronage.[31] Therefore, the king neglected to convene the council of ministers during the summer of 1922, expressed publicly his disfavor with the Liberal-Constitutional Party, interfered in appointments in the administration, and began to patronize political journals.[32] In November 1922 the king organized an anti-government rally at al-Azhar, which accompanied assaults against the liberals in the press and in the streets. Tharwat resigned and was succeeded by Nasim. The removal of the liberals from power left the monarchy in a position to influence the final draft of the constitution, which was revised to enhance royal powers. Also, the tactical alliance with the Wafd meant that the Wafd press represented the monarchy in a positive light, thereby enhancing the image of the king in the popular imagination.

Constitutional debates raged in the press during Nasim's tenure as premier. One issue was that during this period the constitution was revised so that it applied only to Egypt, effectively excluding the Sudan from the new Egyptian state. This was interpreted by radical nationalists as surrendering to Britain a territory previously administered jointly by Britain and Egypt – the 'Condominium'. The Sudan was regarded by some Egyptians as an integral part of the Egyptian state. British policy was to concede national self-government to Egypt while removing Egyptian personnel from the Sudan.[33] Nasim resigned on the Sudan issue. When Yakan refused to form a ministry, the British had no alternative but to turn to the monarchists. The new prime-minister, Yahya Ibrahim Pasha, was subject to royal influence and therefore brought the revised constitution into legal effect. The Minister of Justice in Ibrahim's government was Ahmad dhu al-Fiqar, a client of the king who said that the powers given the king in the final draft of the constitution were 'not in contradiction with the origin of the Islamic monarchical and absolutist governments'.[34] These powers included a veto of any legislation in absence of parliament, the power to prorogue the assembly of deputies (*majlis al-nuwwab*), to appoint two-fifths of the members of the assembly of shaykhs (*majlis al-shuyukh*) or senate, as well as the power to appoint the president of that assembly, the power to confer civil and military rank, decorations and titles, to appoint and dismiss military officers and diplomats, and, finally, control over religious endowments (*awqaf*) and institutions. The final draft of the constitution fell short of the king's ambitions to establish unassailable autocratic powers; however, it conceded far more than initially envisaged by the liberals. 'Abd al-'Aziz Fahmi alerted public opinion to the revisions of the constitution in letters to political journals, notably *al-Siyasa* (Politics), which was edited by the leading liberal ideologue of the interwar era, Muhammad Husayn Haykal. Indeed, liberal and independent journals were the foremost critics of the constitution on political principle, whereas the Wafdist journals claimed that the constitution was a manifestation of 'colonial ambition', whilst avoiding open confrontation with the monarchy.[35] 'Abd al-'Aziz Fahmi voiced the reformist aversion to the shades of Oriental despotism evident in the constitution, pointing to the way autocratic powers were inserted into the constitutional document on religious pretexts.[36] The liberal intervention, combined with British supervision, ensured that the king was blocked from completely dominating parliament by limiting his ability to control the senate or to arbitrarily dismiss or appoint ministers, likewise his control of religious institutions was subject to interpretation once a responsible ministry was elected.[37]

As a consequence of these constitutional struggles, the elections of 1923 were a meaningful contest for political power between various political parties representing divergent political programmes. But the contest was not entirely free and open. In the run-up to elections, the successive governments of Tharwat, Nasim and Ibrahim had attempted to stack the administration with their partisans, using the existing police controls and limitations on freedom of speech and assembly to suppress their opponents. This at times violent political struggle involved the liberals, led by Yakan and Tharwat, against monarchists, led by Ibrahim, who had the tactical support of Nasim. The Wafd covertly supported the monarchy while openly attacking the liberals in electoral campaigns.[38] The tacit accord between the monarchy and the Wafd was designed to destroy a common enemy. As a consequence, the Wafd Party won an overwhelming majority in the elections of 1923, with the Liberal-Constitutional Party utterly defeated. Zaghlul showed himself a moderate and cautious political leader from the outset, forming a coalition cabinet that included well-known conservative-minded statesmen like Muhammad Sa'id and Tawfiq Nasim. However, after the convening of parliament, the Wafd leadership had difficulty imposing party order upon the deputies in the assembly. The Wafd Party was composed of various interest groups and each alike tested the Wafd's solidarity on questions dealing with treaty negotiations with the British, particularly the issue of the Sudan, as well as constitutional questions, such as individual freedoms.[39] There was also controversy on the issue of electoral reform, including women's rights.[40] Discord on these issues destabilized the Wafd government, but the party did not crack until Zaghlul failed to reach a negotiated settlement with Ramsay MacDonald, the Labour Prime Minister and Secretary of State for Foreign Affairs, in the late summer of 1924. The king capitalized on Zaghlul's weakness by asserting his powers of patronage at al-Azhar and the Ministry of Religious Endowments. Meanwhile, Zaghlul moved to a more radical position to mobilize the core of his support within the party.[41] In the midst of these events the British commander (*sirdar*) of the Egyptian army in Egypt and the Sudan, Sir Lee Stack, was assassinated by unidentified assailants on 19 November 1924. Allenby severely punished the Wafd government for the assassination, imposing an indemnity, seizing the customs house in Alexandria, withdrawing all Egyptian military units from the Sudan and arresting Wafd activists in Cairo. Zaghlul's government resigned.

The Labour government in Britain also fell in that year on a separate issue. With the assassination of Stack and the removal of the Wafd, British policy was reconsidered. Winston Churchill, the Chancellor of the Exchequer, rejected Allenby's policy of conciliation claiming that the British were confronted with a choice between evacuation and annexation.[42] He favoured the latter, which he described as crown colony status with the Egyptian king serving as an instrument of imperial control. However, British advisers to Allenby in Cairo were ideologically committed to the idea of finding a middle way between the 'power of the throne' on the one hand and 'mob rule' on the other.[43] Likewise, the Foreign Office argued that British influence had always depended on the collaboration of a sector of Egyptian political society. Thus, with the failure to build a solid body of 'moderate' opinion behind the liberals, the Foreign Office favored the formation of a 'conservative' party loyal to the king. As a result, Allenby and the new Conservative Foreign Secretary, Austin Chamberlain, worked with the Egyptian king to organize a political party to contest the Wafd in the next round of elections. The basic tactics and principles of British policy remained consistent, which is to say the quest for a middle ground between the extremes of revolutionary disorder and full scale royal autocracy. The means to do so was the government of Ahmad Ziwar, a premier appointed by the king.

The monarchist party, *hizb al-ittihad* (Union Party), was organized by Hasan Nash'at, whose political career began as one of the more militant Wafdists. Nash'at had acted as a liaison between the king and the Wafd in 1923 when he was an undersecretary in the Ministry of Interior. In 1924 Nash'at was transferred to the Ministry of Awqaf where he was able to use his influence with the *'ulama'* to rally demonstrations by religious students against the Wafd government in November. Moreover, in the course of the trial of those accused of assassinating Stack, it became clear that Nash'at had some part in the inspiration of that political crime.[44] Stack's assassination was carried out by members of the Black Hand, a secret society active from before the war. Nash'at's association with members of that society suggests a monarchist plot to undermine Zaghlul and the Wafd by diverting Allenby's policy from conciliation and negotiation to repression. Also, as the agent responsible for the organization of the king's secret service, Nash'at led the campaign to bring a faction of the Wafd into the monarchist party.[45] It was the open confrontation between Zaghlul and the king in November 1924 that began the defections from the Wafd; however, the assassination of Stack and Zaghlul's fall from power resulted in considerably more. Many of the monarchists were rural landholders, mostly educated in Arabic rather than French, and concerned with access to political patronage. But Nash'at represented younger monarchists, including 'Ali Mahir and Mahmud Abu Nasr, who were motivated by the desire for power afforded by proximity to the throne. For both types, there was deep distrust of Zaghlul's populist style of politics and his mobilization of lower class groups and youth. The Ittihad Party was founded not only on money or power interests, but on a significant political divide between those who regarded kingship as legitimate authority against the Wafd's 'veiled Republicanism'.[46]

The monarchists were a political organization, not simply a vehicle for the king's dynastic ambitions or colonial power. Indeed, the British had an ambivalent attitude toward the monarchy. John Murray, the head of a newly formed Egyptian department in the Foreign Office, compared King Fu'ad to the last of the independent khedives, Isma'il Pasha, known for his despotic propensities. Murray therefore advised that the British government would have to rely on the constitutionalists to counter royal autocracy. The Foreign Office envisaged that the Ittihad Party would elect a party of rural notables who were representative of solid conservative opinion and therefore equally distrustful of radicalism and unbridled royal power. The monarchists would benefit from the powers of the king, without being necessarily entirely subservient to the king. But the autocratic character of the royalist government militated against this outcome. In the ensuing election campaign, the monarchists employed tactics similar to those that had brought the Wafd to power in 1924, which is to say manipulating the bureaucracy, exerting the king's powers of patronage and coercion.[47] A prominent politician loosely allied to the Liberal-Constitutional Party, Isma'il Sidqi, was appointed Minister of Interior. He purged Wafdists from ministries and departments. Sidqi also supervised a revision of electoral constituencies and regulations for the elections to increase the administration's power to manipulate the results.[48] After the elections of 1925, the parliament was divided between government supporters, including Ittihad, Liberal-Constitutional, and independent deputies, as against a nearly equal number of Wafdist deputies.[49] Many prominent liberals won seats – including Tharwat, Isma'il Sidqi, Muhammad Mahmud and 'Abd al-'Aziz Fahmi – while some of the most renowned Wafdists lost seats. 'Ali Mahir, who was to become a staunch monarchist throughout the interwar period, joined the Ittihad Party after it had thus proven itself in the elections. The king was therefore able to build a significant body of support. Nevertheless, the monarchists, like the Wafd, had difficulty establishing party discipline in the assembly of deputies. The Ittihad government was defeated in the first vote in the assembly. Loath to bow to the deputies, the king dissolved the parliament in March 1925 after it had sat for only one day.[50]

At this juncture the Ittihad-Liberal government formed a committee to redraft the electoral law. It also restricted freedoms of association and the press. However, a faction of the liberal party, led by 'Abd al-'Aziz Fahmi, protested the autocratic style of politics of the king and his agents, particularly Hasan Nash'at, as well as the trend toward exploiting religious issues as a platform for the Ittihad Party. The controversy surrounding the well-known political treatise of 'Ali 'Abd al-Raziq was the immediate cause of the collapse of the Ittihad-Liberal coalition. Raziq scandalized opinion at al-Azhar by arguing that there was nothing in the Qur'an to support the idea that religious law had any part to play in the organization of politics and the state. These opinions resulted in his expulsion from the ranks of the 'ulama'.[51] The controversy opened up ideological differences between monarchists and liberals, royal autocracy and constitutionalism.[52] Torn as they were by the religious question, some liberals abandoned the coalition whilst others changed their colours to join the Ittihad camp. These events were critical for establishing the monarchy and religion as integral to debates on political modernity in Egypt.

Before his resignation in mid-1925, Allenby commented that Egyptian politics was divided between three 'forces': the palace, the aristocratic and the democratic. The first drew its power from 'traditional authority' and persistent political manouevering between the other two powers. The second, the Liberal-Constitutional Party, monopolized intellectual ability, professional acumen and the monopoly of wealth. The third power, the Wafd, was driven by 'evolutionary' forces of discontent and ambition of a social or national type.[53] It was significant that Allenby identified social and cultural issues as important bases for political mobilization and division, rather than viewing the parties only as vehicles for elite politicians. But Allenby gave way to a new high-commissioner, Lord George Ambrose Lloyd, who resembled Cromer in his dim view of the Egyptian capacity for self-government, particularly parliamentary institutions. Lloyd differed from Allenby in his willingness to intervene in Egyptian domestic affairs and assert British imperial controls. However, in line with mainstream British colonial theory, Lloyd sought a median between 'absolute monarchy' and the 'forces of anarchy'.[54] This meant dismantling the autocratic and repressive political machine constructed by Nash'at while keeping the Wafd out of power.[55] Nash'at was dismissed. Ahmad Muhammad Husayn was appointed as the new president of the royal diwan as a more reliable liaison between the British agency in Cairo and the Palace, a role played by Husayn throughout the interwar period, until he was succeeded by 'Ali Mahir. According to Wafdist critics, the high commissioner's intervention was designed to play upon the division between the political parties and thus rule the Egyptians through the king.[56] While this position represented conventional interpretations of colonial strategies, it was not an accurate assessment of British policy. The monarchists had already proven themselves unruly. Indeed, it was Nash'at's autocratic style of politics, as well as his likely involvement in political violence, that prompted his dismissal. The monarchists represented a political force autonomous from the British, created by younger bureaucratic professionals including Hasan Nash'at, Mahmud Abu Nasr and 'Ali Mahir, all of them initially adherents of the Wafd.[57]

The rise of the monarchists forced the Wafd to compromise with the liberals. The publication of the new electoral law in December 1925 symbolized the monarchist attempt to revise the democratic system; thus liberals and Wafdists formed a coalition in defence of the constitution. The course toward an elitist type of politics was evident when Zaghlul met with his old political rivals, Yakan and Tharwat, to form a coalition against the king's party in preparation for the third round of elections. The liberals thus shifted from alliance with the monarchists to the Wafd within a year, indicating a maneuvering for office characteristic of elite politics. There was also a shift in the Wafd's tactics. During this coalition phase, the Wafd avoided mobilizing the street and repressed the activities of its more militant supporters in favour of a programme based on legal precedent and constitutional law, which was of course more acceptable to the liberals.[58] Zaghlul was reconciled with Yakan in December 1925 and with Tharwat in February 1926. The coalition ensured that the monarchists were defeated in the elections of May 1926 when the Wafd took approximately three quarters of the parliamentary seats. However, the assembly now included significant numbers of opposition figures, as well as uncertain coalition partners, alongside the stalwart Wafdist deputies.[59] Zaghlul was excluded from the cabinet to avoid a rupture in the coalition.[60] Perhaps this outcome was the result of colonial interference or even the conventions of elitist Egyptian political society. Alternatively, it might be argued that Egyptian political society oscillated between radical and autocratic, democratic and monarchist alternatives, motivated by interests of a class, cultural or ideological character. Zaghlul recognized the fickle character of public opinion by adopting a more pliable political posture, no longer seeking radical political change; rather he accepted the elitist preferences of a certain sector of Egyptian political society. The Egyptian monarchy easily adjusted to the new elitist framework, using its powers of patronage to dilute the political differences between the parties. The king was a key political player. Only he had sufficient powers of patronage to draw support away from the Wafd and neutralize the powerful statesmen and the wealthiest notables. In this way the monarchists won over Husayn Rushdi, Muhammad Sa'id, Ahmad Ziwar, Yahya Ibrahim, Yusef Qattawi, Muhammad al-Shawarbi and Sulayman Abaza, as well as members of the liberal and Wafd parties such as Yakan, Tharwat, Isma'il Sidqi and Muhammad Fathallah Barakat.[61]

Yakan led the coalition government from June 1926 until April 1927. Tharwat headed a ministry from April 1927. Zaghlul died in the summer of 1927 and was succeeded as leader of the Wafd by Mustafa al-Nahhas. Tharwat resigned in March 1928 after the parliament rejected the terms of a draft treaty negotiated with Chamberlain. Therefore Nahhas formed a government with a parliamentary majority. However the intervention of Wafdist deputies in the normal routine of the administration was the subject of liberal and monarchist critiques of the Nahhas government. The king dismissed his government in June 1928 and prorogued parliament in July. After Isma'il Sidqi rejected the offer to form a government, the new leader of the Liberal-Constitutional Party, Muhammad Mahmud, formed a coalition government with the Ittihad Party in the absence of parliament. The Wafdist opposition pronounced Mahmud a tyrant. This was an effective enough argument to scuttle any possibility of treaty negotiations between Mahmud and the Labour Foreign Secretary, Arthur Henderson, in the summer of 1929. The episode also brought an end to Lord Lloyd's career as high commissioner after Henderson determined that his policy had effectively frustrated negotiations.[62] Yakan, who was now an independent rather than a liberal politician, was restored to the premiership in October 1929, and served long enough to supervise elections that brought the Wafd to power in December 1929.

The return of an elected Wafd government with 90 percent of the seats in parliament in 1929 resulted in a renewed contest between the monarch and the elected deputies in the parliament. As in 1924, the major issue was the question of treaty negotiations and the constitutional powers of the king. A coalition of liberals and monarchists protested Nahhas' government's failure to come to a treaty agreement in another round of negotiations with Arthur Henderson, who had made significant concessions. These developments, together with the king's refusal to accept legislation that would have reinforced the constitutional powers of the ministers against those of the king, led to Nahhas's resignation. The king had proven again the inflexibility of his will.[63]

The Wafd was replaced in 1930 by the government of Isma'il Sidqi, which included many Ittihadists. Ostensibly a liberal, Sidqi ruled unapologetically as a pro-palace 'strong man'.[64] Sidqi dissolved the parliament, abolished the liberal constitution and drafted a new constitution that increased the powers of the monarch. The ministers were made responsible to the king, not the parliament. The electoral law was redrafted to enhance the candidatures of the rural notability against the professional middle classes. Sidqi then formed a 'People's Party' (*hizb al-sha'b*) to muster votes in the elections of 1931. A coalition of Wafdists and some liberals boycotted the elections; therefore only the Sha'b and Ittihad parties fielded candidates. Public rallies were broken up and voters intimidated by the police. Ninety percent of the seats went to government candidates. Sidqi's regime lasted from 1931 to 1934. Public protests were met with more draconian measures, including press restrictions and a revised penal code that increased the state's power to imprison its opponents. These measures cost Sidqi political legitimacy and the support of some monarchists, notably 'Ali Mahir, leader of the Ittihad Party, who quit the government in 1932. But it also seriously weakened the Wafd. Shut out of office, many Wafdists abandoned the party and looked to the other political organizations as alternate avenues to government office and political influence. Throughout the period of the Sidqi regime the British government observed a policy of non-interference, strictly applied by the British high commissioner Sir Percy Lorraine, who served from 1929 until 1934.[65] Ironically, upon his departure from Egypt in 1934 Lorraine mused that the only solution to the Egyptian question was that Britain formally incorporate Egypt into the empire.[66]

Sir Miles Lampson assumed the post of high commissioner in 1934 at a moment when the 'strong man', Sidqi, had resigned and parliament had been dissolved. The king ruled supreme through a Sha'bist cabinet and a monarchist premier, 'Abd al-Fattah Yahya. At this juncture, British opinion in Cairo turned against royal absolutism.[67] Lampson therefore abandoned Lorraine's policy of non-interference with the overthrow of the king's favourite, Yahya, and the appointment of Tawfiq Nasim in November 1934. Nasim demanded the suspension of the 1930 constitution and thus the swing from the monarchists to the democratic nationalists was assured. In January 1935 the Wafd convened a congress of opposition parties that called for a restoration of the 1923 constitution. The congress was accompanied by unruly student demonstrations that persisted and intensified throughout the year of 1935. Under these pressures Tawfiq Nasim was able to convince the king to restore the 1923 constitution and the electoral law that had been drafted by the Wafd government in 1924. By the end of 1935 a 'United Front' of Wafdists and liberals had formed, demanding treaty negotiations. These events, together with the great revolt in Palestine and the rise of fascism in Germany and Italy, led British policy toward compromise with Egyptian nationalism.[68]

A monarchist, 'Ali Mahir replaced Nasim as premier in January 1936. In April the king died and was succeeded by Faruq, still a child. Elections were held in May and the Wafd took a majority of the seats in parliament. With the monarchists much weakened, Nahhas was left alone on the political stage and had little to lose by making the necessary concessions to bring about a treaty settlement with the British government. Likewise the international context meant that the British were also willing to make concessions. This was the policy of the two main proponents of the treaty, Antony Eden, the Conservative Foreign Secretary, and Lampson. The Wafd relented on its customary demand for a complete military evacuation, conceding the existence of British military bases in the Canal Zone. In return, Cairo and Alexandria were to be evacuated. The Capitulations (extra-legal rights for foreigners) were terminated within a year and thus the privileges of the resident European colonies were erased. The treaty was signed in August 1936.[69]

The treaty had seemed to promise the Wafd primacy over the monarchists; however, Nahhas' opponents in the palace quickly rallied behind the leadership of 'Ali Mahir. The last contest between an elected Wafd government and the monarchy in the period before the Second World War involved the old issue of the king's constitutional powers, in this case the question of royal patronage over military officers. Consequently, the place of the officer corps in politics was debated, as was the question of whether the allegiance of the officers belonged first to the king or the elected government. This dispute also involved debates on the form and setting of the official coronation ceremony in 1937. The monarchists wanted the coronation to take place in a religious setting and the oath to follow a religious rather than secular formula. The resulting controversy led to yet another palace coup. Nahhas was dismissed from the premiership in December 1937, already weakened within his own party by his attempt to impose draconian controls over the party membership. Thus, in the elections of 1938, the Wafd Party split again. The new Sa'dist Party, led by Ahmad Mahir and Mahmud al-Nuqrashi, took 84 seats; the Liberal-Constitutional Party under Mahmud, 90 seats; whereas the Wafd marshaled only 12 seats. The results seemed to confirm the idea that one party could not dominate political society. A coalition cabinet was formed with 'Ali Mahir at its head.

The fracturing of the Wafd Party and the aristocratic elitism of political society resulted in the emergence of new political forces, including the Communist Party, the proto-fascist organization Misr al-Fatat (Young Egypt), and the Muslim Brotherhood.[70] Sidqi resigned as president of the Sha'b Party in the summer of 1939, declaring in a statement to the chamber of deputies that the utility of the democratic experiment, elections, and party politics had passed.[71] In these troubled circumstances, the autocratic vision intensified. 'Ali Mahir moved from the premiership to the head of the royal cabinet, where he sustained the power of the monarchy by exerting royal patronage through the normal channels, such as al-Azhar and the senate, as well as building clienteles among the military and Misr al-Fatat.[72] The monarchy also had amorphous ties with the Muslim Brotherhood. Politics was changing in the run-up to war, but shifting alliances and rotations of ministries defined the period from 1919 to 1939.

CHAPTER 3

DEMOCRACY, ARISTOCRACY, AUTOCRACY

Histories of the interwar period define Egypt's political community narrowly. 'Abd al-Rahman al-Rafi'i's histories, which began to appear in the 1930s, argued that the divergent ideological orientations of the period after 1919 were implicit in political programmes defined by the concepts of 'evolution' (*nahda*) and 'revolution' (*thawra*).[1] Normally the term *nahda* was translated as national renaissance or awakening; Rafi'i interpreted *nahda* in this way to underline the collaborative relationship between moderate, liberal nationalists in Egypt and British colonial agents, whereas *thawra* was associated with the uncompromising nationalism of the radicals. The political party differences originated in the period before 1919 when the *Umma* (People's) Party represented the evolutionary orientation. The leading ideologue of the Umma Party was Ahmad Lutfi al-Sayyid. Although resistant to the British military occupation, Lutfi al-Sayyid accepted the idea that Egypt was on an evolutionary path toward modernity; therefore British tutelage was not altogether unacceptable.[2] Whereas Lutfi al-Sayyid spoke of progress, Rafi'i and the *Watani* (Nationalist) Party were proponents of revolutionary political change. The differences between the two parties were largely tactical because the *nahda* and *thawra* positions were equally modernist, seeking a break with archaic aspects of Egypt's political community, which modernists associated with dynastic rule, the Ottoman Empire, and Islam.[3] The modernism of these political parties also informed the policies of new parties that formed during and after the First World War, although again there were differing tactics in relation to the British occupation. One trend in historical scholarship from the 1920s thus underlined the republican and populist character of the nationalist organizations, particularly evident in the Watani and Wafd parties, and the inevitability of the republican triumph.

For mainstream nationalists like 'Abd al-Rahman al-Rafi'i, Western cultural models like narrative, national histories were one of the marks of advancement. In his histories, Rafi'i charted the Egyptian 'movement' toward national autonomy and sovereignty. Within this framework there was no room for a backward glance; rather the nation was viewed as a single actor marching toward an inevitable historical conclusion: nationhood, independence and modernity. In Rafi'i's histories Mustafa Kamil, the founder of the Watani Party, was the exemplary exponent of nationalism. Rafi'i described Kamil as belonging to a new generation (*jil*) of Egyptians embodying the spirit (*ruh*) of the age and the nation (*watan*). The modern idea of generation was formulated during the French Revolution for exactly this purpose, to identify the nation with youth and vigor and regiment a party of supporters by ideological commitment to the nation. Arabic and Islamic terms were adjusted to the new language of nationalism. Kamil thus identified the future of the nation with youth and appealed to the students (*talamidh*, having the double meaning of trainees and disciples) to instill in the younger generation a sense of the rights and obligations of nationalism (*wataniyya*). Revolutionary nationalism was the vehicle to transform inert subjects into active citizens. Kamil thus made his 'call to *jihad*' in 1906 not as an incitement to religious war, but rather to inculcate in the youthful nation the spirit of patriotism, to uplift (*yanhadu*) the classes (*tabaqat*), and secure the rights and properties of the majority of the Egyptians. He imagined Egyptian modernity as democratic and egalitarian: 'families, classes, sects, and faiths' all would have equal rights.[4]

Purely ideological, the idea of the new generation addressed the ills associated with an ancient, disorganized heterogeneous society overwhelmed by the cultural and technical powers of the European nation-states. Unsurprisingly other types of ideologies were muted by this dominant model of historical advancement through reform or revolution. The progressive historical paradigm was drawn out also in histories of the cultural *nahda*. Albert Hourani, for instance, described three generations of cultural development from Tahtawi's translations of Western concepts into Arabic in the mid-nineteenth century to Muhammad 'Abduh's equation of Islamic legal precepts with liberal ones in the last quarter of the century. In Hourani's scheme these processes culminated in a third generation, typified by Taha Husayn, who wrote critical historical reflections on the Islamic heritage. Taha Husayn's identification with the West was complete. In his writings in the 1930s Egypt had become identical with European modernity.[5] By adopting the ideological point of view of liberal, progressive nationalism, such interpretations failed to do justice to the ideological and cultural divisions in Egyptian political society. Throughout the interwar period, the monarchy acted as patron of conservative cultural organizations, including Muslim groups, and sponsored cultural works in a programme to enhance the prestige and influence of the monarchy. To bring to the fore the cultural policy of the monarchists, this chapter considers the historical and political imagination of monarchists like Zaki Fahmi and Diaeddine Saleh. White Ibrahim's writings on similar subjects provide a liberal or republican counter point. But the comparison involves more than a straightforward contrast between monarchists and republicans, conservatives and liberals because whereas Saleh defended the autocratic powers of the king and Ibrahim the 'natural rights' of the citizen, Zaki Fahmi, in his case writing in Arabic not French, occupied the middle ground by presenting the case for rule by king and aristocracy. Fahmi's position was ambiguous as it resembled colonial and Egyptian liberal opinion, at least as manifested after the demonstrations and confrontations between 1919 and 1921. The liberals and the British were committed to blocking the participation of the 'people' in the political process while also imposing limitations on the powers of the Egyptian king.

It is important to identify the monarchist ideological current, conservative and traditionalist, which existed alongside the modernist. In spite of operating under the rubric of 'tradition', this trend was a creature of modernity. As monarchist histories insisted, modernity in Egypt was initiated by the royal family, beginning in the early nineteenth century with Muhammad 'Ali. By making this claim, monarchists like Fahmi and Saleh confronted the problem of how to fit a modern form of government within Egypt's social and cultural 'traditions'. The historical problem was acute because the monarchists were aware that Muhammad 'Ali had torn down social hierarchies and disrupted cultural forms in the process of building the modern state. Modern journalistic, political and historical forms of writing were developed alongside indigenous literary formats, such as the annals, chronicles, surveys (*khitat*) and biographical dictionaries (*tabaqat*), all of which persisted in spite of the modernist preference for Western forms. Zaki Fahmi's *Safwat al-'Asr* resembled a tabaqat. Such indigenous literary forms were not remainders or last gasps of a dying cultural heritage. Indeed, the cultural processes underway were quite complex. For instance, in the latter part of the nineteenth century 'Ali Mubarak used the medieval *khitat* literary form toward modern ends by employing it to document the accomplishments of the modern bureaucratic state.[6] The example of Mubarak is instructive because his *al-Khitat* or 'The Plan' (first published in 1887) is an essential source of information on the state project of late nineteenth century Egypt. It is strange, therefore, to find Zaki Fahmi reversing that process of cultural change a generation later. Whereas Mubarak used a traditional literary form toward modern ends, Fahmi inverted this trend by using a traditional form, the tabaqat, not to speak of Egypt's cultural or political progress but rather to represent Egyptian politics and society as continuous and unchanging. Fahmi's writing questioned the dominant historical model of change as a progression from 'tradition' to 'modernity', as it was promoted by the exponents of the Arab cultural *nahda*. The cultural and political model that Fahmi promoted was based on a combination of medieval Islamic political thought and concepts associated with European modernity. At its core his writing envisaged the Egyptian national identity not in a West-oriented future, but in the Islamic heritage. The de-linking from the Ottoman past was not manifest in Fahmi's writing, conversant as he was in the language of the national community and the 'Eastern' or Ottoman community. His writing was clearly influenced by the language of Muslim reformers such as Muhammad 'Abduh, which is evident in his application of the thought of 'Abd al-Rahman Muhammad Ibn Khaldun (1332–1406). Ibn Khaldun had said that throughout Islamic history politics was dynastic, not essentially religious. That interpretation was attractive to liberal nationalists in Egypt, including Taha Husayn and 'Abd al-Raziq, because it countered the idea of the Islamic state or a restored caliphate as promoted by the *salafiyya* (a return to the practices of Muhammad and his immediate followers). Fahmi's reading of the Islamic heritage was closer to the medieval idea that the *umma* owed allegiance to the ruler, Islamic or not, as a precaution against rebellion or social fragmentation.[7] In a significant development, Fahmi's writing represented an ideological formulation of 'tradition' typical of periods of social and cultural crisis when there was anxiety or strain concerning the consequences of modern change. He referred explicitly to Montesquieu in his history of constitutionalism. Montesquieu was of course specifically concerned with the inquietude that accompanied the formation of the modern state, particularly the erosion of civil society institutions like the church and social corporations like the aristocracy. Similarly, Edmund Burke valorized England's 'ancient constitution' at the time of the French revolution, fearful as he was of the social leveling brought by revolutionary democracy. Although Burke was not specifically mentioned by Fahmi, the tone of his writing owes something to conservative thought in the West, alongside medieval Islamic scholars like Ibn Khaldun. Fahmi pointed to the twin threats posed by modernity: autocracy and democratic anarchy.[8] Likewise, the ideological purpose of Zaki Fahmi's work was far from traditional in the sense of following historical patterns of political thought or practice. Instead, Fahmi combined elements of Islamic and Western ideology to form the basis of a new traditionalism. In doing so, Fahmi was particularly intent on identifying the threat posed by democracy to religiously sanctioned monarchy and aristocracy, which, in his appreciation, were the pillars of an ancient constitution. His critique of a West-oriented modernity therefore expressed a very modern anxiety.[9]

Bonapartist Monarch

Monarchists imagined Egypt's political constitution as one that protected the rights of the ruler as overlord, patron of communities and arbiter of political factions. The problem for the monarchists was that the Egyptian constitution of 1923 was written by an Egyptian commission with British legal advice. Its final form was a compromise between liberals and monarchists, with the more radical democrats shut out of the process. The constitution was critically examined in 1925 by White Ibrahim in *La Nouvelle constitution de l'Egypte* (The New Egyptian Constitution). The Egyptian constitution of 1923, he said, did not enshrine the 'rights of man' but only the rights of the few. Ibrahim's solution was revolutionary: the convening of a constituent assembly to guarantee the citizens' 'natural rights'. The historical example of the French Revolution and the declaration of the 'rights of man', said Ibrahim, had a special appeal for developing nations because it had the seeming perfection and completion of a 'philosophical doctrine:', whereas the Egyptian constitution of 1923 was counter-revolutionary because it compromised on the republican model by retaining the symbols, laws, and practices of the autocratic *ancien régime* (ancient regime).[10] The case for a radical constitutional reform was made again in 1926 in his *Police Judiciare en Egypte* (Judicial Police in Egypt) wherein Ibrahim discussed the history of the formation of a bureaucratic hierarchy over the previous century. Historically, there had neither been constitutionally defined executive, judiciary or legislative bodies, nor protections for individual rights and freedoms. Ibrahim attributed this outcome to the failure of the Egyptian legislators to institute Montesquieu's theory of the separation of powers.[11]

Diaeddine Saleh also analyzed the Egyptian constitution of 1923. In his *Les Pouvoirs du roi dans la constitution Egyptienne* (The Powers of the King in the Egyptian Constitution), which appeared in 1939, Saleh denied that a constitutional formula founded on European, particularly French, models could be transplanted to Egypt. Written constitutions founded on Enlightenment theory were an 'abstraction' without any basis in Egyptian society or its cultural heritage.[12] According to Diaeddine Saleh, democracy was purely theoretical, never reality in the Egyptian context.[13] Saleh rejected the idea that the theory of 'natural right' might be written into a constitutional text, claiming instead that constitutions had to be founded on social structures, historic traditions, and elites. Citing Edmund Burke and Friedrich Carl von Savigny, Saleh said that constitutional law was inherent in a nation's history and could not be imposed by a theoretical assertion. He therefore implied that Egyptian constitutional law needed to be revised based on analysis of Egyptian history and society, rather than founded, as was done typically by Egyptian intellectuals like Ibrahim, on the political doctrines of the French Enlightenment.[14] As he said, modern Egyptian legal and constitutional regulations did not constitute the essential traits of the monarchical regime, but were only a mantle thrown over it. In an argument typical of monarchists, Saleh asserted that Muhammad 'Ali, the founder of the dynasty, was the architect of Egypt's modern destiny. He founded the khedival regime, destroyed the power of the ancient lords, mamluks (Turkish military aristocracy) and pashas (Ottoman overlords), while engendering a modern public order to better organize the resources of the state for the benefit of the people.[15] The 'khedival regime' marked the transition from 'Islamic power', as represented by the Ottoman Caliphate, to a modern regime. And although Saleh regretted the separation of political authority from religion, only by these methods, he said, was a modern regime instituted wherein the welfare of the national population was primary rather than a war-lord legitimized by Islam.[16]

The monarchical imagination was historical: the legitimacy of the monarchy rested on its century long endeavour to make Egypt a strong and independent state. Therefore, recounting the history of this process was an essential part of Saleh's political theory. The Muhammad 'Ali regime he said traced its genealogy to the hierarchic and centralized Napoleonic state. After the French invasion of 1798, Napoleon introduced the idea of monarchy, which for the first time did not have the authority of religion, but of a person 'like the others'.[17] Napoleon departed from the purely revolutionary concept of the social contract by instituting military rule alongside a consultative assembly or *majlis al-shura*. Napoleon's successor in Cairo, General Kleber organized the Egyptian administration under the headings of legislation, administration, police, government, history, military, commerce and industry, agriculture, geography and hydraulics. Thus the mechanisms for a bureaucratic state and institutions for the development of the economy and national culture were already in place when Muhammad 'Ali came to power. Egypt was divided into 14 provinces (*mudiriyyat*), 8 in Upper Egypt and 6 in Lower Egypt. The provinces were divided into districts (*marakaz*). The administration required a corps of officers, the most important was the inspector-general (*mufattish*) followed by the provincial governor (*mudir*) and city superintendent or governor (*muhafiz*). Each provincial district was headed by a *ma'mur*, an office that corresponded to the French *préfet* (prefect). The urban districts were known as a division or *qism*. The French regime created 8 divisions in Cairo, pulling down the medieval gates that separated the old quarters. Later the number of divisions became 10, subdivided into administrative quarters, known as a *hara*. Urban quarters and provincial villages were headed by shaykhs, normally men with some hereditary status who made the transition to bureaucratic officer. The head village shaykh was the *'umda* or mayor. As Saleh observed on the formation of institutions, foremost in the reorganization of the regime was the mark of French ideas of that époque: hierarchy and centralization.[18]

Far from a democrat, Saleh argued that the counterpart to the French bureaucratic plan was what he described as the constitutional principle of the *coup d'état*. This was a reference to the methods of Muhammad 'Ali, who arrived in Egypt as an officer in an Ottoman military force that expelled the French with British assistance in 1801. He also repulsed a British invasion in 1807. He then set about suppressing the old military and civilian elites. Like Napoleon, he convened an assembly to gain the support of the rural cultivators (*fallahin*) to counter the entrenched power of the mamluks and the *'ulama'*. As Saleh said, Napoleon introduced the modern state, and Muhammad 'Ali instituted it. The new regime was of a Western type, based on the idea of national sovereignty and a liberal economy. Its internal development allowed the 'evolution' of a social group able to govern the nation because, as Saleh argued, the Western state eliminated all particularisms of religion, sect, and locality.[19] On the other hand, Islamic or Ottoman rule had created the conditions for a classic case of despotism: landownership never belonged to the Egyptians and society was divided into communal groups known as the millets. The conqueror took care to respect religious and social traditions but took all the land for himself and his clients, whereas Muhammad 'Ali's 'genius' was to found his legitimacy on services rendered. Order was established, needs were satisfied and general prosperity assured. Lands and properties belonging to the old elites were confiscated. The properties of the military and religious elites were placed under bureaucratic supervision by the new official class, many of them Arabic-speaking Egyptians rather than Turkish. Also, the power of the religious elite was undermined when the *'ulama'* lost the power to nominate judges without the consent of the ruler.[20] Such arguments underlined the way the Muhammad 'Ali dynasty created a state for the people, and not for vested interest, and thus, if not democratic, it was 'representative'.[21]

By instituting property rights, Muhammad 'Ali's successors increased, according to Saleh, the representative character of the state. The fellahin acquired rights of ownership to the land and were thereby 'raised' to the level of citizen. Initially royal clients received land grants known as *ushuriyya* and *kharajiyya* lands. For instance, under Muhammad 'Ali the Abaza descent group was given the right to collect taxes on twenty villages in Sharqiyya. During the reign of Muhammad 'Ali's successor, 'Abbas, these lands were transferred into private landholdings in the form of a tithe (*'ushuri*). Sa'id Pasha, who succeeded 'Abbas, made communally worked lands subject to the *kharijiyya* tax; the richer cultivators eventually monopolized these private landholdings. These reforms dismantled the communal tenure system and brought the fellahin into a 'liberal economy'. By mid-century 85.5 percent of taxable land was in the hands of the fellahin paying the *kharaj* tax. Fellahin living in villages held small plots of land, but also took wage labour on large commercial estates held by members of the royal family and their clientele, known as a *da'ira* or *izba*.[22] Alongside these changes came of course the new system of barrages and reservoirs that enabled perennial irrigation. The market or liberal economy replaced Muhammad 'Ali's monopoly system and wage labour expanded dramatically. As noted by Diaeddine Saleh, Egypt's rural population was largely transformed into wage labourers and sharecroppers under the thumb of tax collectors and large proprietors. The rural peasantry was obliged under the new bureaucratic system to pay '*baksheesh*' to the state official to ensure the irrigation of its lands, whereas previously water was available by the diurnal flood of the Nile. In this way Saleh pointed to the threat posed to public welfare by the rise of an oligarchic class of officials and landholders.[23]

Saleh argued that the 'evolution' of government in the nineteenth century witnessed the replacement of the 'personal' rule of Muhammad 'Ali with more 'representative' government as indicated by the new legal codes that established the property rights of the citizen.[24] Representative government was not democratic; rather, Saleh compared Egypt in the mid-nineteenth century to the 'English system' before the reforms of the nineteenth century when the members of parliament did not represent a specific 'quantitative' sector of society, but rather the general public good. Saleh cited Montesquieu and Edmund Burke's theory that in great states people cannot govern themselves through direct democracy. Rather political representatives govern not strictly in the interest of constituents, but of the community and its laws as an entirety.[25] In due course, the Burkean model of representative government gave way to more democratic forms; thus Jeremy Bentham and Adam Smith theorized on a society governed by the majority of self-interested individuals. Monarchists like Saleh, however, regarded this trend with the sort of concern entertained by European conservatives of an earlier era. While many scholars of modern Egypt have diagnosed the excessive power of the notables resulting from the reform of landownership, the monarchists viewed this as largely the result of democratization. For them, only the king had the power to curb the predatory character of the Egyptian elites because the monarch represented the general interest.[26]

The critical question of the constitutional definition of the modern regime in Egypt first came to a head during the reign of Khedive Isma'il (1863–79). During his reign the dynasty secured its hereditary title to the throne, the new title of khedive (1872), and gained the freedom to borrow on the international financial markets and to develop the army. Also, with legislative autonomy the Ottoman restrictions that made it necessary to observe Islamic law were suspended. As a result, Egypt was the foremost modern state in the Middle East and Isma'il the most West-oriented of rulers. He guarded his absolutism, but undertook economic development on liberal principles and abolished communal differences in matters of state more effectively than the Ottoman Tanzimat reforms of 1839 and 1856. The instrument to achieve 'Westernization' was Prime Minister Boghos Nubar Pasha, who created a modern judicial system that was intended to abolish the multiple judicial, legislative and executive powers of the old regime, which included various types of religious law, the writ of the Ottoman Sultan, as well as the seventeen consular courts representing the European powers in the Ottoman Empire.[27] Saleh said that the 'proof' that Isma'il intended to abolish the ancient regime and replace it with a representative national administration was that he had established a consultative assembly of deputies (*majlis shura al-nuwwab*) in 1866.[28]

For monarchists, the national will and its representation inhered in the ruler's modern reforms. While hardly signaling a move toward legislative powers in the hands of the deputies, the convening of an assembly did mark the search for a new kind of political authority. Saleh argued that Isma'il was not a democrat. He was primarily concerned with ideas that increased his absolute powers. However, he was 'progressive'. He acted as patron of nascent Islamists like Jamal al-Din al-Afghani and Muhammad 'Abduh. As a consequence, the caliphal idea of a state serving the interests of a religious collective, the Muslims, lost ground to Afghani's 'constitutionalism' and subsequently 'Abduh and 'Ali 'Abd al-Raziq's developed theories that equated Islamic and liberal concepts. As Saleh argued, there was a theoretical trend toward government that was representative of the individual citizen, not the religious collective, and conducive to the development of a liberal economy.[29]

After the Egyptian ruler was forced to declare bankruptcy in 1876, a European Commission of Enquiry convened to declare Isma'il's rule despotic: there was not any religious, social or 'contractual' regulation upon the ruler's absolutism. The commissioners noted the abuse of the *corvée* (conscript labour), taxation by will of the khedive alone, and the imposition of unlimited military service. Although the assembly voted on the budget each year, the khedive had the power to confiscate properties.[30] Isma'il responded to the European critique in his well-known speech of 28 August 1878 when he declared the formation of a responsible ministry under Nubar Pasha. As he said, 'Mon pays n'est plus en Afrique; nous faisons partie de l'Europe actuellement' (My country is no longer in Africa; we are currently part of Europe).[31] The monarchist historical narrative claimed that Isma'il conceded some powers to the ministers to stave-off a European takeover. As a consequence, a constitutional monarchy was established. However, the pace of political events outran the ruler. Thus, when the khedive attempted to dismiss the delegates from the assembly in 1879, they refused to go, and Isma'il was forced to form a new ministry under Sharif Pasha responsive to opinion in the assembly. According to Saleh, the Egyptian ruler spontaneously and sincerely abandoned his absolute powers. However, the 'evolution' toward constitutional monarchy was disrupted by the deposition of the khedive by the foreign powers. Moreover, according to Saleh, because Afghani directed his rhetoric against the khedive rather than the real cause of Egypt's troubles, that is to say the foreign powers, the national regime was ruined. The new khedive, Tawfiq, assumed absolute powers under the purview of the 'English consul'.[32]

It is easy to identify the relevance of these arguments to the interwar period when, according to the monarchists, liberals and radicals formed parties that divided the nation by attacking the throne. These divisions led to British intervention. Also, in his history of the khedival regime Saleh argued that the monarchy was the key institution in Egypt's constitutional development: Isma'il led the nation toward constitutionalism. By such argument he rejected the republican logic of the nationalist historians and the Wafd Party.[33]

Saleh's monarchist interpretation of history can be compared with White Ibrahim's. As Saleh said, there was a 'double evolution' afoot in the nineteenth century: the khedival and the national movements.[34]

This interpretation of Egyptian history before 1919 pointed to the central conflict of the interwar period. Each movement, as demonstrated by Saleh, shared a belief in the autonomy of the Egyptian nation-state from the Ottoman Empire; however there was an ideological conflict between the two. The khedival movement established the principle that sovereignty was an attribute of the prince, who held sovereign power as a right. The national movement held to the theory that sovereignty belonged to the nation and as a result argued that there should be contractual or constitutional regulations over the powers of the ruler. In *La Nouvelle Constitution de l'Egypte*, Ibrahim identified three types of political systems: direct democracy where the people decided on all subjects by direct vote; representative democracy where people elected representatives to a legislative assembly with the power to make laws, which were then enacted by a separate executive authority; and finally, the third type where the monarch had the absolute power to exercise sovereignty in perpetuity, normally through some type of consultation with the people. In 1878 the ministry of Nubar Pasha had limited the ruler's power by delegating authority to the ministers; in addition, the *majlis shura al-nuwwab* established its right to vote on laws and the budget. Whereas monarchists and nationalists interpreted the significance of these events differently, they were agreed that these events represented a movement toward constitutionalism, whether at the discretion of the ruler or by the will of the nation. This movement was disrupted by the British. Ibrahim said that the organic laws of Lord Dufferin in 1883 and Lord Kitchener in 1913 reduced the powers of the assembly to consultation only, reverting Egypt to strictly absolutist rule.

For Ibrahim the problem was the persistence of the forms and practices of a 'Napoleonic' regime in Egypt. The argument was repeated in his *Police Judiciaire en Egypte*, published in 1926. Referring to the reforms of the nineteenth century, Ibrahim said that they might have brought new law codes, but these were not representative, but rather were mostly concerned with punishments for attacks on tax collectors and embezzlement of state funds. There was little place for citizenship in the khedival regime. Moreover, Ibrahim demonstrated that after 1883 the British exploited the existing centralized, monarchic state constructed by Muhammad 'Ali to entrench colonial power.[35] Indeed, in 1883 the Egyptian judicial system was described by Lord Dufferin as 'courts of summary justice' and the legal codes as simply the 'laws of Muhammad 'Ali'.[36] Afterwards, the British consul-general, Lord Cromer, argued that autocracy was an essential trait of Islamic society and Egyptian history.[37] To counter these claims, Ibrahim showed that the practice of dispensing summary justice without trial increased during the colonial period when British advisers supervised all departments and ministries. Cromer resisted any attempt by Egyptian ministers, led by Nubar Pasha, to safeguard the separate authority of the Ministry of Justice. Thus, British advisers and supervisors were imposed on the existing Egyptian judicial and police authorities and the adviser to the Ministry of Justice, John Scott, increased the number of European judges in the *ahliyya* or national courts in 1888 while creating a European committee to supervise the proceedings of these courts. Two statute laws in 1889 and 1891 removed the independent powers of the Parquet or public prosecutor's office to try cases. Ibrahim compared the resulting system of justice to a surviving law of Napoleonic France that enabled prefects to assume the powers of judiciary. As in the Napoleonic state: 'En Egypte la centralization est absolue' (In Egypt, centralization is absolute).[38] Ibrahim described how a law of 1895 further restricted the independent powers of the judges, enabling the executive to organize corps of inspectors to 'instruct' the judiciary. The same law created a commission, presided over by the *mudir*, to appoint rural officials. The concentration of power in the Ministry of Interior had the effect of creating a police state.

While Ibrahim was clearly critical of colonial authorities for reestablishing autocratic rule, he noted that these reforms suited the political culture of a sector of the Egyptian elite. In short, the khedival regime under the supervision of the British consul-general involved a compact between the British and Egyptian elites. Ibrahim observed that for *mudirs* and other Egyptian officials, it was incomprehensible that executive power should be weakened by creating a rival authority in the judiciary. Writing in 1926, Ibrahim thus recorded the influence of social structures, elites and hereditary political culture upon the development of the monarchic state in Egypt. Yet according to his commitment to the ideals of the French Enlightenment, he held up the ideal prescriptions of Montesquieu as a measure of Egyptian modernity. For this purpose he cited the dictum: 'Si la puissance de juger est jointe à la puissance exécutrice, le juge pourrait avoir la force d'un oppresseur' (If the power to judge is joined to the executive power, the judge could have the force of an oppressor).[39] With these reflections Ibrahim contemplated the persistence of the Napoleonic regime throughout the period of British rule and, as argued in *La Nouvelle Constitution de l'Egypte*, even after 1923 when the entrenched statute laws of the khedival regime continued to empower a Bonapartist type of state in Egypt.

The Egyptian Constitution

In his discussion of constitutional law, Ibrahim said that the liberal constitution of 1923 was a grant or 'octroi' of the ruler. This, he said, was the weakest base for any such law, whereas the most perfect was the expression of the voluntary will of the people. 'L'octroi est un mode d'establissement de constitution propre à la monarchie absolue' ('The grant is a method of establishing a constitution suitable to an absolute monarch').[40] Examples of the grant were the French constitution of 1814 or the charter of Louis XVIII. Alongside the grant and the popular will, Ibrahim identified a third foundation for the modern representative regime, which he described as the pact. As in thirteenth century England, the pact involved a contract between a king and another authority that more or less expressed the popular will. Parliament and the English king were on par in 1215. Because the Egyptian constitution was founded by grant, the 'new Egypt' involved a contradiction between the liberal declarations of the constitution and the inherent idea that the 'prince' had sovereignty in his patrimony and thus the power to dispose of the constitutional law at his pleasure.[41]

Ibrahim's analysis of the post-1923 constitutional regime found that individual property rights and rights to privacy could be defended in the courts; however, freedom of the press, religion, opinion, education and public assembly were guaranteed only when these did not threaten 'social order'. There was equality before the law but not, for example, before subscriptions for electoral rolls, women being excluded as were certain other 'social classes'. Voting rights were granted only to a 20 percent minority of the population. Moreover, the constitution explicitly forbade any attack directed against royalty, the succession, and any of the constitutionally defined powers of the king.[42] Regardless of the liberal sounding pronouncements of the constitution, the limitations imposed by the clauses referring to 'public' and 'social order' meant that the administrative police had wide powers of interpretation of the civil codes. Liberty was subject to a 'police regime'.[43] Ibrahim concluded that the 'new Egypt' was more autocratic than democratic. Again, as in his arguments in *La Police Judicaire*, Ibrahim argued that the constitution was shaped by the culture of Egypt's administrative elites. In his opinion, the drafters of the Egyptian constitution and electoral law estimated that Egypt could not pass from an autocratic to a democratic system without a transitional period of political education. A significant indicator of the intensity of ideological debates of the era was that Ibrahim, a nationalist highly critical of British interference, concluded that the autocratic character of the liberal constitution had to be understood as a consequence of Egypt's deeply engrained dynastic culture and a history of its legitimization by consultative, rather than truly representative, institutions. But Ibrahim was a revolutionary modernist. He desired the imposition of a new order after a rupture with the past and the fall of the old regime. This was the point of his critique of colonial legal reforms and the 1923 constitution: that they sustained and reified the autocratic state. Diaeddine Saleh, on the other hand, wanted to show that the powers the king secured in the constitution were indicative of Egypt's 'internal' social structures, heritage and political evolution, whereas the demands of the democratic nationalists were driven by the 'external' pressures of imperialism and foreign ideas.[44]

Saleh reviewed the debates of the constitutional commission in his *Les Pouvoirs du roi* to show that the drafters of the constitution were concerned to harmonize the constitutional text with Egypt's political heritage, its constitutional evolution and its existing institutions. Saleh's argument was indicative of the monarchist ideological perspective, showing the intellectual tradition of Montesquieu and Burke as a prescription for representative rather than democratic government. Saleh's review of the constitutional debates of 1922 therefore detailed the controversy revolving around the question of whether the ruler exercised 'traditional' powers or only symbolic power as a constitutional monarch.

The constitutional commission was composed of 32 representatives, mostly founding members of the Liberal-Constitutional Party; however, there were a few democrats recently alienated from the Wafd Party as well as officials appointed by the king. Saleh noted that the Wafd Party had called for the drafting of the constitution by a constituent assembly because the idea of a 'pact' implied possession of sovereignty by the people. Saleh said, however, that the granting of the constitution by royal prescript was typical of Egypt's political history, wherein the state's powers were exercised in the interest of the Egyptian people and justified by the idea of services returned.[45] Thus, the commission only provisionally adopted Article 23 of the constitution: 'Tous les pouvoirs emanant de la Nation' (All powers emanate from the nation). One of the leading democrats, 'Abd al-Latif al-Makkabati insisted upon the article as a precondition for participation in the commission; however, other members of the commission refused to accept its inclusion in the final document. According to Saleh, the article served only as a working principle. 'Abd al-Hamid al-Badrawi and Tawfiq Doss opposed it on the principle that it might lead to future challenges to royal authority. Hence, Article 156 stipulated that constituent powers could not revise the form of government and Article 157 made any constitutional revision subordinate to royal assent. In a traditionalist interpretation, Ahmad Zulficar said of Article 23 that for the first time in the history of the country a constitutional law provided for a representative form of government that was not in conflict with the ideology of Islamic monarchy, wherein laws were generally ratified with express or tacit agreement of the notables.[46]

Equally contentious was Article 48, 'Le roi exerce ses pouvoirs avec le Conseil des Ministres et par son intermediare' (The king exercises his powers with the Council of Ministers and by its intermediary).[47] As Saleh commented, this draft article reflected the tradition of khedival government. As a result, it occasioned debate. Makkabati argued that the king should be excluded from active participation in affairs of state. Makkabati cautioned: 'Nous ne devons pas oublier que nous sommes dans un pays oriental et que le mal qui accable ... et aneantit l'esprit democratique, c'est l'influence des rois' (We must not forget that we are in an oriental country and the evil that overwhelms ... and annihilates the democratic spirit is the influence of the kings).[48] Thus, a leading spokesman of the liberals, 'Abd al-'Aziz Fahmi, took exception to the terminology in Article 48 that described the king as exercising his powers 'with', rather than 'by', the intermediary of the ministry. As he said, the king should be subject to the rule of law. Husayn Rushdi, the chairman of the commission, replied that the king's powers did not constitute a threat because the ministers were responsible to parliament. 'Abd al-'Aziz Fahmi replied that the ministry would become a mere instrument in the king's hands. As a result the word 'with' was replaced with 'by'. Thus, Article 48 of the draft constitution was altered to read: 'Le roi exerce ses pouvoirs par l'intermediaire de ses ministres' (The king exercises his power by the intermediary of his ministers).[49] Yet, Rushdi would not replace 'ses' (his) with 'les ministres' (the ministers), arguing in favor of the king's power to arbitrate disputes among ministers or parties in the parliament. In the subsequent session of the commission, Makkabati questioned provisions that enabled the king to dissolve parliament and argued that the ministry should not be able to stay in office after a parliamentary vote of no-confidence. Rushdi responded with the observation that parliamentary traditions were already established in Europe that favoured the popular will in such situations and that these would equally apply in Egypt, ignoring Makkabati's warning that European precedence would not apply in the 'Oriental' context.[50] Makkabati returned to this point when he said that examples from European constitutional law were irrelevant and that Egyptians should draw their conclusions from their own political history. It was unlikely, he said, that members of an Egyptian legislature would risk their seats by a vote of no-confidence if the ruler had the power to dissolve parliament.[51] Inevitably, conflicts between legislative and executive authority would rebound in favour of the latter. The commission ultimately rejected

Makkabati's argument, securing the power of the king to dissolve the ministry and parliament. Thus, although the constitution declared that all authority emanated from the nation, the king's powers and authority over parliament were firmly established in the new constitutional law.

Saleh claimed that the content of the constitutional debates showed the attempt to impose the British model of constitutional monarch and responsible ministry upon Egypt. It was, he said, ill-suited to Egypt. The British parliamentary tradition involved an 'unwritten' code of political behaviour within a political culture habituated to free government and where there was equilibrium between parliament and cabinet and the king was above political factions. But, as Saleh said, political practice was entirely different in Egypt. His documentation of the constitutional debates displayed the way elite statesmen like Rushdi safeguarded the powers of the king over the legislature and the ministers.[52] Saleh's argument was that royal authority was necessary and the royal decree a legitimate form of government, if exercised in the public interest. The evidence from the debates suggested that members of Egyptian political society entertained similar concerns regarding parliamentary authority. Some members of the commission favoured a traditionalist political constitution that conformed to Islamic historical models wherein the popular will was consultative, not authoritative. As in Islamic political history, the 'prince' exercised his hereditary right to supervise the decisions of his ministers in council and notables in assembly. The French system where ultimate authority was vested in the elected representative was, said Saleh, favored by Egyptians with a Western education; however, democratic elections disguised the real structure of oligarchic rule, which had enabled the Wafd Party to dominate elections and parliament throughout the interwar period.[53] The parliament, as dominated by the Wafd, was a 'spoils system', serving the interest of clan and class, not the public.[54]

The divergent positions of Ibrahim and Saleh indicate the wide ideological spectrum of modern Egyptian political society. For Ibrahim, the constitutional system had not met the ideal of the 'rights of man'. For Saleh, Egypt's constitution had diverged too far from indigenous models that ensured the powers of the monarch as founder of the modern Egyptian nation-state and guardian of the public good. The conflict, as represented by Saleh and Ibrahim, reflected cultural divisions in political society; therefore the monarchy attracted various defenders and promoted a complex cultural programme, evident in Zaki Fahmi's work. Fahmi resembled Saleh insofar as he developed a hybrid of modern and historical constitutional models and pointed to a middle way between the extremes of democracy and autocracy.

The Middle Way: Aristocracy

Ibrahim underscored the hierarchic and centralized state constructed by the Muhammad 'Ali dynasty, and its further institutionalization under the British. Zaki Fahmi emphasized the dynasty's political pact with the notables (*a'yan*). For instance he said that Isma'il's distribution of lands held as religious trust (*waqf*, pl. *awqaf*) among the *a'yan* had the effect of expanding the size and increasing the autonomy of the rural notables. Likewise, while the hereditary ruler was an indispensible feature of the Egyptian political system, according to Fahmi legitimacy depended upon the support of the aristocratic classes, including the Ottoman elite of statesmen (*dhawat*) and the 'cream' of the Egyptian a'yan. Fahmi's history of Egypt in the nineteenth century described the way notables mixed with the *dhawat* from the 1850s and formed a bureaucratic and professional class by the 1860s; as a result, Egyptian political society involved two distinct status classes, *dhawat* and *a'yan*, with the commoners referred to as the *ra'iyya*, literally the 'flock'.[55]

These themes distinguish Fahmi from Saleh because the latter focused on the ruler almost exclusively. It is revealing to contrast Fahmi's interpretation of the events that led to Isma'il's deposition in 1879 and the British occupation of 1882 with other accounts, including Saleh's and republican nationalist, as well as those of colonial agents. For the British financial expert and consul-general, Lord Cromer, Isma'il was a corrupt Oriental ruler responsible for squandering the country's inheritance. The notables were little better. They acted out of property interest, resisting French- and British-inspired tax reforms designed to salvage the country's finances. There was nothing resembling a national or popular will in the notables' opposition to the European Debt Commission of the 1870s.[56] Cromer published his account in 1908. Writing in the 1930s, the nationalist historian 'Abd al-Rahman al-Rafi'i also criticized Isma'il for political tyranny and mismanagement of the finances; however, he found the underlying problem in the dynasty's dependence upon European powers and financiers. Therefore, it was his opinion that resistance to the European Debt Commission in the 1870s was a manifestation of nationalism.[57] In the same period monarchist historians and political thinkers like Diaeddine Saleh, Georges Douin and Angelo Sammarco credited the political reforms of the era to the sagacity of the ruler, with the main threat to the political community being the foreigners and irresponsible nationalists, like Afghani and 'Abduh.[58]

Zaki Fahmi's interpretation of the same events pointed to the political agency of the notables, both those from religious and state institutions, equally representative of the national community. Unlike subsequent, more dogmatic monarchist narratives, Fahmi did not identify the monarch as the sole embodiment of modern Egypt; nor did he adopt the nationalist idea that the essential drama of Egypt's modern history was the confrontation between European imperialism and Egyptian nationalism. Rather, Fahmi placed himself within a genre of Islamic political writing that held up a mirror into which the ruler and elites might gaze and reflect upon their attributes, known as the 'manuals for government' or 'mirrors for princes'. By adopting this form, Fahmi showed that he was more than a publicist for the monarchy. On the movement toward representative government, Fahmi referred to reforms such as the new legal code (*al-qada' al-ahli*) of 1876 and the grant of ministerial responsibility in 1878. Whereas monarchists regarded the khedive as the author of these reforms, Fahmi was critical of the khedive and praised Nubar Pasha. According to Fahmi's account, it was the confrontation between Nubar and Isma'il that led to the dissolution of absolutist rule in 1878 when Isma'il was forced to countenance a responsible ministry. The domain lands of the ruler were ceded in that year. On the crisis that brought about the khedive's deposition, Fahmi, unlike Saleh, found the 'disease' was in the designs of a ruler too proud to have his hands tied by ministry or majlis. Fahmi equated khedival autocracy with unjust rule and throughout his account of the national movement, led by Ahmad 'Urabi, he implied that just rule required the political engagement of the elite, *dhawat* and *a'yan*. In the run-up to the British invasion, there was consensus between the civilian leadership (*a'yan*), the military party (*al-hizb al-askari*), and the delegates (*wufud*) in the majlis. Also, in deference to religious opinion he said that 'Urabi consulted with the *'ulama'* of al-Azhar, which he described as the 'centre of speech'. Fahmi also said that 'Urabi was distinguished by his moral qualities, particularly his devotion (*ikhlas*) to the nation. As a result he was nominated as the 'greatest Islamic leader'. It was on this basis that 'Urabi won the support of the nation, whereas, said Fahmi, other adherents of the movement failed to impress.[59]

By making the will of the nation central to his narrative, Fahmi clearly showed his familiarity with the doctrines of political modernity. His discussion of the notables as intermediaries between ruler and the general population highlighted the influence of the political thought of Montesquieu. The emphasis upon the political agency of the notables suggests a concern that tyranny had increased with the formation of the modern Egyptian state by removing aristocratic checks on the power of the monarch.[60] These ideas were also apparent in Islamic reformist thinking, an important component in the Egyptian national *nahda*. As a cultural strand independent of the royal court, the Islamic reformists proposed constitutional reform, including parliamentarianism.[61] Jamal al-Din al-Afghani developed a type of political thought wherein the moral corruption of the ruler was responsible for the weakening of Islamic states vis-à-vis the imperial powers of Europe. Arguing in this vein, Fahmi opposed the virtuous 'Urabi to the unjust Isma'il. The influence of Islamic reformism upon Fahmi's theory was apparent in his desire to reconcile monarchical rule with representative government. This was evident in the terminology he used. For instance, Islamic reformists combined the French republican idea of the 'people' (*sha'b*) and the Muslim idea of a community of believers (*umma*). They also equated Islamic concepts like *shura* with modern ones like democracy. Fahmi's work was conversant in this modern political vocabulary, but the monarchy and the aristocracy took centre stage in his discussion of politics, indicating that his thought was grounded in conservative thinking. The new king Ahmad Fu'ad was praised by Fahmi for supporting a government that had pledged to found a constitutional regime. The objective said Fahmi was to create a system that ensured the involvement of the people (he used the term *umma*) in the administration of the country (*bilad*) while laying down the principles of ministerial responsibility that would preserve (*tura'a*) the traditions and customs of Egypt.[62]

Fahmi belonged to a school of monarchist cultural workers that showed deference to the king, their benefactor. The king subsequently sponsored other national histories, such as those written in French by Angelo Sammarco, Georges Douin, Gabriel Hanotaux, Joseph Cattaoui (Yusef Qattawi), Etienne Combe, Jacques Bainville and Edouard Driault.[63] Many promising scholars found their way into the royal court. As Donald Reid surmised, the royal cultural programme was undertaken to 'burnish the image of the prince'.[64] Historical writing under royal patronage created the myth of an enlightened Egyptian dynasty, responsible for all the benefits of modern civilization in Egypt. The book by Fahmi, a monarchist, fits the purposes characteristic of Sammarco and other royal panegyrists. His history of the dynasty founded by Muhammad 'Ali Pasha al-Kabir (the Great) includes portraits of Napoleon, Sulayman Pasha al-Faransawi (Joseph Sève, a French colonel in Napoleon's army employed by Muhammad 'Ali to reorganize the army), and Ferdinand de Lesseps, the financier of the Suez Canal. King Fu'ad's cultural work was represented as an extension of the imperial ambitions of his grandfather, Khedive Isma'il, the last independent ruler of Egypt. Fahmi chronicled Egypt's civilizing mission in Africa during Isma'il's reign, as would subsequent histories written under royal patronage. He noted that Isma'il revived the Institute d'Egypte (a scientific institute initially founded by French savants) and acted as patron of the first national library (*dar al-kutub*), the school of administration (*madrasa al-idara*), the opera, the parliament (*majlis shura al-nuwwab*), and the geographical society. Fu'ad likewise acted as president of 12 charitable societies, mostly Islamic. Fu'ad's reign saw a resurgence of French culture at the Egyptian university where monarchists combated British influence. The discovery of Tutankhamen's grave goods was given a prominent place in Fahmi's narrative, suggesting continuity between pharaoh and king. The image of modern Egypt that emerges is as broad and grand as the dioramas and African artifacts housed by the National Geographical Society at the parliament buildings in Cairo. Accordingly, Egypt was all at once modern, European, Pharaonic, Islamic, Arabic, and African; neither ethnically nor religiously bounded, nor territorially defined because in 1926, the imperial question of Egypt in Africa remained unresolved.

As Reid has said of the monarchist school: 'That most of these works were in French by Western authors suggests that Fu'ad saw the security of his throne as more dependent on the West and the francophone Egyptian elite than on the majority of his countrymen, who read only Arabic or nothing at all.'[65] Certainly, this was a weakness of the monarchist cultural campaign. However, firstly, the monarchy definitely reached out beyond the French educated elite for political support, and, secondly, the monarchist cultural campaign was aimed broadly at the Egyptian elites, from rural notable to urban effendi, mostly Arabic-speaking. *Safwat al-'Asr* was written in Arabic; it resembled the 'mirror for princes' genre and the *tabaqat* literary form, rather than the historical narrative method preferred by those writing in French. This showed an appreciation for indigenous cultural forms as well as the accepted function of the Islamic scholar to record the qualities or virtues of the elite. While Albert Hourani has suggested that this function was destabilized in the modern period when rulers increasingly appeared 'alien in ways of thought', the *tabaqat* literary form adopted by Fahmi went against that trend, if such it was, by praising the ruler and the elite in the tradition of medieval chroniclers such as Ibn Khaldun, Maqrizi, Sayuti and Ibn Iyas, as well as the nineteenth century Egyptian chroniclers, 'Abd al-Rahman al-Jabarti, Mahmud Fahmi and 'Ali Mubarak.[66] Hourani argued that the 'men of the old culture' were oriented toward the preservation of the 'heritage of Islam through history', whereas a modern cultural worker like 'Ali Mubarak aspired to change, rather than preserve that culture.[67] Fahmi used a traditional form toward what might be called post-modern ends: an affirmation of the medieval view of the prince as the constitutional formula for Egypt in the modern age. Hence, Fahmi's thinking also marks a break in the straight-forward progression from tradition to modernity as described in Hourani's *Arabic Thought in the Liberal Age*.

Fahmi differed from the francophone chroniclers in that his work avoided Western forms, but the book included alongside the biographical dictionary a political treatise and a chronicle of the 'age'. The political content resembled the 'manual for government' genre of writing in so far as it offered a portrait of the just prince. Using moral categories, Fahmi described the character and functions of the monarch, which amounted to the constitutional rules of government. Ann Lambton said of this type of writing in medieval Islamic cultures: 'Politics are not separated from morals, and ethics, rather than politics, are the subject about which they write. The state is a "given" and there is no attempt at its justification and control.'[68] Hourani also observed that 'books of practical advice for rulers' were prevalent after the fall of the classical caliphate when philosophers were forced to reconcile the fact of kingship to the ideal of the *umma* and *shari'a*.[69] The assumptions of this type of advice literature recurred throughout Ibn Khaldun's *al-Muqaddima* (The Introduction), which was produced in the fourteenth century. Significantly, that work declared that Islamic law was not necessary for the existence of the state, although religion could provide the social cohesion and unity of purpose necessary for state formation.[70] Indeed, the 'mirrors for princes' as a literary genre pre-dated Islam, having its source in the Sassanian and Byzantine empires where of course the primary concern was with the fact of kingship as it actually occurred in the world. Fahmi, likewise, concerns himself with Egyptian kingship, which he related to medieval Islamic and modern Western political concepts. Given this attempt at synthesis, it is worth noting that such writings were also existent in Europe. Relying on Aristotelian categories for a description of ethical rule, Erasmus' *The Education of a Christian Prince* and Machiavelli's *The Prince* adopted the 'mirrors for princes' form. *The Prince* could be seen as a subversion of the genre, pointing to the importance of the political, as opposed to the moral, qualities of the prince.[71] It is significant that Fahmi, when referring to monarchical rule in general terms sometimes used the word 'prince', transliterated into Arabic as 'brins', as if he wanted to record his engagement with modern European political theory.

Fahmi's political message was clearly stated: the main threat to the nation was factional conflict, as a consequence of democratization and political party formation. The prescription to avoid democratic anarchy was elite, aristocratic rule. Employing classical Islamic concepts, Fahmi said that that there should be consensus (*ijma'*) and consultation (*shura*) among the elite classes only. Such ideas were fitted to modern politics by the Islamic reformers Afghani and 'Abduh. Afghani had taught that society resembled a body, requiring cooperation between its various parts, based on a reading of Islamic philosophers like Abu Nasr al-Farabi, a tenth century commentator on Plato's idea of rule by the philosopher prince.[72] Farabi can be compared to the jurist-theologian Taqi al-Din Ahmad Ibn Taymiyya, who made a more orthodox prescription for a hierarchy of *'ulama'* and prince in his *Al-Siyasa al-Shar'iyya fi Islah al-ra'i wa al-ra'iyya* (Legal Policy for the Improvement of the Shepherd and the Flock).[73] Ibn Taymiyya's theory of consultation between ruler and *'ulama'* implied that the ruler should respect the civilian elite. Farabi and Ibn Taymiyya together advanced the theory of equitable relations between ruler and notables, including the *'ulama'*, as guardians of the social mass or flock (*ra'iyya*). Another important influence on modern Islamic political thought was Ibn Khaldun; his history of 'civilization' (*'umran*) reckoned that the rise and decline of Islamic 'umran could be measured by the factors of tribal or religious cohesion (*'asabiya*). Fahmi's arguments rehabilitated Ibn Khaldun. He identified the *'ulama'*, notables, and king as the best authorities for the political community. The justification for a hierarchical arrangement of classes was viewed as nothing less than the preservation of 'civilization', for which Fahmi used Ibn Khaldun's term 'umran.[74] Adopting the medieval world view of preservation within a cycle of rise and decline of civilization in effect refuted the evolutionary sequence of progress or advancement (*tattawur* or *taqaddum*) held up by the West-oriented modernists.

Fahmi observed that the individual was subject to desires and passions and that this underlined the need for education in the virtues of charity, effort and self-sacrifice.[75] The emphasis on moral virtue was found also in the sociology of Ibn Khaldun, in which civilization persists, coheres or falters according to these virtues. The prince was distinguished by his virtues. The image of the just prince was mirrored in the elite, which in Fahmi's description resembled the elite of medieval Islamic society when patrons dominated city politics through corporations or brotherhoods with an expectation to observe social obligations understood in a moral sense.[76] As for the rural population, the notables were bound by equally close ties to 'their' fellahin. The elites were entrusted with the welfare of the royal subjects (literally flock, *ra'iyya*) according to the principle of patronage (*ri'aya*). By using these ideas, Fahmi propounded a theory that was not obscurantist, but engaged with the problem of incorporating Egypt into political modernity in a manner consistent with the political culture of Egypt. According to Fahmi the constitutional commission of 1922 was only able to come to a consensus by royal arbitration. Fahmi's emphasis upon the king as arbiter and the recourse to indigenous political models prefigured Saleh's thinking. Identifying the king as a moderator among political factions was like Rushdi's commentary in the minutes of the constitutional commission.[77] Before the constitution was published, said Fahmi, two laws were passed that secured the powers of the king and his family's hereditary claim to the throne. Fahmi said that an authoritative form of government was the basis of freedom (*hurriyya*) and justice (*'adl*). All these principles were declared in the introduction to the constitution, which founded a constitutional monarchy through the principles of consultation (*shura*) and representation (*niyabiyya*).[78] The concept of *shura* points to the influence of reformist Islamic ideology, indicating that Fahmi's thinking involved a dialogue between Islamic and Western political ideology: 'the great ones and the news of others'.[79] Like European conservative thinkers, Fahmi's arguments implied that unfettered freedom was associated with social disorder, a scenario that informs Fahmi's history of constitutionalism and representative government.

Fahmi's history of constitutionalism appears in the book as an introduction to his account of the opening of the new Egyptian parliament in March 1924. Fahmi began by setting up a typology of political systems, not unlike those proposed by White Ibrahim. Fahmi said that political rule might be by an individual (*fard*), a social group (*aristuqratiyya*), or by the people (*sha'b*). It is interesting that Fahmi transliterated 'aristocracy' into Arabic script, rather than use an Arabic synonym. This was a sign of the syncretic nature of his thought. The political concepts he chose would appear to be a selection from Aristotle's political typology in which the virtuous types of monarchy, aristocracy, and polity were opposed to the unjust types of tyranny, oligarchy, and democracy. By selecting three types from the opposed categories, Fahmi seems to suggest that only aristocracy conforms to a just type of government. Rule by the individual (*fard*) suggests autocracy and rule by the people (*sha'b*, rather than *umma*) democratic anarchy, that is to say unjust types of government. The typology pointed by default to aristocratic rule. To prove the point, Fahmi carefully distinguished between just representative government and democratic anarchy in his brief constitutional history. The narrative began with Rome, which he said evolved from republic to empire and that Roman law later enabled the rule of the feudal prince. This inverted the historical progression characteristic of modern history, beginning with the American and French revolutions where imperial and monarchical rule gave way to the republic. Fahmi however recognized that in the modern period the spirit of nationalism (*qaumiyya*) brought with it the idea that the lower classes should not be servants, but rather participants in politics. This idea manifested itself in the French Revolution, where lower class people (*sha'b*) grasped hold of power. But Fahmi said that it was in England that the contemporary meaning of representative government was born, following a decree of King Edward I in 1290 that called upon the princes and important men of state (*kibar rijal al-dawla*) to look into the ills of the country and how best to alleviate them. Two men from every region, city, and estate (*da'ira*) were called upon, men known for their wisdom (*hikma*), devotion (*ikhlas*), and competence (*kafa'a*), and they were given responsible power to make decisions for the good of the country and with the general agreement of all. The English system established the oldest parliament in history. It was, he said, this model that the constitutions of America, France, and all other countries have copied (*taqlid*).

The example has survived through the centuries and has therefore been the source for subsequent laws.[80]

This history might suggest that Fahmi was influenced by British political culture, perhaps as indoctrinated at the law school in Cairo; but that hardly fits his insistence upon cultural authenticity and national independence. Rather, it might be assumed that his thinking betrayed an education in modern political thought, beginning with Montesquieu, acknowledging that European culture had an impact upon the development of Egyptian modernity. The point was not to emulate Europe, but rather to promote a modern, political constitution that adhered to Middle Eastern and Islamic 'tradition' (*taqlid*). While White Ibrahim had pointed out that French political ideas had a unique appeal to Egyptians, like other developing nations, Fahmi expressed an equally deeply felt fear that French- inspired republicanism threatened social anarchy and civil war. Therefore Fahmi explicitly referred to Montesquieu's study of the representative institutions as the best model for modern Egypt. Fahmi noted that political scientists (*'ulama' al-siyasa*) like Montesquieu had shown that the constitutional separation of powers is the superior type of government and that limited (*muqayyad*) monarchy with a parliament divided into two chambers as in England, Italy, Egypt and Japan was the best political system in the age. It was a safeguard against instability (*taqallubat*), protected tradition (*taqlid*) and honour (*'izz*), while representative ministers took responsibility for the affairs of state as in all republics.[81]

Apparently for Egyptians like Fahmi, monarchy and aristocracy came to represent political and cultural continuity. Thus, when speaking of the constitutional monarch, he implied that electoral politics had to be founded on a combination of Western innovation and medieval, Islamic models. Repeatedly Fahmi underlined the importance of the elite classes in the constitutional system. However, unlike liberals Fahmi did not challenge religious authority by arguing for a separation of church and state or reform of religious law. Instead, by adopting the medieval model of political consultation between virtuous elites and ruler, he seemed to endorse the political role of the *'ulama'*. As he said, the notables and princes were the best guides for Egypt's political community.

Fahmi celebrated Zaghlul's achievements as a representative of Egypt's indigenous, Arabic-speaking elite (*a'yan*) describing him as leader (*za'im al-umma*) of the 'revolution.' (The term *nahda* was used because Fahmi avoided radical, revolutionary vocabulary like *thawra*.) Zaghlul was a hero (*batal*) of the struggle for independence and Fahmi credited him with heroism and 'uncompromising politics' (*siyasa al-jafa'*).[82] But even as he praised Zaghlul's fame (*shuhra*) and 'leadership of his nation' (*za'ama qaumhu*), Fahmi implicitly questioned populist politics. Only a virtuous life (*al-hayat al-khalida*), said Fahmi, was a guard against the ignorant (*jahil*), who are easily infatuated by appearances. Individuals cannot win fame without effort (*nasab*) and resolute dedication to the political struggle (*jihad*).[83] Without explicitly denying that Zaghlul had these qualities, Fahmi identified them with the aristocracy, rather than the popular hero. His commentary was inflected with religious terminology, implicitly suggesting that Zaghlul's methods followed a Machiavellian political calculation, rather than selfless dedication to the cause.

To conclude, the conservatism of Saleh and Fahmi was grounded in medieval Islamic political thought, as well as modern European conservatism. Historical Islamic political models can be divided into two dominant types, one a society united under the political and moral headship of a charismatic Islamic teacher; the other a society where political and religious elites were distinct estates, with the latter guardians of religious law and values. In the second type, the prince was in essence a secular ruler, although sure to respect the religious authority of the '*ulama*'.[84] Indeed, Zaghlul did adopt the role of charismatic religious leader during the 1919 revolution. Naguib Mahfouz's childhood recollections of the 1919 revolution indicate that among the *baladi* neighborhoods of Cairo, Zaghlul was regarded as a moral leader of the community, a 'shaykh'.[85] Likewise, Reinhard Schulze's study of the 1919 revolt distinguished between the millenarian movements of 'Oriental societies' and the modern political organization and ideology of the Egyptian '*afandiya*'. He observed that the effendis had expanded their authority with the formation of a modern bureaucratic state; however, the nationalism of the effendiyya did not correspond to the culture of the Egyptian masses. Among the lower classes, 'nationalistic propaganda' was made to correspond to the religious millenarianism of the charismatic leader.[86] Monarchists like Diaedinne Saleh and Zaki Fahmi rejected such appeals to the masses as dangerous. Like other conservatives within the elite, they preferred the monarchic or aristocratic political models. Conservative monarchists engaged with a very modern problem, not unlike proto-Islamists the conservatives used historical cultural concepts to construct a model that was fitted to modern politics. Thus, the historical example of Islamic societies wherein the prince consulted with the civilian elite – the latter group having a great degree of autonomy and control over civil affairs – was adapted to modern representative government.

CHAPTER 4

EFFENDIS AND NOTABLES: THE ELECTIONS

'Les Deux Saads' deceived the people. That was the opinion of an article in a French language colonial broadsheet, *La Bourse Egyptienne*, after the election of a Wafd government in early 1924.[1] Sa'd ('Saad') Zaghlul was on the one hand an effendi politician representative of bureaucrats, professionals, students in the new government schools, and all those like-minded individuals who demanded that the government recognize their rights as citizens.[2] But Zaghlul's second persona had its origins in a class of rural notables who sought first of all to protect their status as the leaders of their local communities, popularly known as the shaykh. The article emphasized the duplicity of a national leader who, by speaking in more than one idiom, conjured the fiction of the 'people' from fragmented social groupings. Colonial narratives thus sustained the negative image of nationalism as unrepresentative of the 'real' Egypt. While this was more colonial fantasy than reality, it was certainly accurate to say that the ambivalence of Zaghlul's posture was founded on the localized nature of social groupings and the cultural distance between the effendi and notable sectors of society as a consequence of the building of a modern bureaucratic state. The ambiguous national/local posture of the political leadership was a necessary adjustment to social structures. A political society at once bifurcated between effendi and notable, and also highly hierarchical in its social relations, provided an opening for the Wafd's opponents. The liberals, and subsequently monarchists also, attempted to capitalize on these social characteristics by formulating electoral laws, party organizations, and ideology that would draw power away from the charismatic leader. This chapter therefore moves from intellectual, as recounted in the previous chapter, to practical modes of shaping social relations.

According to many interpretations, the building of a modern Egyptian state involved the ruler and his administrators in the molding of a new type of political subject or citizen; or at least a new relationship between government and citizen. Diaeddine Saleh recounted this process, but it has been the subject of many studies of modern Egypt. As these studies have shown, the results were problematic.[3] To use a phrase from one study of the modern political method, it had the effect of making 'a world that would now seem to be divided in two'.[4] The modern regime created a cadre of Egyptians (effendiyya) that viewed the remainder of Egyptian society as if it were another society. In cultural works effendi intellectuals often associated the fellahin with the opposite of the modern: archaic, primitive, superstitious, disorganized, or in a word 'uncivilized', however invested with some organic or authentic attribute of the Egyptian identity.[5] The effendi had the capacity for modern political discourse, the fellah did not; therefore the fellahin had to be represented in culture, and in politics, because the fellahin were incapable of representing themselves. The process recalls Marx's observation on the rural notability of France in *The Eighteenth Brumaire of Louis Bonaparte*: 'They cannot represent themselves; they must be represented.'

The terms 'effendi' and 'notable' are problematic. While normally associated with the rural landholding class, the term notable has been applied to the wealthiest class of landholders that also constituted the elite of political society. Hence, Malcolm Yapp refers to the interwar period as 'The Years of the Notables'. The period might equally be defined as 'The Years of the Effendis' as it was those notables who had attained a modern education and thus status as effendis who organized the national political parties and formed governments. Nevertheless, those with high status normally carried the honourific title of pasha, rather than effendi, and did not belong to the 'middle class' that is normally associated with the effendiyya. The term effendi is used here in the generic sense of a cultural type, as it was applied in Egypt to a 'class' of people created by the process of modern change, particularly descriptive of social divisions in the period between the late nineteenth century and the Second World War. Through education and modernization the effendis separated themselves out from the rural notability, with the latter often viewed by effendis as little removed from fellahin culture and society. By the interwar period, the idea of the notable can thus be taken as a generic type also, as it was applied to those without a modern education and with status in their local communities, rather than the state administration. As Nathan Brown said of the rural notables, 'The group is of the village and not above it.'[6] With reference to urban social groups, historians of the Egyptian urban working class have also shown that the term for trade union, *niqaba*, was a fluid one, applied equally to unions, guilds and cooperatives, which is to say new and old labour institutions. The guilds and cooperatives had long traditions of corporate identity, specific to local neighborhoods in the cities. Often these corporate identities had a religious dimension, hence the notion of the elder or boss having the status of a shaykh or leader of a religious brotherhood.[7] These notables, urban and rural, were mostly men with status as leaders of corporate groups, whether urban quarter or rural village. The notables could enable or, if necessary, suppress the political engagement of the lower orders, which meant they were essential to national politics.

The cultural divisions were complicated by status distinctions, with the effendi attaining high status as bureaucrat and professional, whereas the *fallah* cultivator, rich or poor, had less status in the context of a modern bureaucratic regime, more so in his local domain.[8] The merging of rural notables into a political organization dominated by the effendis in the 1920s and 1930s provided one basis for political division because the effendi and notable types represented quite distinct social roles. The effendi can be defined by reference to Max Weber's sociological categorization of the typical managerial bureaucrat whose acts were directed toward 'rational' institutional ends.

The effendi was thus an exemplar of modernity. However, the typical notable led historical communities of village or urban quarter by virtue of religious education and ascribed (acquired at birth) status. The ubiquity of these role models, effendi and notable, suggests that they were ideal types: 'They are, so to speak, the moral representatives of their cultures and they are so because of the way in which moral and metaphysical ideas and theories assume through them an embodied existence in the social world.'9 The two ideal types operated according to two diverging principles; on the one hand the effendi followed the legalist-universalist script of the modern bureaucratic state and on the other hand the notables followed an 'organic' moral code, hereditary and specific to status class and local custom. The distinction is Weber's.10

The division of political society between notable and effendi was an issue central to political mobilization and social control. The effendis were more prepared by technical training to operate the bureaucratic state; as a result the effendis dominated the Wafd Party leadership. Their purpose was to impose political party organization upon society. As this process worked itself out in electoral campaigns, society broke down into constituencies that elected local notables with hereditary power, whose support for the party was conditional upon the maintenance of their status in their local communities. There was thus a potential conflict of interest. This conflict pointed, of course, to the distinction between state and community, gemeinschaft and gesellschaft, another hallmark of modern sociological theory.11 If the great transformation that came with the formation of a modern regime was the integration of the Egyptian 'fellah', effendis and notables (*a'yan*), into the old 'Turkish' (*dhawat*) political society, any split between the two types could undermine the political party organization and ultimately the 'new Egypt' conceived as a nation-state.12 The problem was compounded by the fact that the Wafd's opponents also regarded the cultural distance between effendi and notable as the best method to dominate and control political society. The first to engage in this strategy were the liberals, secondly, the monarchy. Behind each of these political eminences were the British, with a deep-seated belief in a two- party political system and an electoral landscape grounded in the predictable grades of a hierarchical society. It should be underlined that many Egyptians held similar beliefs.

The tensions within a political community composed of effendis and notables were summed up in an academic controversy discussed in the works of Roger Owen and Robert Springborg. These scholars focused on the question of whether the primary category of analysis in Egyptian politics should be the state or the family. Owen was critical of Springborg's methodology, which centred on elite social structures as the key factor in Egyptian politics. Springborg dispensed with the usual categories of political analysis, particularly those premised on ideas such as government directed toward public ends and rational or efficient administration. Rather, politics should be understood as personal power over dependent persons, with the basic mechanism of control being patronage. As Springborg argued, the political associations of Egypt were essentially unlike the occupational associations of European civil society. Instead of civil society, the important political groupings in Egypt were the descent group, extended family, tribe or religious community. Families with their origins in the rural notability monopolized a complex set of social relations, property, markets, and bureaucracy by capitalizing on personal relations of family, age cohorts, and connections through political patronage. In the introduction to his book *Family, Power and Politics in Egypt*, Springborg envisaged a methodology unbiased by European political and social theory (particularly Marxism and its influences) through a 'prosopographical' approach: the identification of the important social and political actors and their modes of political agency. As he said, political actors formed cliques (*shilla*) tied together by primordial bonds of family and friendship or else based upon the clientele of a landlord or government official. Political power was not determined by horizontal class associations, but vertical connections of the descent group, ethnic group, communal or religious associations, or graded administrative hierarchies. Politics involving the lower social stratum was therefore highly localized. The point was relevant in the national political arena also, where political actors were motivated by immediate self-interest or the interest of their political clique. Politicians sought to increase their personal power and status through control over dependents and resources.

In this manner Springborg argued that whereas Marx characterized the state as a committee for managing the affairs of the bourgeois class, in the Egyptian setting the state was autonomous from society.[13]

In sum, politics was very much reduced to material interest and primordial social bonds. The political class was defined by lordship over clients. Its power founded on monopolizing access to rewards. Politics in this form bore some resemblance to Weber's description of the politics of the pre-modern patrimonial state. Nor was it unlike the negative interpretation applied by colonial agents, who focused on factors like corruption, nepotism, and self-interest. In Weber's interpretation of the patrimonial state politics was reduced to the ruler, his family, and his 'political subjects'.[14] Another way to express this is oligarchy, a common critique of Egyptian political society voiced by colonial agents and Egyptian critics of democratization. Indeed, Roger Owen was critical of Springborg's methodology because, he said, it restored the methods of Orientalism by accentuating the role of primordial social groupings, while discounting the importance of social classes and the state.[15] In his book *State, Power and Politics in the Making of the Modern Middle East*, as distinct from Springborg's *Family, Power and Politics in Egypt*, Owen demonstrated that the state provided a new arena for politics. This was represented in the political vocabulary, where for instance the word that historically designated religious community, *umma*, was equated with the modern idea of the nation-state. Yet, Owen was sensitive to the complex and contradictory results of state formation in the modern Middle East. To a degree, Owen's analysis therefore supported elements of Springborg's conclusions by identifying, to use a term applied by Sami Zubaida, the 'specificity' of state formation in the Middle East wherein ethnic, religious, and patrimonial interests took a prominent role.[16] There was less opportunity for the state to penetrate society through the imposition of state administrative regimes, such as military conscription, tax collection, education, and a state law code to replace customary types of social regulation.[17] Ultimately, the positions of Owen and Springborg were not very far apart. Politics involved new associations and cohorts thrown up by the modern state; however, the important associations were cliques, families, and lordship over local fiefdoms, whether bureaucratic or regional.

These theories can be related to colonial and Egyptian ideology of the interwar era. The British officials in Cairo and their liberal allies were the first to identify the potential conflict between the rural and the urban or the notable and the effendi as the best weapon against the Wafd Party. A prominent liberal ideologue, Muhammad Husayn Haykal, described Egyptian society as divided along cultural lines. Haykal's account of the 1919 revolt did not refute a national narrative premised on unity; all parts were joined together as a single body, but the social body was not a collection of equal parts, not a nation of citizens, but of cultural types, gender difference, and diverse communities.[18] Haykal's theoretical works also emphasized that the national community was a composite of differing members; some elevated above others, and thus only certain sectors were 'naturally' fitted to lead.[19] This view of social relations was evident in the first electoral law drafted by the liberal government of 'Abd al-Khaliq Tharwat, which was premised on the idea of constructing an administrative regime to control the involvement of society in politics. The electoral law reflected the idea of a structured, hierarchal political landscape, with the notables acting as barriers upon the flow of political participation. As it turned out, this type of electoral process also served the political practices of the Wafd, a party of notables as much as it was a party of effendis. Indeed, the prevalent culture of patronage and communal, localized political organization was evident in the Wafd Party's organization. It is important to outline the liberal vision of social relations in the electoral law, just as it is to trace the ambiguous character of the Wafd's tactical and ideological positions in the elections. The Wafd's dependence upon patronage, elite relations, and the administrative machine provided fertile ground for a conservative, authoritarian regime premised on the very idea of graded and hierarchical social relations.

Electoral Blueprints

The graded political landscape was built into the electoral law published on 30 April 1923, as drafted by the government of 'Abd al-Khaliq Tharwat and the European legal department in the Ministry of Justice. However, this was not the first Egyptian electoral law, but rather evolved out of a long history of representative institutions in Egypt, all of which were grounded in Egyptian-Ottoman political culture. Khedive Isma'il's *majlis shura al-nuwwab* had been designed, according to Jacob Landau, to extend the authority of the ruler over the rural notables. Indeed, after the first elections the majority of the representatives in the majlis were rural notables with the status of village mayor or *'umda*. In 1870 the *'umdas* made up eighty percent of the majlis.[20] It has been argued that the interests of the ruler and the rural notables were consistent, equally concerned with maintaining elite privileges and status.[21] After 1882 the British built on the existing model. In 1883 Lord Dufferin described the 'Chamber of Notables' as composed of 'large landed proprietors, rich townspeople and village Sheikhs'. While these types, he said, were 'indifferent to the fellahin' the 'idea of the elders of the land assembling in Council around their Chief' was a tradition 'instinct with evolutionary force'.[22] The justification for a highly graded electoral landscape was Burkean in its assumptions: hierarchy fitted Egyptian political culture and ensured the survival of existing social structures, most importantly the hereditary authority of the ruler and the notability. Modern change would be long term or 'evolutionary'.

The electoral law of 1923 likewise prescribed for an electorate of notables, great and small, who were described in the correspondence of Edmund Allenby as lords over 'tenants' and 'sub-tenants'. In his analysis of the situation the electoral campaigns of prominent liberals, such as 'Adli Yakan, relied upon government patronage and popular support among rural notability: 'They [the liberals] count, through the backing of the landed classes, upon the election and support of a strong country candidate in all or nearly all of the rural constituencies, and upon a sweeping victory over the Zaghloulists.'[23] To ensure this outcome, the electoral law required that all candidates had to be domiciled in their constituencies so that the rural notable would outnumber the effendi.[24] There were property holding requirements for the electorate, but not educational qualifications because it was believed that the unlettered voter was more likely to vote for landholding notables, rather than effendi politicians. The electoral law was designed to leave the final election of deputies in the hands of a 'few' susceptible to the pressure of 'rich notables, while the elected senators were chosen from a severely restricted field'.[25] Election by the 'few' was legislated by electoral stages. The electoral law provided for a vote by universal suffrage of the male population over 21 years of age; however the election of deputies (*nuwwab*) took place in two stages and those of senators (*shuyukh*) in three stages. The first stage involved a unit of 30 electors voting for an elector-delegate of at least 25 years of age. In a second round, the elector-delegate cast a ballot for a deputy of at least 30 years of age. Therefore, the design of the electoral law was not to give citizens a direct vote for parliamentary candidates, but to construct a system of locks that controlled the flow of political participation.[26]

The new law also involved the redrawing of electoral boundaries. Cairo had eleven districts: Shubran, al-Wayli, al-Azbakiyya, Bulaq, Abdin, Bab al-Sha'riyya, al-Gamaliyya, Darb al-Ahmar, al-Khalifa, al-Sayyida Zaynab and Masr al-Qadima. Alexandria had six: Muharram Bey, al-'Attarin, al-Laban, Karmus, al-Gumrak and Min al-Basil. The governorates of the Canal Zone, Suez and Damietta had one seat a piece. Thus the urban constituencies had 20 seats out of 214 in the assembly of deputies. Typical of an agrarian economy, the system was weighed heavily in favour of the rural provinces (191 seats). The provinces – Qalyubiyya, Minufiyya, Daqhaliyya, Sharqiyya, Gharbiyya, Beheira, Giza, Beni Suef, al-Fayyum, al-Minya, Asyut, Girga, Qena and Aswan – were subdivided into electoral districts. This apparent electoral advantage for the rural notables was strengthened by the fact that the provincial districts had a clear administrative definition. In the lists of provincial districts there were as many as 105 and seldom fewer than 50 administrative sections, usually villages, in each constituency. The villages were corralled into electoral districts where a few, normally two or three, notable families dominated the local region. These families normally held the post of *'umda* and therefore operated the local administration and influenced local opinion. They could be counted upon to deliver votes to a candidate chosen by government or political party committee. Urban constituencies were less coherent in the sense of not having as clearly defined localities. Each urban district had as few as three to five defined administrative sections, although the populations were similar. Leonard Binder noted this phenomenon in his study of the elections of 1959, claiming that the distinction between the rural and urban was 'due to the unarticulated belief that the regions of the country and the village represent more meaningful or significant diversities, whereas the cities were not thought of as diverse but identical'.[27] The 'belief' was clearly articulated in the electoral law of 1923, premised as it was on the idea that the notables were the shepherds of their local flocks. The 'belief' was widespread. *La Liberté* voiced the opinion that the electoral law favoured rural 'reactionaries' over urban 'intellectuals'; however, government intelligence reports indicated that this line of criticism was not picked up by other papers, Liberal-Constitutional or Wafd, because 'the landed element was strong in every organized political body'.[28] On the same day *La Liberté* commented, 'So we remain alone to combat the feudal and medieval text evolved by the [Electoral] Commission.'[29]

Following the logic of a distinction between the organic and the legalistic types of community, the local community and the bureaucratic state, the electoral law was premised on the idea that the organic community of village or urban quarter was the base of a social and administrative hierarchy. The electoral system was constructed on an organic base, but supervised by legalistic officials. The rural electoral committees were presided over by a district commissioner, the *ma'mur*, a delegate appointed by the governor or *mudir*, and an *'umda* selected by the *ma'mur*. The village *'umda* and the shaykh of the urban quarter (*shalykh al-balad*) were responsible for drawing up the lists of electors and organizing the lists into units of 30 responsible for electing the elector-delegates. These officials also supervised the casting of ballots. In cases of illiteracy, not uncommon, the name of the chosen delegate or candidate was communicated to the president of the electoral committee. There was no secret ballot. Voting was a communal exercise, with the conscience of the individual clearly in public view, which meant in effect under the supervision of the officials and the large landholders. As reports of the elections indicated, normally the electors were securely under the thumb of the government officials and the notables, who, between the two, had already worked out the result of the vote. In the absence of such agreements, there were normally violent altercations between political party committees supporting rival claimants for election.³⁰

In the first stage of elections in 1923, 58 percent of those eligible voted. The lowest percentages were in the modernized sectors of the Canal Zone and Suez. These regions were mostly composed of migrant workers without well-established localized identities. The migrant communities were settled in 'Arab' quarters of what were largely modern, European towns. In the Canal Zone, 13.2 percent of the population voted; in Suez 22.2 percent voted. According to the logic of the electoral law, these percentages must have reflected the absence of communal identity within the modern urban social sectors. Cairo and Alexandria had of course experienced rapid social change in the modern era also. These cities were dominated by the effendiyya and the foreign colonies. They had been the site of massive demonstrations between 1919 and 1922. Yet, these cities saw the lowest percentages of voter turnout after Suez and the Canal Zone. Voter turnout in Cairo was 27.4 percent; 23.4 percent in Alexandria.

Overall percentages of the suffrage that voted by province and governorate:³¹

Sharqiyya	70.5 percent
Beni Suef	68 percent
Minia	67.2 percent
Menoufieh	65.7 percent
Fayoum	64.1 percent
Daqaliyya	64 percent
Qalubiyya	63.27 percent
Gharbiyya	62 percent
Behera	59.6 percent
Giza	59.3 percent
Assiut	53.1 percent
Girga	49.37 percent
Qena	49.37 percent
Aswan	38.68 percent
Cairo	27.4 percent
Alex	23.4 percent

Suez   22.2 percent
Canal   13.2 percent

The elections conformed to the expectations of colonial officials and their liberal allies, with the voting largely taking place in the rural sector where voters were securely under the supervision of the rural notables, unlike the cities, which had been the scene of the unruly demonstrations. As the percentages indicate, the prospect of a Wafd government was met with indifference, fear or incomprehension by the majority of the urban electorate. The figures suggest that the 'belief' that the cities constituted a less coherent political field was indeed an accurate assessment. The Wafd electoral victory was not the result of broad based popular support, but a political victory in a highly graded landscape, mostly rural, wherein the notables controlled the outcome of the vote.

Electoral Tactics

The elections were designed to put the vote in the hands of the notables, who were supposed to serve the interests of the big landholding families as represented by the Liberal-Constitutional Party. The utter failure of the liberals in the elections occasioned reanalysis of the situation. The conclusion in British commentary was not that the philosophy behind the electoral law was faulty, but that the Wafdists and the monarchists had more successfully mobilized the rural vote by exploiting bureaucratic advantage. The king threw his considerable powers of patronage behind the Wafd Party, ensuring that officials under his sway were placed at the levers of the administration. He was warned against this policy by British agents; for instance, John Scott advised the king that a Wafd victory in the elections would bring to office men without any stake in the country and therefore unlikely to adopt a conservative policy. There would be 'mob' rule. The king responded that the political future of the country would be found not to reside in radical or liberal nationalists, but in the great bulk of the rural population, which he described with the English phrase (he normally communicated in French or Italian), 'country gentlemen'.[32]

The king was confident that the deputies would be repelled by the effendi leadership of the Wafd once parliament sat. Therefore, parliamentarians would be open to royalist guarantees of stability and order. The king was thus in theoretical agreement with the British and the liberals on the nature of the Egyptian political landscape; however, he took an independent political course.

The defeat of the liberals by the allied forces of the king and the Wafd involved the politicization of the administration. The liberals and the Wafd (with royal backing) battled for control of administrative positions with the full knowledge that influence over the government electoral committees responsible for voting procedures would be the key to electoral success. Therefore, the elections involved a major shake-up of the Egyptian administration as constructed by the British and inherited by the government of Tharwat. As a result, British observers developed a political analysis that contrasted colonial bureaucratic order with democratic disorder. The reports indicate that the breakdown of administrative order was a complex process, with roots in a wartime policy that had, according to British reports, ruined the pre-war colonial system. During the First World War, the British Protectorate delegated greater powers to the *'umdas* to facilitate the provision of the British army through conscription and forced labour. This measure was to the benefit of the notables, large and small. The notables, loosened from strict bureaucratic controls, emerged as so many petty tyrants in their localities. The analysis thus sustained the idea of the tyranny of the Egyptian notability over the fellahin, with the British viewing themselves as the protectors or guardians of the fellahin. However, analysis at the British Residency was also critical of the Protectorate regime. It had been despised by all, Egyptian and British officials, as well as the fellahin. It had operated by the use of military force, whilst degrading the once respected Egyptian official class. At the same time the Protectorate regime had empowered the notables, who were loath to give up their newfound local autonomy after the war. This dynamic between the central state and the local communities complicated political contests. Thus, during the electoral campaign of 1923, the Wafd represented itself as a party of the people (the notables) vis-à-vis the central government. In the situation reports of the Egyptian intelligence service in the Ministry of the Interior (where there was British staff) the Wafd's campaign tactics were described as the breakdown of order and a drift into an uncharted area of democratic disorder.[33]

Colonial reports exaggerated democratic anarchy by characterizing the political party contests as the exploits of 'brigands' and 'adventurers' let loose by the failings of a weakened bureaucratic state. On the contrary, acts of brigandage were coordinated by the Wafdist and monarchist political opposition with the specific objective of capturing the state. Whereas liberal patronage was apparently less effective because it represented particular interests of family and clique, the Wafd and monarchists dominated the administration. Patronage as practiced by the opposition coalition was founded on centralized, national organization and planning, whereas the liberal government of Tharwat revolved around particular interests of family, friend or client; thus, the characterization of liberal patronage as 'nepotism' in British reports. The liberals gave few political speeches during the campaign and did not set up a political party organization in the districts; that is to say beyond the organizing capacity of the territorial magnate in his own fiefdom. The influence of the local notable, however rich, was undermined by the tactics of the opposition. The Wafd and king took advantage of local rivalries, pitting one notable family against another, which tended to unbalance, if not cancel, the organic style of politics at the local level. Latent regional feuds flared up in villages and districts as the possibility of political rewards were opened up to new players through the electoral process. Meanwhile, the less politically minded notables hedged their bets and waited to line up behind the likely winner of the contests.

The Wafd and monarchists set about winning the elections in a rational, bureaucratic style typical of the effendi bureaucratic cadre. The tactic was first of all to take control of the state machinery, which could then be used to ensure electoral victory. To do so, the Wafd formed links with the monarchists, who, in 1923, were battling the liberals over the final shape of the constitution. The royalist prime minister, Yahya Ibrahim, who was also Minister of Interior, was in a position to instruct the Under-Secretary of State for the Ministry of

Interior, 'Ali Pasha Jamal al-Din. The Department of the Ministry of Interior responsible for drawing up electoral districts was under the supervision of Zaki Bey Ibrashi and Mahmud Fahmi Nuqrashi. Ibrashi was a client of the king. Nuqrashi was a confident of Zaghlul. These two together subverted the electoral blueprints provided by Tharwat's government and its British advisers, drawing up the constituencies to the advantage of the Wafd's candidates.[34] A department set up in 1923 to organize the agricultural cooperatives, initially for the purpose of controlling the vote of farmers, was staffed by bureaucrats sympathetic to the Wafd-Palace opposition.[35] There was also the *'umda* and shaykhs commissions, which fell under the control of members of the Wafd and remained so until the monarchists seized power in 1925. The agricultural cooperatives enabled the Wafd to influence the smaller landholders. Likewise, the *'umda* and shaykhs commissions were in a position to influence the government electoral committees supervising the casting of ballots.[36] Altogether, these bureaucratic instruments enabled the opposition to overawe many powerful notables during the electoral campaigns.

This description of electoral tactics was drawn up by personnel at the Egyptian Ministry of Interior (including a European department), which advised the Residency on events on the ground. The Residency in turn advised the Egyptian government in Cairo and the Foreign Office in London. However, under the conditions of the 1922 declaration, the Residency could only observe without effectively policing the implementation of Egyptian government policy. Thus, reports indicated that the preferred British policy of establishing administrative order succumbed to a political party contest within the administration. Tharwat's government offered honours, positions, salaries, pensions and titles in return for the support of influential officials and notables in its campaign against the Wafd. Also, prominent liberals like 'Adli Yakan used their influence to neutralize the opposition.[37] However, the liberal campaign failed to meet expectations. A British report from April 1922 noted, 'Some of the Governors and Omdas and other provincial officials who stood by Sarwat [Tharwat] Pasha during Zaghloul's campaign complain that their services had not been adequately recognized. It will improve the Ministry's prospects in the elections ... if this complaint is remedied betimes.'[38] According to British reports, Tharwat's government filled bureaucratic positions with favourites 'to score off their enemies in the last Ministry'.[39] The administration was purged for political party reasons, which had a negative impact upon bureaucratic efficiency and long term political strategy. A report produced by the Residency on Tharwat's policy claimed that the 'Ministry gave way to nepotism and in their attempts to gain Government posts for their friends and relatives they earned great unpopularity and provoked discontent among the important administrative officials in the provinces on whose exertions the maintenance of public security depends'.[40] The British view, therefore, was that the liberal government failed to use patronage as a device to maintain the interest of the central authority over particular, local interests. For example, positions in the departments of the Ministry of Interior that required police work in the local communities were not distributed to government supporters because such positions were a source of unpopularity and therefore were not regarded as a political favour.[41] At the same time, those passed over for rewards agitated for improvement of pay and pensions.[42] Thus, as it was said, in securing the support of one person, the liberals cost themselves another fifty.[43] Most disappointed were those minor officials who had regarded the declaration of 1922 and the dismantling of British controls as a sign that hoped-for employment opportunities would be realized.

The weakening of government controls had a widespread impact upon the population. According to one informant, the 'fellahin' were no longer the 'apathetic and docile people' they had been 'a few years previous to the revolt'.[44] The Wafd successfully channeled these resentments along political lines. As the bureaucracy loosened its hold, local personalities and their followers challenged government officials through vendetta. The public security department in the Ministry of the Interior reported that local police (*ghafir*) in the provinces had fallen victim to reprisals at the rate of seven per week.[45] Wafd activists, it was said, incited the 'lower classes' to assault 'Omdehs and Notables'. 'Usually the victims are chosen from amongst personal enemies of the assailants.'[46] John Murray at the Foreign Office read these reports and noted that the responsible officials in the provinces, *mudirs*, *ma'murs*, and *'umdas*, preferred to absent themselves from the field rather than face assaults and petty battles. Indeed, even the under-secretaries of the ministries, government appointees who had replaced the out-going British officials after 1922, had, he said, fallen idle.[47]

Officials and police surrendered the political field to partisan electoral committees supporting designated candidates, mostly Wafdist. The committees mobilized the more 'rowdy' elements of the population to intervene against liberal candidates. Two liberal candidates in Sharqiyya province, Ibrahim Dasuqi Abaza and Ahmad Abaza, put forward their candidatures in the teeth of such disturbances.[48] *'Umdas* were threatened with dismissal if they did not collect votes for Wafd candidates.[49] In Asyut it was reported that the sub-*mudir* and sub-commander of police compelled the elector-delegates to sign papers in support of the Wafd candidates.[50] Mustafa al-Khayyat, local shaykh and executive member of the Wafd, entered the mosque and took the pulpit at the conclusion of prayers to deliver a political address in support of Zaghlul.[51] In Cairo and Alexandria, the Wafd co-opted the embryonic trade unions against the efforts of Kamil Husayn to establish a Labour Party. Husayn was described in government intelligence reports as 'a lawyer and shepherd of the Syndicate of Tramway Workers'.[52] A rally organized by Husayn in Cairo was broken up by a Wafd committee. In the industrial districts of Karmuz in Alexandria 'bands of roughs' attacked the political meetings of the Watani Party.[53]

The contest for control of the administration seemed to presage a more general civil conflict, which was described in British reports as endemic to the unprecedented democratic experiment in Egypt. With the formation of the ministry of Yahya Ibrahim on 15 March 1923, the British advised his government on the importance of maintaining strict hierarchical order, apparently unaware at this point that Ibrahim and the king would use their influence over the administration to deliver votes to the Wafd. Robert Furness, the Oriental Secretary at the Residency, submitted this summary of a conversation with Prime Minister Ibrahim: 'I have been rubbing into him the necessity of impressing himself on the *Mudirs*, they on the Mamours and so on (or we shall get into another period of intimidation); and he had them all up last week and talked to them properly that he must impress upon the *mudirs* their duties.'[54] But liberal nepotism had, according to British analysis, already undermined the government's authority. Thus, the *mudirs* and their subordinates had to win the favour of the 'notables, village headmen and brigands'. One British official concluded that for the Egyptian official 'the world is upside down'.[55] Authority had passed from government to local bosses. One characterization of the new political practices borrowed a term from the American democratic lexicon by describing the Egyptians as having learnt to 'filibuster'.[56]

Contemporary British reports thus described the degree to which the tactics of the Wafd-Palace coalition had upset existing hierarchies, to the detriment of the great landholding notables. Electoral contests meant that there were larger numbers of political players vying for future positions of influence. As a result, notables had to manoeuvre to establish political party connections. The ambitious politician sometimes sacrificed local connections with notables for a Wafd candidature on the gamble that a Wafd victory would bring influence.[57] In the second stage of elections, at Asyut, Jurji Khayyat defeated 'Abd al-Rahman Mahmud, brother of the prominent liberal, Muhammad Mahmud. The Mahmuds were one of the most powerful families in Asyut, yet Khayyat controlled 400 of the 465 elector-delegates in the Mahmud stronghold. The defeat of the Mahmud family reflected the power of the administrative machine, as deployed by the Wafd and monarchists, over the vested interest of notable families. The breaking of historical practices wherein the great families dominated the lesser indicated that electoral politics was not organized simply on the organic solidarity of the local community. The process was more complicated, with the effendis attempting to impose central political party control upon society.

For critics in the British colonial press, the Wafd's tactics created a 'voting market'. Many elector-delegates sold their votes to the highest bidder, with the result that many reaped a 'rich harvest'.[58] Independent journals also pointed to the deals struck between local notables, often the village *'umda*, and politicians. The power of the notable to act as intermediary or broker between the local electors and candidates was graphically displayed in a cartoon produced by the journal *Kashkul*, entitled 'Kish Kish Bey and a Free and Dashing Deputy'. Kish Kish Bey was a character from Egyptian folklore, dressed in the long flowing robe (*gallabiyya*) common to fellahin and rural notables, whereas the candidate for the assembly of deputies appeared in Western-style suit and tarbush of the effendi. The cartoon offered a caricature of an effendi candidate, Sinut Bey Hanna, who commented to Kish Kish Bey that he feared that the elector-delegates would discover that he had no hand in writing a single word of the political slogan, 'Patriotism is our Religion'. Kish Kish responded that there was no need to worry because he was happy to deliver the votes of the village of Kafr al-Ballas to Hanna and ensure his election to the assembly.[59] The cartoon from *Kashkul* reflected liberal and colonial opinion: Local notables, usually the *'umda*, were in a position to take bids from government or opposition electoral committees and then 'pledge' the votes of the district to one of the parties (or in some cases both) after accepting bribes or other forms of enticement from the political party committees. The pledges were then taken by the committees to the party leadership to be sold on a political 'market'. Becoming a Wafd candidate meant a significant investment, as much as 1,500 to 2,000 Egyptian pounds. The sale of a pledge was sometimes made to a prominent notable willing to pay; however, in many cases the Wafd Party was able to impose a candidate upon a constituency, which contradicted the idea of organic solidarity within the localities. This process also showed the complicated relationship between effendi and notable, state administration and locality.

For example Joseph Piccotto, a Jewish notable from Alexandria, was able to demonstrate that the elector-delegates of his district supported his candidacy for one of the elected seats in the senate. However, his candidature met with resistance from the Wafd leadership. Piccotto travelled to Wafd headquarters in Cairo to appeal personally to Zaghlul. He was received by Fathallah Barakat who told him he was required to pay 1,000 Egyptian pounds to stand as a Wafd candidate. Piccotto refused and offered his services to the king instead, who included him in his list of nominees to the senate.[60] Piccotto's plight was recorded in the English and French colonial press. Similarly, monarchist intelligence agents reported that this type of subscription payment to the Wafd was the 'cost' of conversion to the Wafd Party.[61] The commentary underlined the corruption, however petty, of the electoral system. Such payments also pointed to the increasing confidence of the Wafd Party organization in the latter stages of the 1923 elections.

The coalition with the Palace enabled the Wafd to dominate the administration and thus join the party machine to the power of the state. However, the importance of family connections and the notables' influence over their localities cannot be discounted. The prevalence of family networks in the larger national organization of the opposition coalition was for instance clearly demonstrated in the marriage of William Makram 'Ubayd to Aida Hanna in November 1923, the high point of the first electoral campaign. Aida was the daughter of Marqus Hanna Bey, the president of the *ahliyya* (indigenous, or in colonial parlance, 'native') bar association and a Wafd candidate for the Cairo seat of Azbakiyya. The wedding marked the political alliance of two of Zaghlul's closest supporters in the Wafd Party, as it did that of two wealthy and influential Coptic families from Upper Egypt. The list of guests at the wedding also illustrated the ramified interests of the effendi bureaucrats, rural notability, and the palace. Tawfiq Nasim was present. He was at that time acting as intermediary between Zaghlul and the king. Also attending was Hasan Nash'at, undersecretary of state in the Ministry of Awqaf. Nash'at was an effendi with close associates in the Wafd organization, particularly its militant wing. He was, however, a convert to monarchism. Three representatives of another family from Upper Egypt, the Khayyats, were present. Also there were relatives of Zaghlul, including Atif Barakat Pasha. Wafd candidates attending included of course Marqus Hanna, as well as Hamid al-Basil, Ahmad Mahir, Najib Iskander and Ibrahim Ratib. Ostensibly a religiously ceremony, the wedding also represented a family compact between Coptic notables from Upper Egypt and a political performance that demonstrated the coalition of Wafdists and monarchists. Those attending were the wheels of the Wafd-Palace political machine.[62]

Electoral Rhetoric

The liberal and colonial presses asserted that electoral misconduct was driven by personal ambition and a base desire for power. The Wafd refuted these charges by describing the liberals as a party of provincial families of 'reactionary tendencies and education – to the exclusion of the intelligentsia'.[63] Thus rhetorical flourishes during the elections represented the democratic contest as one that pitted the modern against the primordial, the effendis against the regional lords, or the virtuous against the corrupt.

A publicist in the employ of the king, Leon Castro, defended the effendis against the hereditary power of the great notable families when he recalled that the Wafd candidate for the constituency of al-Wayli in Cairo had broken the powerful Abaza family when he was the *mudir* of Sharqiyya province. Zaghlul also reminded the voters that he had fought against the tyranny of the notables when he was a reformer in the pre-war Egyptian administration. Upon his return to Egypt in 1923 Zaghlul explicitly attacked the Abazas as one of those families who chose to deliver the Sharqiyya vote to the liberals rather than to the Wafd. That the Abazas claimed Circassian origins and had historically been tied to the house of Muhammad 'Ali made them obvious targets of nationalist slogans. Indeed, a Foreign Office file from 1930 on the Egyptian political elite described the Abazas as a Circassian 'tribe', indicating that the family maintained a somewhat autonomous power base in Sharqiyya well into the twentieth century. The report said that one family magnate, 'Abd al-'Aziz Abaza, had little respect for either the Wafd or the king, and, typical of elitist attitudes, was contemptuous of the Egyptian capacity for self-government. The family put its own interests first.[64] Zaghlul's attack on the Abazas thus betrayed the sort of antipathies that existed between effendis and notables, with the one imagining the political community as a universal state (equal for all) and the other defending family power from a regional base.

In 1923, the Abazas put forward four candidates for the Liberal-Constitutional Party in Sharqiyya, all of whom lost. Thereafter, party solidarity was broken, but not 'tribal' cohesion. After 1923, Abaza family members stood for parties in opposition to the Wafd, in spite of the Wafd's power. The Abazas continued to show a preference for the Liberal-Constitutional Party. A monarchist intelligence report from 1931 showed ten Abaza family members on a list of 149 Liberal-Constitutionals running in the national elections of that year.[65]

The liberals complained bitterly of the way the Wafd used its contacts with the palace, as well as its influence over notables and officials, to seize control of the levers of the state administration. The liberal politician Tawfiq Doss made the point that in 1922 the government had been 'offered to us without our seeking it'. But, as he said, the liberal government stuck to its principles by establishing a fair and open democratic process. Meanwhile, the Wafd built up an 'artificial majority' based on 'personalities, not principles'. He cited cases where Wafd committees had assaulted and threatened candidates. In the 1923 campaign the imam of Manfalut was stopped from leading a prayer when a Wafdist forced him from the pulpit, claiming that liberals were not worthy prayer leaders. When Doss held a rally 'both for those who were for me and those who were against me', the 'soldiers of Saad' broke up the meeting. Doss bemoaned the fact that the principle of freedom of speech was enlisted by the Wafd to suppress free speech, whereas the liberals sought to persuade without influence, a sign, he said, of the true democrat.[66]

The liberal paper *al-Siyasa* claimed that in the final stage of the elections, Wafd 'terrorist bands' wandered the districts in the presence of government agents, compelling voters to pledge themselves to Wafd candidates and preventing those who would not from reaching polling stations.[67] British intelligence reports also showed that voters were asked to make oaths of fealty to the Wafd elector-delegates. These pledges, it was said, bound voters and elector-delegates to the Wafd candidates 'beyond reconsideration or recall, often by drastic methods'.[68] The acting high-commissioner in November 1923, Ernest Scott, observed that 'Zaghlulist agents, accompanied by students and "notary", have been reported as visiting the houses of elector-delegates, and practically forcing them to subscribe to a written acceptance of such candidates as the Wafd chooses to impose.'[69] In an electoral speech, Tawfiq Doss said that these methods enslaved the conscience of the voter, rather than leaving it free to make a choice on individual preference.[70]

While the liberals attacked Zaghlul for abandoning his liberal principles, the Wafd responded with manifestos accusing the liberals of influencing the elector-delegates by deception, by promises, or by threats. 'The people, however is always strong in its faith, unshakeable in its resolve, and the elector-delegates are fully conscious of the national will which they are labouring to realise under the guidance and counsels of the Wafd'.[71] Zaghlul accused the liberals of representing nothing less than privilege. As he said, 'The Wafd has no glittering gold to give, and no official posts and no personal influence of a nature to corrupt conscience.'[72] This rhetoric recalled a century of state-run patronage to the benefit of a few notable families, many of them comprising the liberal leadership. However with the king as ally, the Wafd also used bribery and the promise of rewards, alongside moral influence, to sway the voters. Those who did pay subscriptions to the Wafd did so with the expectation that they would be rewarded once the Wafd Party took power. This was at least the critique publicly thrown at the Wafd by the liberals. When the Wafd leadership denied charges made in *al-Siyasa* that prospective candidates to parliament made money payments to the Wafd, *al-Siyasa* responded with the claim that while evidence of political influence peddling was not likely to be forthcoming from the candidates, the proof would be forthcoming when parliament met: 'for those who had bought seats would not remain silent with the goods undelivered'.[73] Indeed, the king exploited this sort of resentment among notables to build up a body of political support after the election of the Wafd government.

Whereas the political machine of the liberals relied on patronage, the political capital of the Wafd Party involved influence and ideological commitment. In either case, the Wafd executive sought to control the distribution of constituencies. The Wafd executive sometimes favoured prominent notables with cash over those with a record of service to the Wafd Party, but not always. Thus, Doctor Hasan Kamil had to cede his Cairo electoral district to Najib al-Gharabali Effendi, whose political credentials were based on his organization of demonstrations in Tanta in 1919 and 1921, as well as his arrest and imprisonment in 1923.[74] However, a payment to the party treasury could secure a decree from Wafd headquarters that bestowed the rank of 'sincere patriot' and the guarantee of a sole and uncontested candidature in a constituency. *Kashkul* claimed that Shahin Siraj al-Din paid 1500 to the Wafd Party for a constituency in Gharbiyya. His candidature was challenged by a local, 'Abd al-Halim al-Biyali Effendi, a lawyer who put himself forward in the same constituency. The effendi's claim to represent the constituency was founded solely on his reputation as a 'hero' of the revolution, whereas Siraj al-Din had gold to give.[75] Wafd headquarters was obliged to pay the effendi 500 pounds and offered him instead the Wafd candidature in Old Cairo. To do so, the Wafd had to shunt aside yet another one of its supporters: Afifi Husayn al-Barbari, described in Zaki Fahmi's biographical dictionary as a 'devoted hero' (*al-batal al-mukhlis*) of the national *nahda*. Barbari gave up his candidature in Old Cairo to Biyali Effendi and in return was promised a Wafd seat in the senate.[76]

The Wafd leadership therefore had to engage in considerable brokering to build up a political party organization that included party activists and notables with local influence. These deals were not lost on critical observers among liberals or future political adversaries in the royal palace. The riposte of the Wafd was that the constitutional commission had rejected direct election by universal suffrage and introduced a 'feudal' system of election by intermediate stages, which afforded ample opportunity for pressure to be brought to bear on the elector-delegates by the government. Such pressures were clearly part of the liberals' tactics. That the Wafd also resorted to these methods resulted in controversy and political jockeying. From October, deputations of elector-delegates travelled from various electoral districts to Wafd headquarters (Zaghlul's house) for the purpose of submitting names of candidates for whom they proposed to vote.[77] A British report on the process said, 'Numerous complaints are stated to have been received by the Wafd against certain of its members on the ground that, from purely personal motives, they have been favouring, especially in the Provinces, the candidature of persons who have no claim whatever on the Wafd's support. In connection with such complaints the following are named: Fathalla Pasha Barakat, Hamad Pasha el Bassil, Mohammed Bey Abu Shady and Elwy Bey el Gazzar.'[78] When the Wafd attempted to draw up an 'Official List' of all Wafd candidates in the districts there were 'serious disputes within the Wafd itself' and 'trouble in the constituencies'.[79] As a result, the Wafd gave up on the idea of an official list and left constituencies open for the nomination of several Wafd candidates.

Ultimately, the will of the party leadership was tested by the notables in the constituencies. This provided a rhetorical opening for protests against the tyranny of the Wafd central committee. An organization was formed by the name of 'The partisans of liberty of opinion'. It consisted of Liberal-Constitutional Party, Watani Party and Wafd Party supporters. The organization claimed that the Wafd's executive leadership had too ruthlessly subordinated the wishes of the electors to what the executive considered the 'general advantage of the nation'. The chief speaker at the second meeting of the organization was Muhammad Husayn Haykal, editor of *al-Siyasa*, who dwelt on the extortionate sums levied for candidatures in the provinces and related instances of corruption. The Wafd student organizations responded by visiting the offices of Liberal-Constitutional and Watani newspapers and, with threats, prevented any further reporting on the story.[80]

Because of the fine balance between notables in the constituencies and the effendi leadership of the political organization, winning a constituency involved political brokering, not only of money, but of honour or political status. Much of the rhetoric thus involved the condemnation of self-interest while praising the selfless devotion of the patriot. The ascribed status of the notable was weighed against the effendi patriot or soldier (*jind*). Indeed given that the notable and effendi represented two types of status or honour, either type might be translated into electoral victory. The liberals defended elite status. In a speech of 13 November 1923, Muhammad Mahmud said that 'political ferment' had a 'degenerating' effect. 'It has sapped the principles of some of those engaged in politics ... . This political crisis had had a harmful effect on the character and the consciences of many people, so that now they perform any ignoble acts without feeling the least shame.'[81] Like other elitist critiques of the democratic process, 'Adli Yakan credited the Wafd leadership with purely selfish motives, the quest for personal power by any means. Zaghlul was the exemplar of this Machiavellian disposition: 'When Zaghloul saw that here was a prospect of success he could not sink his individuality for the good of the nation. Whereas the Liberals saw in electoral success the good of the nation, Zaghloul only saw his personal ambition.'[82] Yakan offered a similar analysis of the new style of politics: 'The unity which is based on the adulation of an individual will not last long. ... If we have a definite aim, it is the greatest mistake to suppose it be good policy to use any means, lawful or unlawful, to attain that end. In time of stress and change there is a danger of revolutionary ways of thinking becoming prevalent.'[83] In another speech Muhammad Mahmud defended the 'rights' of the notable. Campaigning in the village of Gharib for Isma'il Sidqi, Mahmud described Sidqi as a 'man who knows you', whereas his opponent was a 'lawyer and poet'. As it transpired, Sidqi lost his seat to the patriotic poet-effendi.[84] Patriotic status sometimes displaced the claims of established notables and signified the power of the political party organization, as well as the arrival of new political types. There was an ideological cohesion among radical nationalists that carried considerable currency, particularly in the urban electoral districts. The Wafd's best electoral results were in the cities where the radical effendi had the greatest social influence and where the least number of citizens actually voted.

The liberals were defeated in the 1924 elections, but support among the rural notables for the Wafd was not overwhelming. The Abaza family territorial base in Sharqiyya resisted Wafd hegemony throughout the elections of the 1920s and 1930s. This involved the Abazas in contests with effendi patriots, like 'Ali Shamsi, and petty notables who viewed the elections as a means to challenge the Abaza's monopoly of power in Sharqiyya. This did not necessarily mean adherence to the Wafd's policies or ideology. For instance, the Mar'i family of Sharqiyya took advantage of the electoral process to establish itself as one of the new political families of the region. Yet, indicative of the fickle temper of the rural notability, the Mar'i family abandoned the Wafd after it failed to win seats in the 1923–1924 elections. Likewise, the Abaza family hedged its bets after the weak performance of the Liberal-Constitutional Party in those elections. In 1926, Abaza representatives stood as Ittihadists, Liberal-Constitutionals and Independents. Thus, 'Ali Shamsi instructed the Wafd journals to vent the party's "hatred" for the Abazas'.[85] There were complaints that Muhammad Bey Sadiq Abaza, previously a liberal, disregarded his 'constitutional' duty to support the nation (the Wafd) by turning to the monarchist Ittihad Party. But royal patronage assured Sadiq Abaza a safe seat in parliament and thus satisfied family ambitions. Such manouevering meant that the Wafdists regarded the Abazas as corrupt, inveterate schemers.

Liberals and monarchists preferred to rely upon the patronage clientele of the great family patricians to secure electoral districts. Patronage was a safe bet, given a political structure securely founded on social hierarchies and thus, according to theory, not subject to the competitive claims that marked the Wafdist campaigns. In the elections of 1925 and 1926, the Ittihad Party delegated recruitment to notables, who carried a number of cultivators in their districts, who in their turn carried a number of tenants. Take for example an electoral list of the notables of Aswan in the Abdin files. None of the four names on the list were declared as Ittihadists, yet a note attached to the list suggested that by gentlemanly agreement the four notables would cooperate to ensure that their clienteles would collectively vote for the Ittihad candidate. The agreement was not based on ideological commitment to the Ittihad Party, although it might demonstrate antipathy to the Wafd; rather the four notables expected to profit collectively from resultant access to government patronage. Elite consensus and consequent expectation of social order inherent in such deals also pointed to conservatism, the ideological foundation of the monarchist party.[86]

To recapitulate the argument: in an organic political field, party organization and ideology constituted, according to the theory, a fiction cloaking the actual structure of politics. The rules of organic politics recognized the absolute authority of the notable within the boundaries of his locality. The electoral law of 1923 was based on this vision of social relations. Therefore, the liberals expected to dominate the vote by the exercise of government patronage through the rural notables. To counteract the liberals, the Wafd and monarchy deployed an arsenal of administrative, financial and rhetorical techniques of influence and persuasion, even if this meant opposing many powerful notables in the field. However, this opened up opportunities for the monarchists, who used similar methods in subsequent elections with some success. Also, the Wafd's liberal opponents were able to undermine the Wafd's claim to the moral high ground by pointing to its corrupt practices, which sustained the bitterness of ideological disputes between liberals and the Wafd nationalists. Finally, the elections laid bare a conflict of values at the heart of Egyptian political life. It came with the creation of a modern administration in which the notable, the lord possessing prestige and power in his own right, had to negotiate with the bureaucrats, whose legitimacy and authority was founded on control over the administration. With the introduction of democratic elections, the conflicting interests between the two took on the aspect of a contest of political values between privilege and patriotism, social rectitude and political ambition, which evolved into an ideological contest between conservatives and democrats.

Party Ideology

A comparison of the political vocabulary of nationalist historical writing and the language of electoral slogans or manifestos lays bare the duality in the political practices and ideology of the effendi leadership of the national political parties. The modern political discourse of the histories contrasts with the societal motifs and ethics of the campaign slogans. Hence *La Bourse Egyptienne* compared Zaghlul with a *jinn* or genie who took a multiplicity of forms because he spoke in these two idioms. There was the idiom of republican Europe that was directed toward the effendiyya, a type of person adept in modern political discourse. But the political discourse prepared by the effendi for social consumption was replete with religious and social meaning. Modern political ideology is enshrined in the political histories of 'Abd al-Rahman al-Rafi'i, in which political legitimacy was derived from the 'will of the people' (*idara al-sha'b* or *idara al-umma*) and by a 'movement' (*haraka*) of the 'masses' (*jamahir*), imagined as one and the same political actor, a sacred totality (*ittihad muqaddas*), with a soul or spirit (*ruh*).[87] This language is prescriptive, not descriptive, by conceiving the nation as unanimous and invested with a natural right to self-determination. It also suggests that society was organized into national associations, like political parties and other civil society organizations. Rafi'i's references to the people were like those of the French republican historian Jules Michelet. But as Georges Rude's study of the urban crowd in the French Revolution showed, the republican categories tell us very little about the actual mode or motive of political association, sometimes referred to as the structure of politics.[88] Indeed, for the Wafd leadership the dissemination of the national idea required the submission of the hierarchical and diverse structures of social relations to the politically prescriptive category of nation. On the other hand, indicative of existing social structures, there was a political vocabulary that found its relevance in moral language that represented social relations in terms of locality, gender, status, family and tribe. In practice, moral language pointed to the 'primordial' forces in apparently modern political movements.[89] Such language reflected the diverse types of political actors and their customary modes of association that hardly conformed to republican formulas of national unity or the engagement of the 'people' in the political process. Rather, large sectors of the 'people' imagined politics only according to localized notions of identity, such as the fellah or *ibn al-balad* (terms for rural and urban locals) or the leadership types that dominated these groups, like the shaykh or *futuwwa* (urban gang leader). Building on the insights of Rude, Sawsan El-Messiri argued that these micro-political types in Egypt were not political party activists, but generally were acting according to localized ideas of social values that exalted moral example, cunning or bravado. The effendis led these types, without necessarily indoctrinating or integrating them into the national movement.[90] Nevertheless, the engagement of these types in politics might bring about a cultural transformation, so that locals entered into national politics in moments of enthusiasm and even entertained a new national consciousness. Many were exalted as a national hero (*batal*) or a martyr (*shahid*). However, it is not clear that social structures such as the social authority of the notables over their communities were altered through this process of engagement.

On the contrary, the language of political manifestos suggests cultural continuity, as much as change. A term like *jihad* might refer to the sort of self-sacrifice and dedication to the cause required of the political activist in a 'movement'. *Jihad* in this sense could be indicative of cultural change, with the religious connotations sublimated. However, terms like forbidden (*haram*), referred to family or religious taboo, as well as respect (*ihtiram*), which designated the type of deference due to the notables. There were also the values that tied society together, *thiqa* and *ikhlas*, trust and devotion, which were commonly used to transfer identification from the micro-local to the macro-national realm of meaning. Thus, as Louis Joseph Cantori observed, Zaghlul appeared to the majority of Egyptians as a shaykh, a role he replicated in each locality across the 'nation', and accordingly invented, just as he represented, the national community.[91]

This correspondence between local and national was evident in Wafdist political manifestos as they appeared from the first outburst of revolutionary enthusiasm in 1919 through the election campaigning that began in 1923. Take for example a manifesto published 22 March 1922 after Zaghlul had been exiled by the British to the Seychelles and a military guard placed around the headquarters of the Wafd, which was also Zaghlul's private residence and known as *bait al-umma* (house of the nation). The manifesto was signed by the core of the Wafd Party in the absence of Zaghlul: Hamid al-Basil, Wisa Wasif, Marqus Hanna, 'Ali Shamsi and Wasif Ghali. These men were the principal organizers of collective action through covert bureaucratic channels at the ministries, government departments and schools, but they were equally concerned to mobilize a broader section of Egyptian society. Thus, the vocabulary of the manifesto identified the motive for political action with the societal values of a local community, the Sayyida Zaynab district of Cairo. Addressed from the Wafd to the nation (*min al-Wafd ila al-umma*), it read:

> Do not put down your weapons, but attack the men of steel who surround the house of the nation and prohibit the people (*sha'b*) from visiting it. The house of the nation is the fire that lights the nation (*watan*). In the house is Sayyida, the name that represents the mother of the Egyptians and the people must be faithful to her. The men of the nation must come and surround the house of her seclusion. Nor should the people countenance her separation from her husband, sent to a far land while she is

secluded in her room (*kidr*), Egyptians! Your sons and daughters were prevented from visiting her. Force and aggression can only suppress personal freedom. Indeed it can only destroy the honour of women.[92]

Although the terms *umma* and *watan* clearly signify the nation, the 'house of the nation' was associated with the local community and the familial house. Safiyya Zaghlul had taken an active role in the organization of the Wafd and as 'mother of the Egyptians' had won a public role for herself in the political leadership. However, the men who wrote the manifesto used her as a symbol of family honour. The family obligation to safeguard the honour of women was transferred into a public and political obligation to resist the British and the government of Tharwat. In addition, the term *Sayyida* referred to one of Cairo's most popular saint festivals, that of Sayyida Zaynab, the granddaughter of the Prophet Muhammad and daughter of 'Ali. Zaghlul's home constituency was named after her, which provided an additional means to engage and mobilize the community. The idea of family and religious honour created a link between the political leadership and the 'mass' or at least to the people of this Cairo quarter. The connection between communal values and nationalism gave the latter social meaning, which according to Reinhard Schulze it otherwise lacked among the wider population. But family solidarity was a value around which the community could unite and other influences rejected. Separating women from the Europeans and their collaborators was separating and preserving an Egyptian cultural identity, conceived at the same time as national, familial and religious. In short, the manifesto normalized republican formulas by paying deference to the moral authority of the patriarchal family and religion. The local notables could thus mobilize their communities in an effendi-led national campaign, which had the effect of resolving the conflict identified by Schulze.[93] The Wafd leadership, through such ideological statements, had remarkable success in the integration of diverse classes, communities, corporations, religions, men and women, into national politics.[94]

To communicate their political message to the Egyptian population it was necessary for effendis to combine nationalism with the value systems of local communities. However, the dominant discourse in the

Wafd manifestos was nationalist, muting without erasing the ideas or values associated with family, tribe, or religious community. A manifesto published in *al-Ahram* on 9 January 1924 illustrates the point. It was entitled 'The Nation's Conscience and the Elections' and addressed to *a'yan* and *'umdas*, which was to say rural notables. The manifesto said that during the elections there would be a 'group of people' (presumably, the government or liberal party) claiming that a 'notable' (*al-'ayn, al-dhat*) or personality (*al-wajih*) had promised the community's votes to a particular candidate. It went on to claim that the *'umda* would assure the villagers that the votes of the village would be in favour of the chosen candidate. The manifesto thus reflected the 'belief' that voting followed the logic of communal consensus; the village acted as a corporate body following the edicts of the notable. Yet at the same time, the manifesto underlined the new, nationalistic ethic by warning the villagers that they (the elector-delegates) had made pledges to safeguard the affairs of the nation, not their personal interests. Patriotism, it read, was a crucial value now that the 'ship of state' was in a sea of troubles, tossed to the left and right. The ship needed a captain, *rabbani*. The manifesto concluded with the Qur'anic verse, 'The slaves of the virtuous shall inherit the earth.' Religious ideas emphasized the message that the Wafd represented the people and the government represented privilege. The concept of political community was redefined according to the patriotic idea, although always keeping in view the necessity to fit nationalism within familiar social or cultural references.[95]

A Wafd manifesto published in *al-Ahram* on 10 January 1924 underscored the submission of the individual to the national struggle. However, the manifesto is loaded with religious terminology. The manifesto made a call to awaken the conscience of the nation in the coming elections (*damir al-umma wa al-intikhabat*) by appealing to the active youth of Egypt (*ila shabab misr al-nahid*), its perseverance and efforts (*ijtihad* and *juhud*). The dominant idea was of a political ethic or conscience in so far as the manifesto expressed the obligations of the individual to the nation, particularly the political virtue of activism. The idea of a new, active generation recalled the ideology of Mustafa Kamil, which juxtaposed a new generation to the old status classes. The manifesto thus emphasized community and action, to instill a sense of movement. But the idea of an active nation had strong religious undertones. *Ijtihad* was a term used by Islamic reformers to refer to the interpretation of religious texts, but in the context of the manifesto was closer to the idea of effort or movement. Juhud evoked the idea of *jihad*, although it literally meant efforts; nevertheless it appeared in the text alongside other terms such as *kifah* and *tadhiya*, which meant struggle and self-sacrifice. It was therefore difficult to ignore the religious imagery, although in this context such themes pointed to the need to activate (*nashita*) the national spirit (*al-ruh al-qawmiyya*).[96]

The debt of the radical Wafdists to the legacy of Mustafa Kamil was clear in such manifestos and would be echoed in the national histories of 'Abd al-Rahman al-Rafi'i. Yet, it is remarkable to what degree the Wafd's electoral politics also fitted within historical social custom and cultural beliefs. Consensus was prized, factional conflict, or even individuality, despised. Personal honour was highly valued. Electoral meetings involved public displays of devotion, loyalty and solidarity. Elections where Wafd candidates stood unopposed were celebrated as a demonstration of political consensus. Rather than this being viewed as against the spirit of democratic contests, it was regarded as an essential testament to the candidate's excellent character. Forty Wafdists secured election by this type of unanimous acclamation in 1924, referred to as *tazkiyya*. Evidently, the idea of an electoral majority was a novel one. The term majority itself was not an established concept in Arabic; thus, the relatively new terms of *akthariyya* or *aghlabiyya* were used. The national narrative of 'Abd al-Rahman Rafi'i referred to unanimous election as *aghlabiyya mutlaqa* (absolute majority), erasing specific references to the practice of *tazkiyya*.[97] Yet given the terminology used by the Wafd, it is not unreasonable to compare unanimous election to historical practices in Islamic cultures. The term *tazkiyya* had the historical meaning of the verification of integrity of character or honourable record. Islamic *fiqh* law involved a process of investigating the character (*tazkiyya*) of witnesses to judge a case and ascertain truth. The concern with personal character in electoral politics seemed to reflect this historical practice. Moreover, virtue or an established good character was historically an indicator of social cohesion and thus political community.[98]

In electoral campaigns the Wafd's ideology was a mix of social and religious values, which were however subsumed under nationalist, political objectives. In one manifesto Zaghlul beseeched the elector-delegates to ignore the temptations of 'wicked people'. He warned that 'you will grieve Allah and his prophets, will degrade your land and insult the national martyrs. Furthermore you will stand convicted before your ancestors as sons devoid of obedience, and will go down in posterity as sons unworthy of your ancestors.'[99] Such manifestos were described as Qur'anic in British intelligence reports produced at the Residency, yet the ethic expressed was not simply Islamic, but societal, speaking of family bonds across generations. Another Wafd manifesto reproduced in the French press heralded election day as a great awakening in Egypt. The manifesto concluded with the warning that whoever soiled his hands with money from the hypocrites committed a crime against the family, the country, mother Egypt and the martyrs, the sincere and true adorers of God.[100] Such language, together with the method of elections, indicates that social and religious values underpinned political groupings. Patriotism was the dominant theme; the inclusion of religious and social themes widened the appeal and meaning of nationalistic slogans. In subsequent election campaigns the monarchists reversed the imagery, by making religion the dominant idea and the overarching symbol of the political community. Likewise, monarchists asserted that the notables were representative of Egyptian political society to the exclusion of the radical effendis. This was a tactical move, but also suited monarchist or conservative ideological beliefs. However, it should not obscure the understanding that the basic political tactic of the monarchy was directed toward capturing control of a bureaucratic state.

In sum, electoral politics involved control of the bureaucracy and 'meaningful' social relations. Effendis and notables were therefore essential actors in making the population vote. Liberals were determined to uphold 'meaningful' social relations wherein local communities were corralled by their shepherds, the notables, out of a concern for moral propriety, social status and material interests, or, in other words, to sustain the elite structure of society. 'Meaningful' social relationships were represented in patriarchal or paternalistic language, a sure foundation for political order, according to the liberals and the British. The radical nationalists, however, challenged this view of social relations by rhetorically defying the 'rights' of the notables; however, electoral practices indicated that the Wafd combined the ideological 'fiction' of the nation with the functional language of social ethics because the Wafd Party was also largely composed of notables. Yet the cultural or ideological tension between the effendi administrator and the local notable was clearly evident in the election campaigns, compromising the nationalist idea of the nation-state as an undifferentiated sacred totality. It must have been instructive for conservatives to witness the way that the authority of the notables was able to draw power away from the effendi leadership of the Wafd. Indeed, the monarchist campaign as it emerged after 1923, with tactical support from the liberals and British, was premised on the idea that effendis and notables, radicals and conservatives, diverged on basic ideological or cultural orientations.

CHAPTER 5

RADICALS AND CONSERVATIVES: THE PARLIAMENT

A persuasive interpretation of politics in the interwar era is known as the 'politics of the notables'.[1] From that point of view, party and ideological politics was a secondary if not a negligible factor in any interpretation of political behavior. Politicians were relatively autonomous players, having their own political capital through their control over local fiefdoms, which were easily transferred into power through the democratic electoral process by means of patronage. Political parties were largely vehicles for the patrician's personal power. Nomination for election was recognition of the notable's status in the local community, whereas national party politics had very little impact on politics at the local level. Politics was not class based, nor were political parties composed of a broad base of the population. Rather than class, according to this theory imagine society divided into segments representing the local power holdings of the patricians or notables. This type of political landscape is a fertile ground for the application of political patronage, if carefully distributed to create blocs or coalitions that supported one of the notables as over-lord or first among equals. John Waterbury applied the term bet-hedging to describe the motives of political actors in this kind of landscape. Alliances were almost always provisional, based on a calculation of cost/benefit, but never uncompromisingly made on political principle or ideological orientation.[2] The politics of the notables, or the elite model of social scientific analysis, is remarkably similar to British colonial analysis of Egyptian politics. It was the preferred political model of the liberals, who collaborated closely with the British. Indeed, although the liberals failed in the elections, the Wafd's electoral victory was dependent upon the power of local lords over their localities, proving the utility of the elite model of political relations. That model was sustained in Egypt in the post-1919 period. Thus the revolutionary events of 1919, and its aftermath can only be said, in the words of Louis Joseph Cantori, to have amounted to a 'mild social revolution' that brought greater numbers of middle stratum notables into political society.[3]

Yet, ideological factors should not be dismissed. There was an absence of consensus on the basic rules of the political game, which had been apparent from the first split in the Wafd Party in 1921. Although modernist, the radicals of the Wafd Party developed a cultural nationalism that rejected the evolutionary thinking of the liberals, looking instead to internal signs of Egypt's cultural identity, such as patriarchy and Islam, to formulate a kind of ethnic nationalism. This orientation promised to appeal to a larger sector of Egyptian society. For the liberals, it marked a betrayal of a modern, secular ideal of political community.[4] Ethnic or cultural nationalism also opened the door to religious nationalism. In the period after 1919, these trends were all visible, particularly so in the contests that emerged with the convening of the first parliament in 1924.

The Wafd parliamentary majority was unstable, as will be demonstrated in the following account of the first elected Wafd government. A conventional explanation for the weakness of the Wafd government was that it was subject to British interference through a kind of divide and rule tactic. But to implement such tactics, the British exploited divisions that already existed within Egyptian political society; they did not invent or even control those forces. The turn to ethnic or cultural nationalism opened opportunities for the Wafd's opponents on cultural and social issues, notably the question of the participation of women and the masses in the political process. The disquietude occasioned by these questions suggests that political parties were more than vehicles for the political interests of elite politicians and their British collaborators. British tactics initially centered on the Liberal-Constitutional Party. When the liberals failed, the British were willing to countenance a more robust monarchy as a counter to the Wafd. But monarch as autocrat was not a colonial policy objective, nor were the bitter ideological disputes between religious nationalists and the liberal constitutionalists that manifested themselves after 1924. On the other hand, monarchists were ideologically oriented toward autocracy and the liberals toward elitism. Consequently, there were significant efforts to adjust the political system from the democratic toward the autocratic and aristocratic models. This took the form of a constitutional struggle, largely between the king and the Wafd, with the liberals maneuvering so as to steer the state along a moderate course.

Rather than legislation on social or economic problems, the Wafd Party in power concentrated on its organizational strength, party unity and its monopoly of bureaucratic positions. P. J. Vatikiotis flatly stated that Zaghlul's record in office did not 'justify faith in him'.[5] Jacques Berque also noted the autocratic character of the Wafd and the absence of meaningful legislation.[6] In his estimation, the failure of the democratic experiment was that it was a 'model rather than a functioning instrument'.[7] Berque's argument mirrored the analysis of Diaedinne Saleh, who said that the liberal constitution cloaked the actual form of the political body. Indeed, the first Wafd administration was the beginning of what would be described by the liberals and supporters of the king alike as democratic tyranny. Nevertheless, Berque observed that there was a deputies' report on the misuse of land by concessions to religious endowments and public utilities. The former was an area monopolized by the monarchy, the latter the preserve of colonial business; thus the Wafd initiated a direct attack at royal and colonial privilege from the outset. Also, the passing of a new electoral law in August 1924 was a declaration of the Wafd's democratic principles. The law provided for election by universal suffrage of all men over 21 years of age, voting for deputies in one stage rather than two. Senators were elected in two stages, rather than three.[8] These reforms indicate that the Wafd was a populist party committed to democratic elections; however, women were excluded because of the

Wafd's concern not to show any disrespect for religious or patriarchal values. Such moves disappointed the radicals and hardly served to dispel the concerns of the conservatives. To follow these contests, this chapter traces the attempt of the Wafd leadership to retain its grasp on power, beset as it was by disputes on treaty negotiations and cultural issues from the left and right of the political spectrum. These pressures led to the fracturing of the Wafd Party and the formation of a conservative political party.

Wizara al-Sha'biyya

The government's official journal announced the formation of the first 'people's ministry' (*wizara al-sha'biyya*) on 29 January 1924. The ministry's populist credentials were more declamatory than real. There were 196 Wafdists, 15 liberals, and 3 Watani deputies in the assembly of deputies; however, although the Wafd Party had 90 percent of the seats, it had only about 50 percent of the popular vote.[9] Moreover, electoral victory had depended upon a coalition with the monarchists. As a result, the king could pressure Zaghlul to exclude some of the more radical Wafdists from the cabinet. For instance, the king blocked the appointment of 'Ali Shamsi Bey. The people's ministry was therefore a coalition of the radical core of the Wafd (Mustafa al-Nahhas, Marqus Hanna, Wisa Bey Wasif, and Najib al-Gharabali Effendi) and politicians under the sway of the king (Tawfiq Nasim) or else at least of conservative tendencies typical of elite political society (Muhammad Sa'id).[10] Likewise, the solidarity of the Wafd's majority in parliament was illusory. From the first sitting of the parliament, there was potential for division, as the English colonial press predicted, between those 'discontented with the existing state of things and those with a distinctive distrust of change'.[11]

The leadership of the Wafd Party was dissatisfied with a constitution that limited the powers of elected representatives of the people. Thus, Zaghlul asserted the power of the elected ministers over hereditary authority in a statement in the official journal that announced the formation of the ministry. It said that an act whereby the king invested power in the government should not be understood to repudiate

Egypt's natural right (*haqqaha al-tabi'i*) to national sovereignty. The Wafd's preference for French republican models was apparent in the assertion that a constitutional government should be founded on the 'will of the people' as represented by an elected assembly and not a concession or privilege granted by royal decree. The people's ministry went on to say that the elections demonstrated the consensus (*ijma'*) of the nation. The deputies placed their trust (*thiqa*) in the Wafd Party and the natural right of Egypt and the Sudan to complete independence. Previously, the nation, it read, viewed the government as the prey regards the hunter, but it was necessary to replace mistrust with confidence, to reduce struggle between individuals and families, and to unite races and religions.[12] The rhetoric of 'natural right' in the speech had two dimensions. It clearly signaled to the British that the new government would reject on principle the 1922 unilateral declaration in so far as it limited Egyptian independence and effectively separated the Sudan from Egypt. But beyond the struggle between Egyptian nation and imperial power, there was the question of political authority and where it was invested – in the nation or the monarch. This was a fundamental constitutional issue that set up the conflict between the king and the ministry.

The first monarchist counter-stroke came during the convening of parliament on 15 March 1924. The speech from the throne had been drafted in a committee, but the final version was composed by Zaghlul. Controversy ensued when Zaghlul removed references to the Sudan from the final text. The king won considerable political capital when he avoided reading the speech himself and, by default, forced Zaghlul to deliver the address. The sessions of parliament that followed resulted in uproarious debates, led by Amin al-Rafi'i of the Watani Party on the language of the throne speech. A group of 40 deputies led by Ahmad Muhammad Khashaba lined up behind Rafi'i, which amounted to a split in the Wafd to the advantage of the Watani Party. The bloc demanded that the government restore the references to the Sudan that had been in the original draft of the speech. The demand was punctuated with the cry, 'Long live the King of Egypt and the Sudan.'[13] The king thus exploited the question of the Sudan to divide the Wafd Party.

Zaghlul attempted to redress the damage with a speech wherein he reminded the deputies that the speech from the throne required interpretation (*tafsir*) because it was the responsibility of the ministers to judge if the statements were in accordance with the opinion of the deputies. It would be vain to accept words without understanding. The purpose of *tafsir* was to clarify and, by doing so, challenge the 'adversary'.[14] Zaghlul thus attempted to unite the deputies against a common enemy, although his speech was vague as to whether that enemy was the king, the British, or a sinister combination of the two. By implication Zaghlul suggested that these forces, but perhaps primarily the king, was the source of political discord: 'We, the ministry, are not foreign to you, we are part of you.'[15] Zaghlul also instructed the deputies on parliamentary procedure in an attempt to impose order on the sessions. Apparently many of the deputies found these lectures unconvincing. The bloc of forty, mostly Wafdist deputies, called for a 'statement of principle' from Zaghlul on negotiations with the British. Rafi'i argued that negotiations with the British implied acceptance of British terms, including the separation of the Sudan from Egypt. 'Ali Shamsi, who like many Wafdists had previously been a member of the Watani Party, attacked Zaghlul for his supposed conciliatory attitude toward the king. Denied a seat in the ministry, Shamsi had an obvious grievance against Zaghlul.[16]

Meanwhile, the Wafd leadership attempted to stifle the dissenters. Amin al-Rafi'i's views were published in the Watani Party newspaper, *al-Akhbar*. The government responded by having the public prosecutor's office use the press law drafted by the government of Yahya Ibrahim to prepare a case against the Watani mouthpiece. The paper responded with articles accusing the Wafd government of suppressing free debate. It was a curious episode given that *al-Akhbar* had within the previous year condemned the royalist government of Yahya Ibrahim for passing laws designed to repress political dissent. These were now instruments of the Wafd Party.[17] Meanwhile, the Wafd student committees organized attacks upon the offices of *al-Akhbar*. There were shouts of 'Down with the Sudan' and Amin al-Rafi'i was denounced as a 'traitor'. Other opposition papers were also targeted.[18] These events cost Zaghlul support among liberal-minded Egyptians, a significant sector of elite Egyptian political society, in spite of the failure of the Liberal-Constitutional Party in the elections.

The members of the opposition bloc in parliament were motivated by nationalistic issues, favouring as they did an uncompromising position in treaty negotiations. Yet, the bloc also represented a distinct regional and cultural dimension in Egyptian political society. The bloc was composed of notables from Upper Egypt. These notables exercised considerable leverage over the party because they controlled so much of the rural vote. The notables of Upper Egypt were fewer in number in relation to the total population of their districts and had a more pervasive influence over their constituents because there was less competition for positions of political leadership.[19] In addition, whereas Lower Egypt was more integrated into the state bureaucratic structure and thus came more strictly under centralized control, this was not true of Upper Egypt. The deputies from Upper Egypt were more independent. They could more easily threaten to take their constituencies to the opposition. Indicating their relative autonomy, these deputies successfully put forward a candidate for the vice-presidency of the assembly against Zaghlul's favourite, Wisa Wasif. The bloc's candidate was Ahmad Muhammad Khashaba, a notable from Asyut, who defeated three other candidates, including Wisa Wasif, Hamid al-Basil, as well as the liberal candidate, Tawfiq Doss. Khashaba therefore put the 40 deputies at the service of Rafi'i and 'Ali Shamsi to form a bloc in opposition to treaty negotiations. However, the notables were not only motivated by the treaty issue. Political motivations blurred into the cultural: the notables were resentful of the power of the urban effendiyya at the core of the Wafd Party, many of whom, like Wasif, were Coptic Christians. This cultural dimension of Egyptian politics was depicted in a cartoon in a popular journal, *Kashkul*, entitled, 'The illiterate deputies take their Parliamentary examination'. The parliament was portrayed as a classroom. Zaghlul appeared as headmaster dressed in the effendi attire of suit and tarboosh, lecturing an unruly 'class' of rural notables dressed in *gallabiyya* and turban. The cartoon played upon cultural differences between the Westernized effendis and rural notables, with the latter clearly suspicious or contemptuous of the effendiyya. The evidence would seem to suggest that politicians could manipulate cultural differences between effendi and notable to build political factions. Political opposition with a basis in cultural differences found its expression on the issue of foreign policy (Rafi'i) and the powers of the king (Shamsi). In each case the deputies from Upper Egypt rallied to challenge the power and authority of the Wafd executive, as represented by Zaghlul.[20]

One way to assess the impact of cultural attitudes upon national politics is to consider the reaction of political society, especially the Wafd Party, to feminist demands for women's emancipation. Feminist activism had complex cultural and political ramifications. Huda Sha'rawi, founding member of the Wafdist Women's Committee and the Egyptian Feminist Union, had been active in promoting women's rights from 1919. In 1922 she tried to influence the drafting of the constitution. In June 1923 there were reports, mostly in the European press, of Sha'rawi, Nabawiya Musa and Zeza Nabarawi meeting a deputation of female pupils from government schools. The speeches at the meeting blamed British educational policies for the absence of schooling for Egyptian girls and women. At the same time, Sha'rawi's comments to the press underlined the favourable reception her work received among religious notables.[21] Other issues discussed by the Egyptian feminists were the raising of the legal age of marriage to not less than 16, the financial obligations of parents to their daughters, as well as greater social mobility for women.[22] Yet, there were few reports of these activities in the Arabic press, indicating perhaps that feminist demands were politically sensitive. When a feminist delegation presented its views to Prime Minister Yahya Ibrahim in July 1923, there was open hostility expressed on the part of a 'certain sector of al-Azhar'.[23] Religious opinion found a voice in the political journals: 'The reform of the law of marriage and divorce, and the limitation of the husband's rights in regard to the latter, are the business of theologians, not social reformers.'[24] In an article in *Wadi al-Nil*, it was noted that Egyptian opinion was suspicious of the influence of European feminists upon Egyptian women, regarded as foreign interference in questions of Islamic reform. Yet, the article concluded: 'Nevertheless, the present time is perhaps opportune for breaking certain chains, these being probably the invention of theologians and other meddlesome persons, whereas the religion of Allah is all for tolerance, and its commandments are based on common sense.'[25]

Such commentary suggested that opinions on feminism and Islam were divided. Huda Sha'rawi's activities therefore placed the Wafd Party in a difficult position. In the event, the Wafd leadership chose to compromise on its liberal and Islamic reformist principles in deference to the opinions of its broad base of support among the notables, particularly the middle stratum with less exposure to such manifestations of Egyptian modernity. The phenomenon was recalled by Sha'rawi in her memoirs where she recorded that Wasif Ghali attempted to dissuade her from publicly unveiling at the port of Alexandria in July 1923. As Wasif Ghali said, 'The people would never accept it.' The unveiling of Huda's face (not hair) occurred on the ship that returned Zaghlul to Egypt after his exile. But while Zaghlul was supportive of women's emancipation on principle, his own wife, Safiyya, disembarked the ship wearing a face veil.[26] Sha'rawi's memoirs indicate that Zaghlul and Ghali were aware that prevalent cultural values did not correspond with their own. Unveiling could be accepted on liberal principle, but not in society. At political gatherings and rallies during the electoral campaign of 1923, women were carefully segregated from men, sitting in separate marquees, and veiled.[27]

Sha'rawi was frustrated that such restrictions were imposed upon women, hence her agitating early in the electoral campaign during meetings with the prime-minister and the shaykhs of al-Azhar. At the opening of parliament in March 1924, she led a protest demanding the vote for women. The Wafd Party stalled in its reform of the electoral franchise and ultimately revised the electoral law in August 1924 to the exclusion of women. In response, Sha'rawi pressured the Wafd leadership by exploiting treaty negotiation issues. After a debate in parliament on 25 May, Sha'rawi rebuked Zaghlul for failing to make an unequivocal statement concerning the status of the Sudan. Sha'rawi, like Shamsi and Rafi'i, had her own motives. She did not renounce her commitment to the national cause as a result of the Wafd Party's ambivalent position on women's issue. Instead, she became a vocal critic of Zaghlul on nationalist issues, placing the women's movement securely on the side of unflinching patriotism while challenging

Zaghlul's commitment. The contest between Zaghlul and Sha'rawi was depicted by *Kashkul* in a cartoon that showed Zaghlul as an old, tired organ grinder parading in the street, whilst Sha'rawi leaned from the window of her residence emptying a slop bucket on his head. The image enraged Zaghlul, who had the editor of the journal arrested and imprisoned.[28] The cartoon is noteworthy because the image itself reinforced patriarchal notions of women's place within the home, as opposed to aging patriarchs, who paraded in the street.[29] Nevertheless, the cartoon indicated that Sha'rawi would make Zaghlul pay a political price for his retreat from liberal principle on gender issues. The constitutional controversy and electoral processes had made patriarchy more than just a system of cultural values, but a political issue that fitted into national debates.

Radicals like Sha'rawi, Shamsi, and Rafi'i pushed Zaghlul toward a more uncompromising position in negotiations with the British, but by radicalizing his position, Zaghlul alienated others. The problem was noted in British intelligence reports during the early months of the Wafd government, which showed that Zaghlul had adopted a conciliatory posture toward the British as he had with the king. He was therefore subject to accusations of 'moderatism' from the radicals.[30] A moderate position was increasingly hard to sustain after the convening of parliament when Zaghlul came under pressure from political opponents both within and outside of the Wafd Party. By April, Zaghlul's position was tenuous. In a conversation with Allenby, he described the parliamentary opposition as 'tres rouge' and said that the radicals 'bound his hands' in any future treaty negotiations.[31] The reports produced by Allenby and his staff at the Residency did not advise the British government to manipulate the actions of the radical opposition to ruin the Wafd government; that would be the strategy of the monarchists. Rather, Allenby reported to the Labour Prime Minister and Foreign Secretary, Ramsay MacDonald, that Zaghlul would overcome the radicals in the parliament if the British government made concessions in treaty negotiations. He advised the government to withdraw British troops from the Nile Valley, Alexandria and Cairo, and concentrate forces in the region of the Suez Canal. He also suggested conceding sovereignty of the Sudan to Egypt. These reports suggest that Allenby and Zaghlul had come close to finding common ground for negotiations. The problem was that sectors of British and Egyptian political societies did not favour compromise. A War Office committee on imperial defence advised the establishment of air bases at Heliopolis and Helwan, which were suburbs of Cairo. Meanwhile, the Foreign Office denied that Allenby's private discussions with Zaghlul on the treaty negotiations had any bearing upon government policy.[32]

Alongside bleak prospects in any negotiations with the British, the Wafd leadership had to contend with an unruly political base. Reports produced by Residency staff credited political disorder to a toxic combination of political corruption and revolutionary radicalism. Some parliamentarians had spent as much as 2,000 Egyptian pounds to gain a seat. For many, their first concern was to profit from that investment. Indeed, according to the logic of the rights and obligations of the patrician, the notables owed it to their local constituents to repay faithful followers in the home constituency with services or spoils of office. Therefore many notables remained relatively autonomous from the political leadership of the party and were more interested in satisfying their own, localized interests. It was reported that the majority of Wafdist deputies had opposed Zaghlul's selection as prime-minister because they believed this would involve him in questions of international relations and distract him from domestic issues, such as the distribution of bureaucratic positions or the flow of other forms of state largesse.[33] The British adviser to the Egyptian Ministry of Education, Reginald Patterson, distinguished between 'dedicated' and 'undedicated' members of the Wafd Party. The 'undedicated' belonged to those sectors of Egyptian society that had 'always been jealous of education'. Patterson observed that although the edifice of modern Egypt had been largely constructed by British staff, it had always relied upon the support of Egyptian families and these had come to represent an influential social body, what he called 'educated Egypt'. However, the 'undedicated' were largely motivated by political rewards, not bureaucratic routine and efficiency, nor even the struggle for complete independence.[34]

On the other hand, Patterson reported that the activities of the 'dedicated' Wafdists also had a negative impact on bureaucratic efficiency. Particularly the ministries of Interior and Education, which were equally vital for the maintenance of bureaucratic order, had 'deteriorated' as a result of the imposition of Wafdists carrying the 'badge of allegiance'.[35] As he said, the 'dedicated' deputies occupied the government offices and issued orders without any consultation with the responsible bureaucratic officers. The new modus operandi was for the deputies to receive payments from supplicants to sponsor various types of petitions. Armed with these petitions the deputies compelled *mudirs* to carry through orders (for example diverting water resources) under the threat of dismissal. Water and other government services were used as weapons against liberal sympathizers in the bureaucracy or notables sympathetic to the liberals. Many officials resigned their positions rather than face these pressures. Others were purged. Hilmi Isa Pasha, formerly *mudir* of Gharbiyya, was replaced with a Wafdist, who then fired Isa's staff. Muhammad Mahmud was condemned in parliament and a new sub-*mudir* appointed to his home constituency, Asyut, with the purpose of dismantling his local power base.[36] The rural estates of the *mudirs* of Gharbiyya and Minufiyya were attacked by groups carrying revolutionary banners calling for the redistribution of land to the fellahin. These assaults upon officials were clearly politically driven. Typical of colonial narratives, Patterson said that with the dismantling of bureaucratic order, democratic anarchy ensued. As he said, what had previously been government by 'superior order' or the advice of the British gave way to the badge of allegiance and the political ticket.[37]

When Zaghlul radicalized his position, he placed his political fortunes in the hands of the 'dedicated' Wafdists and abandoned the 'moderatism' and coalition-building that had marked his politics in the early months of office. Student committees, previously restrained, were unleashed to stage demonstrations during the festivities marking the king's birthday in April. Likewise, fellahin were involved in assaults upon the rural estates of liberals in March and April. There was also increasing activity among the labor unions of Cairo and Alexandria. Zaghlul seemed to endorse these activities with a speech to the organizers of the tramway workers union when he praised the work of 'Abd al-Rahman Fahmi, who had taken over the political mobilization of the unions after the nascent Labour Party had been crushed.'[38] Zaghlul identified the Wafd Party with the working classes in the speech, referring to the working class as the *ra'a*, or *canaille* as it appeared in the French translation. *Ra'a* had had the derogatory meaning of riff-raff in Egypt's elite political discourse, but Zaghlul used the term to identify the Wafd Party with the commoners and restore his image as the leader of a radical revolutionary movement. Zaghlul claimed that the class of commoners (*tabaqa al-ra'a*) was the most numerous and had a 'natural' attachment to the principle of patriotism (*mabda al-watani*). The lower classes had a political devotion that the upper classes lacked. In his rhetorical declaration 'I am one of you,' Zaghlul identified his party with the 'people'.[39] Zaghlul also praised 'Abd al-Rahman Fahmi for his dedication to the national cause – which 'you venerate' (*tuqaddasun*) – by his steadfast devotion to it. It is significant that Zaghlul concluded this speech by defending his position against those 'who say that one should not honour persons ... but rather that one should honour principles. This is wrong. Because principles do not exist except in persons, principles are meaningless when abstracted from persons.'[40] According to this logic, Zaghlul and his ring of effendi activists in the Wafd leadership co-opted working class organizations into national politics; thus, the effendis no more imagined that workers would transfer loyalties from patrons to labour organization any more than that the fellahin would form autonomous communes. It is unlikely that Zaghlul's rhetoric was directed at workers (none were present at the meeting). Rather such language was designed as a challenge to the British, the liberals and the monarchists because even a limited rhetorical allusion to radical working class politics was a dangerous assault upon the values of elite political society. Liberals and conservatives certainly did not underestimate the implications of the speech in the context of the recent student demonstrations in Cairo, the labour rallies in Alexandria and Cairo, or peasant assaults upon notables in the provinces. Allenby noted the revolutionary implications of Zaghlul's speech when he reported on Zaghlul's reference to the divergent roles of the 'Pasha class' and the 'workmen' in the national struggle.[41] In the opposition press, Zaghlul was dubbed 'King of the riff-raff'.[42] *Al-Siyasa* viewed Zaghlul's speech as a 'direct incitement to

Bolshevism and as being designed to stimulate class hatred.'[43] Shortly afterwards, an unknown assailant attempted to assassinate Zaghlul.

Zaghlul's compromises with the king and other members of the established ruling group from January 1924 had been designed to improve his chances in bilateral negotiations. But a moderate position was increasingly hard to sustain after the convening of parliament, when he came under pressure from political opponents both within and outside of the Wafd Party. Subject to accusations of 'moderatism' and the absence of meaningful concessions on the part of British government, Zaghlul was forced to take a unilateral position in negotiations with the Labour Prime Minister of Britain, Ramsay MacDonald, in the summer and fall of 1924.[44] After negotiations broke down in mid-October, Zaghlul made a speech at the San Stephano Club in Alexandria with only a perfunctory declaration of loyalty to the king. The language he employed in the speech suggested that the cost of failed negotiations might be very high. He concluded the speech with the line, *'Ina kanat hayati qasira fa inna hayat al-umma tawila'.*[45] Literally, my life is short, but the nation endures. It echoed the French republican formula, 'I am mortal, but the nation is eternal'.[46] Typical of Wafdist ideology, it was a call for political action, movement, and evoked the idea of martyrdom to the national cause.

Zaghlul formed a 'Zaghlulist ministry' in October. He appointed some of his closest associates to ministerial position, including Fathallah Barakat, Mahmud Nuqrashi, and Ahmad Mahir.[47] While these appointments consolidated the support of his closest adherents, they provoked resistance elsewhere. For many, Zaghlul's turn to his core supporters did not signify selfless commitment to the national cause, but the tyranny of the executive. The Watani Party paper, *al-Akhbar*, asked, 'Where are the heroes?' Zaghlul's government was described as one of 'weakness, courtesy, favouritism, and revenge'.[48] On 2 November a press report appeared in *La Liberté* that supported this conclusion. In a conversation with the editor, Leon Castro, Zaghlul admitted his preference for a political party of 'relatives':

> J'ai beaucoup des parents, j'ai regretté qu'ils ne soient pas competents – car je les aurais nommés partout, nous aurions eu

ainsi une administration veritablement Zaghlouliste en nom, en sens, en sang. ... A égalité de capacité et de competence je suis decidé a préferer toujours un parent. (I have lots of relatives, I regret that they are not all competent – because I would have nominated them [to office], then we would have had a truly Zaghlulist administration, in name, in sense, in blood. ... As to the equality of capacity and competence, I have always preferred a relative).[49]

Zaghlul's statement suggested contradiction between modern political principle, notably equal civil rights and constitutional legality, and the primordial bonds of family, friend and faction. The opposition press was quick to argue this point: 'Is it for this that we have endured six years of martyrdom? That Egypt, which belongs to all Egyptians, should be turned into a farm for Zaghloul's family?'[50] The term 'farm' aptly expressed the practice of nepotism, of which Zaghlul gave a frank admission. It was perhaps not surprising that as national consensus slipped and Zaghlul's hold on the party membership and parliament weakened, he came to rely more upon his family and faithful friends, making his government appear more like a self-interested clique.

By October the various elements that had composed the Wafd Party had split into ideological factions and interest groups. Huda Sha'rawi organized a women's committee to boycott British goods. Shamsi and William Makram 'Ubayd called for a 'bitter struggle' against the colonial power.[51] Shamsi threatened to resign from the party, citing Zaghlul's subservience to the king. Tawfiq Nasim resigned from the government, protesting Zaghlul's appointment of his nephew, Tahir al-Lozi, to the Ministry of Agriculture. Through the agency of Hasan Nash'at, a monarchist clique mobilized some factions of the *'ulama'*. Shaykh Abu al-A'yan organized demonstrations of students from al-Azhar outside the parliament on 3 November with shouts of 'Azhar and King alone'.[52]

The contest between the king and ministry was transformed into a constitutional issue when the king attempted to establish his right to make appointments to the Ministry of Awqaf without ministerial advice or approval. This strategy was aimed at the popular base of the Wafd Party because, although the students of the professional and technical schools had led the revolts in 1906 and 1919, the students of al-Azhar had brought greater numbers and wider social influence to the nationalist demonstrations. The mobilization of monarchists at al-Azhar also initiated a cultural campaign against the Westernized sectors of society. The monarchists sought to eliminate regulations that privileged students from the professional and technical schools over graduates from al-Azhar in appointments to the bureaucracy. In this way, the king's campaign questioned the entire system of effendiyya cultural and political prominence. Friction between effendi and shaykh was longstanding but had continued with the election of the Wafd government when new regulations were passed restricting the access of qadis to government posts. Such laws created grievances among a sector of the students and teachers at al-Azhar and was the cause of demonstrations in May and November 1924.[53] Zaghlul offered his resignation on 15 November after Hasan Nash'at exploited his appointment to the Ministry of Awqaf to initiate a campaign for the king's candidacy as caliph to the Muslim world after the Ottoman sultan and caliph, 'Abd al-Majid, had been deposed by the republican and nationalist government of Ataturk. On 16 November, Zaghlul visited the king at Abdin Palace to demand that the king restrict himself to a constitutional role. Meanwhile, the head of the Wafd's student committee, Hasan Yassin, marshaled demonstrations of students from the government schools with shouts of 'Saad or Revolution' and 'No King but Saad'.[54]

It was this confrontation between the people's ministry and the king that formed the immediate background to the assassination of the top British military official in Egypt and the Sudan, Sir Lee Stack, on 19 November. As commander of British forces in the Sudan, his assassination would seem to have been revenge for British unwillingness to relent on the Sudan issue in negotiations with Zaghlul. Indeed in the days before the assassination, the Wafd leadership appeared to have adopted a militant position, although again it is unclear whether the primary target of this radicalization was the king or the British. William Makram 'Ubayd's speech at Ciro's Club in Cairo on 18 November said that government should be revolutionary: 'Revolution takes the form of belief, annunciation, influence, example, and contagion. It is the fire whose flames must be continually kindled. ... Let us not wait for the conflict, but seek it.'[55] 'Ubayd's speech had a hostile reception from some of those in attendance, particularly bureaucrats, who grumbled about favoritism and the tyranny of the Wafd executive.[56] On the same day Zaghlul received representatives of the Wafd student committees. According to spies in the pay of the British high-commission, Zaghlul called upon the students to 'act and not to talk'.[57] On the following day the students demonstrated in the streets with revolutionary chants. Later that day, assailants identified as 'effendis' assassinated Stack. The course of events seemed to indicate that the assassination of Stack was the work of radical sympathizers of Zaghlul. Allenby presented Zaghlul with an ultimatum of demands including the payment of an indemnity, a ban on political demonstrations, as well as the withdrawal of Egyptian troops from the Sudan. Zaghlul resigned the premiership on 23 November. Meanwhile, the students camped outside Zaghlul's house. On the evening of 24 November, they greeted him by shouting, 'Long live Revolution' and 'Countries are liberated by blood'. Zaghlul told them to go back to their schoolwork and keep quiet.[58] For Zaghlul, there could be little doubt that the real target of the assassins had been the Wafd government, not the British Empire.

Zaghlul's government was brought down by the British; however, the confrontation was staged by the forces of Egyptian domestic politics, not the British. It would seem that the British were easily manipulated in this regard. The high-commission in Cairo drew up a list of Wafdist provocations that, so it was claimed, led to the assassination of Stack. The provocative acts included the speeches made by Zaghlul and other Wafdists. The leading proponents of 'terror' were identified as William Makram 'Ubayd, 'Abd al-Rahman Fahmi and Mahmud Nuqrashi. Allenby accused Zaghlul of appointing to high position 'persons who have been convicted [Nuqrashi] or deeply suspected [Fahmi] of attempted murder of foreign and Egyptian Ministers'.[59] The Wafd leadership was described as having inspired 'secret terrorist societies and a host of revolutionary students'.[60] Indeed, British officials and Egyptian liberals had been targeted by

Wafdist militants, but nothing was said in British reports of the recent attempt on Zaghlul's life. Eventually, arrests were made of members of the 'Black Hand' assassination society and there was a trial of 'Abd al-Hamid Inayat, al-Kharrat, Mahmud Rashid, 'Ali Ibrahim, Raghib Hasan, Shafiq Mansur and Mahmud Isma'il. It was only well after the collapse of the Wafd government and the consolidation of the monarchy that the relationship between the monarchist agent, Hasan Nash'at, and Mahmud Isma'il came to light. Mahmud Isma'il implicated Nash'at in the conspiracy before being executed for his part in the assassination of Stack.[61]

The Monarchist Coup

The assassination cost the Wafd Party not only the confidence of the British government, but of a significant sector of Egyptian political society. Parliament adjourned after Zaghlul's resignation. A Wafd Party petition on 3 December for the reconvening of parliament contained the signatures of 114 deputies, indicating that the Wafd Party had lost 82 seats in the assembly of deputies. Thus, the events of November 1924 provided an opportunity for the Wafd's opponents to seize control of parliament and ministry. The king appointed a government headed by Ahmad Ziwar Pasha and prorogued parliament in December 1924. Meanwhile in London members of the British cabinet and Foreign Office officials considered various new policy options, including dismantling entirely the constitutional system worked out after 1922. One proposal was a return to martial law.[62] There was also the idea of restoring the methods of Cromer, which had involved government by Egyptian ministers with British advisors. Winston Churchill was a proponent of such ideas. He envisaged Egypt with crown colony status and the Egyptian king as representative of 'traditional' authority allied to the British Empire. However, these ideas were rejected. John Murray, head of the new Egyptian department in the Foreign Office, advised the Foreign Secretary, Austen Chamberlain, that Cromerism had died with Cromer and neither Gorst nor Kitchener had been able to revive it. Milner had come to similar conclusions in his report of 1921 and Allenby had made it formally binding with his unilateral declaration of 1922. If Churchill's advice were taken it would mean abrogating the constitution, as 'revolutionary and formidable an operation as annexation itself'.[63] Chamberlain agreed with Foreign Office opinion.[64] Thus, in discussions with the British High Commission in Cairo the policy was adopted of supporting a 'counter organization' to 'collaborate with GB on the basis of the 1922 declaration'.[65]

Ahmad Ziwar's ministry provided scope for the exercise of royal patronage. The king was advised by Allenby to include members of the Liberal-Constitutional Party in Ziwar's government, which would widen his base of support. Accordingly, the king sent out invitations to Isma'il Sidqi, 'Abd al-Khaliq Tharwat, 'Adli Yakan, Husayn Rushdi and Muhammad Mahmud. Only Sidqi accepted a ministerial position; the remainder preferred the relative obscurity of the senate to avoid categorization as 'traitor', which was the term applied to Sidqi in the Wafdist papers.[66] Ziwar's government included younger and ambitious politicians, including Hasan Nash'at and 'Ali Mahir. Nash'at was responsible for organizing the royalist 'counter organization' in 1925. 'Ali Mahir was to become the leading monarchist in the 1930s and 1940s. The new political organization took the name Union Party, *Hizb al-ittihad*, evoking a national coalition. On 9 January, Allenby reported to Prime Minister Neville Chamberlain, 'No leader has yet been found. Nessim [Tawfiq Nasim] still persists in his refusal.'[67] Likewise, Muhammad Sa'id refused to join the new party. As a result, when the Ittihad Party was officially formed on 10 January, it was led by al-Liwa' Musa Fu'ad Pasha, a relatively unknown retired Egyptian military officer of high rank.

According to British analysis, the Ittihad Party was a political organization that represented a more conservative sector of Egyptian political society. In a memorandum to Chamberlain, Allenby said that 'in character it will be strongly in the landed proprietor and tenant farmer interest and in composition mainly notables and others who have been won over from the Wafd or who are naturally opposed to the policy and methods of Zaghlul'.[68] This statement was of course pure theory, showing the British preference for an organic type of political landscape. The monarchist party was more political than this commentary suggests. It was overtly royalist. Hasan Nash'at organized those deputies seceding from the Wafd Party into a coherent monarchist bloc as early as November 1924, beginning with Abd al-Halim al-Biyali, the deputy for Old Cairo. In November Biyali publicly accused Zaghlul of disloyalty to the throne. Biyali was followed by the elected Wafdist senator, al-Liwa Musa Fu'ad. Another defector to the monarchists was one of the few Liberal-Constitutional Party members elected to parliament. He was also one of the largest landowners in Lower Egypt. Muhammad Badrawi Ashur Pasha admitted that he had originally supported the Wafd Party only to secure access to government patronage. Given that landholders of this type had turned to the Wafd to safeguard their property interests in the first place, conversion to the Ittihad Party did not amount to a betrayal of principles.[69]

In January, numbers of rural landholders began to call at Abdin Palace to pledge their loyalty to the king and to obtain instructions 'as to how they should influence electors in their respective districts'.[70] The process was identical to that undertaken by the coalition of Wafd and king in 1923. In charge of the electoral campaign was the Minister of Interior, Isma'il Sidqi, who selected monarchist candidates and placed them in constituencies that would not conflict with candidates for the Liberal-Constitutional Party. To do so, Sidqi redrew the electoral boundaries, shifting villages known to be Wafdist into a combination that gave the monarchist or liberal candidate a better chance of winning the constituency. This was also a strategy initially devised by the coalition of Wafdists and monarchists in 1923. Indicating the determination of the new regime to marshal the vote, government officials appointed by Sidqi were given greater powers of supervision over the casting of votes.[71] By these measures, Sidqi intended to win over those members of the effendiyya who believed that the government should concentrate on domestic policy and bureaucratic efficiency, which, according to British analysis and liberal critiques, Zaghlul had sacrificed to partisan interests and treaty negotiations. The new policy was supported by a wide spectrum of British public opinion, hence an editorial in the *The Manchester Guardian* observed that, 'We must put the Civil Service and the magistrature beyond the reach of party politics.'[72] *The Manchester Guardian* had been sympathetic to the nationalists, but reports of corruption and administrative irregularities impacted upon public opinion in Britain. To restore 'order' in the run-up to elections, Sidqi reinstated Liberal-Constitutional Party appointees removed by the Wafd Party in 1924, consequently purging those officials appointed by the Wafd Party. This was described by Allenby as the restoration of a 'well administered and well ordered' bureaucracy.[73] Rashwan Mahfuz, the *mudir* of Minufiyya under Tharwat, became the *mudir* of Gharbiyya under Ziwar. 'Abd al-Rahman Fahmi lost his Cairo constituency on the grounds that he had a criminal record. Najib Gharabali reported that Sidqi conspired to have eight men murder him and in the event very nearly did murder a man they mistook for Gharabali. Sidqi had Gharabali arrested in March 1925, together with 53 others involved in demonstrations in Gharbiyya province where the villagers had rallied with the cry of 'No King but Saad'. Likewise, elector-delegates were imprisoned for refusing to vote for Hilmi Isa Pasha. In Asyut, Wafd Party supporters were not allowed to socialize together. In Qena, 20 men were employed to 'harry Saadists' with nabouts. In Simballawayn six *ghafirs* were publicly flogged for refusing to give false evidence against Wafd Party candidates. The policing of elections by these methods was described by *al-Siyasa* as the 'collapse of the structure of anarchy'.[74]

The monarchist electoral campaign resembled the Wafd's. There were vendettas, violence and efforts to force the outcome of votes. When the *'umda* in Quesnet offered the village vote to the liberals, he was murdered. There were industrial disturbances in the Karmuz and Attarine districts of Alexandria and student demonstrations in Cairo. The students voiced their support for the Wafd Party, protesting against the new concessions given to students of al-Azhar in qualifications for government positions. Student strikes on 16 and 17 March resulted in a ministerial decree that disallowed student involvement in electoral campaigns. In February a crowd in Mahalla al-Kubra, Gharbiyya, attacked the electoral committees supervising the vote, smashed the ballot boxes, stoned police and stormed the police station and the office of irrigation works.[75] The subsequent government prosecution ordered 125 arrests, of which 71 were tried, convicted, and imprisoned for three to four months. The local Wafd candidate and eight members of the local Wafd committee were also tried. During the trial the local *'umda*, who had been on the official electoral committee, testified that he had formerly been an ardent supporter of Zaghlul but had, since the fall of that party, defected to the Ittihad Party. When asked why he said, 'The town is wholly Saadist; but I have left the Zaghloul party because I have a lot of work to do and am alone.'[76]

The population was divided between government and Wafd supporters. While the theory held that the new party would consist of rural notables, reports showed that the Wafd Party's 'nepotism' and 'terrorism' in 1924 had alienated officials, as well as notables.[77] Sidqi was admired by some as a 'strong man'. Younger monarchist politicians like Nash'at, 'Ali Mahir and Mahmud Abu Nasr assisted in the reorganization of the bureaucracy, ran the Ittihad Party organization and articulated a new conservative ideology. For the latter purpose, the party purchased the Wafd's French language journal, *La Liberté*, as well as creating new Arabic language journals: *al-Ittihad* aimed at elite political society and *al-Sha'b al-Masri* for the working classes. Nash'at and Nasr had been early converts from the Watani to the Wafd Party. Each had been involved in the demonstrations of 1919. Nasr, however, split with Zaghlul in 1919. Likewise, 'Ali Mahir had traveled with Zaghlul to Paris in 1919, split with him in 1921, and was a member of the constitutional commission in 1922. Nash'at acted as a liaison between the Wafd and the Palace from 1922. He was openly a monarchist by 1924. Effendis, these three men had an education in the government schools, political experience in the Wafd, and were in a position to facilitate the recruitment of former Wafdists to the Ittihad Party. Take for example an Ittihad Party membership list, addressed to Nash'at, which contained a declaration of loyalty to the king that included names from the Wafd's general membership, as well as former members of the Wafd Central Committee.[78] Each convert was described as a lawyer in the national (*ahliyya*) court system and each submitted a request for appointment to the Ministry of Justice or the Egyptian Foreign Office, indicating the sort of rewards converts to the Ittihad Party could expect.[79] The Ittihad Party thus counted on support from effendi professionals, as well as from the rural landlords.

It is important to note the diversity of the Ittihad Party membership, if only to guard against taking descriptions of the Ittihad as a party of rural landlords too literally. That view was more ideological than actual.

Like the Wafd Party in 1923, the monarchists had to combine the administrative machinery of the state with the social role of the notables to win seats in elections. The party membership lists support the idea that in electoral practice, the rural notables had a large say in the outcome. In Gharbiyya, Zaghlul's home province, the king could not compete with Zaghlul's kinsmen, the powerful Barakat family; as a result, the Ittihad Party had difficulty placing candidates to stand against the Wafd Party. Minya province was dominated by the liberal 'Abd al-Raziq family. In the previous elections, that province had been divided between the Liberal-Constitutional Party and the Wafd Party. Therefore, Sidqi left the electoral contests in Minya in the hands of the Raziqs. In Sharqiyya province, the electoral lists were dominated by the Abazas. In 1923 the Abazas stood as Liberal-Constitutionals. In 1925 they stood as Liberal-Constitutionals, Ittihadists, as well as independents, indicating an over-all revulsion against the Wafd Party. Powerful families such as the Raziqs and Abazas could exert patronage across an entire region, guaranteeing the votes in villages controlled directly or indirectly by the family. This was the case generally in Upper Egypt, where the notables had greater sway over the constituents. The tactics of the monarchists adapted best to a style of politics that involved an alliance of government officials with notables, which brought the overwhelming weight of the government down upon local officials and the smaller cultivators. Indicative of the localized character of politics, popular resistance to the Ittihad Party was not universal and depended upon local circumstances, certainly in some cases the notables sold their services to the Ittihad Party and delivered their constituencies after a handshake.[80] But with the monarchists firmly in control of the state machinery in 1925, many notables placed their bets on an Ittihad victory in the elections of 1925. Thus the acting high-commissioner, Neville Henderson, said that in spite of the popularity of the Wafd 'the great mass of Zaghlulist sheep will quickly find the gap in the fence by which they can get to the other side of it'.[81]

Localized politics under the umbrella of state patronage was also apparent in the Ittihad Party political organization as recorded in party membership lists. Membership broke down into notable and effendi types, for instance, the generic type of notable can be recognized in categories such as the familiar term for notable, *a'yan*, as well as *muzari'* (small holders of property or sharecroppers), *dhu al-amlak* or *sahib al-amlak* (proprietor or large landholder). The generic type of effendi is apparent in titles such as doctor, lawyer, journalist, and engineer (*tabib, muhami, sihafi* and *muhandis*). Administrative categories were numerous in the Ittihad Party lists, that is to say, categories such as minister, inspector, judge, mayor, police, clerk, and district inspector (*wazir, mufattish, hakim, 'umda, ghafir, katib, nazir al-qism*). There were also significant numbers of members of the *'ulama'*, including the types such as shaykh, qadi, imam, sayyid, and muezzin (*mu'adhdhin*). The lists suggest that the king's party could count on the higher and lower levels of the administrative hierarchy; for example, the Cairo district of Shubra included three lawyers in the *shari'a* courts and three lawyers working in the *ahliyya* courts. In the Cairo and Alexandria constituencies, the most common professional category in the Ittiahd membership lists was that of lawyer, which could have designated lawyers either in *ahliyya* or *shari'a* courts, but whenever specified it was most often given as *shari'a* lawyer (*muhami shar'i*). Unable to win over the majority of the leading political figures (*dhawat*) or of the effendiyya, the Ittihad Party used patronage as a method to enlist marginal members of political society, in addition to the pashas and effendis. This is also apparent in the membership lists. Altogether honourary titles in the lists included pasha, bey, hajj, shaykh, *ustadh* (teacher), and effendi. For example, in a list of all party candidates for the elections of 1925, the Wafd had the greatest number of candidates, 194, and out of that number there were 9 pashas, 62 beys, 94 effendis, and 27 shaykhs. In the same collection, the list of Ittihadists numbered 122, posing the greatest electoral challenge to the Wafd with the total breaking down into 6 pashas, 41 beys, 22 effendis, and 26 shaykhs. The obvious difference between the parties was the larger percentage of shaykhs in Ittihad ranks, indicating the attraction of that party to graduates of al-Azhar. Also, the percentage of effendis was less than that on the

Wafd lists. The Ittihad Party therefore enlisted the support of the rich and powerful, as well as marginal members of the modern state system, particularly Islamic scholars, who sought a way to reestablish their role in government. This accounts for the higher place given to religious ideology by the Ittihad Party.[82]

Monarchist Ideology

The first official expression of monarchist ideology appeared in an issue of the journal *al-Ittihad* that appeared on 16 January 1925. It headlined an essay that warned readers of the dangers of revolutionary, republican politics.[83] The editor of the journal was Taha Husayn, a celebrated liberal intellectual, yet the content of the essay was similar to the constitutional history given in Zaki Fahmi's *Safwat al-'Asr*. Like Fahmi's essay on constitutionalism, the *al-Ittihad* article referred to modern European political history to draw parallels with the Egyptian scene. The revolution in France, it said, had taken power from the monarch and given it to political parties. The parties exploited the naiveté of the masses or mob (*jamahir*) to gain political authority through an elected assembly. In doing so, the revolutionaries committed crimes against social groups. Regardless of the popular character of the revolutionary government, which the writer referred to as *al-sulta bi sibya sha'biyya*, the French republican laws of 1791 removed the rights of representation from the 'sons of the country' (*abna' al-watan*). The reference to 'social groups' and 'sons of the country' would appear to refer to religious and aristocratic classes or 'estates'. Although accepted as an attribute of modernity, revolution and democracy were portrayed negatively in the article. The French Revolution was associated with anarchy through the use of terms such as mob or masses (*jamahir*), controlled by 'factions' (*firaq*), described as evil and contemptible (*aswa* and *fasad*). The article was critical of that aspect of the modern experience that by freeing the individual from social constraints destroyed social institutions. These ideas resembled British colonial and Egyptian liberal arguments that viewed democracy as the greatest threat to liberty. Indeed, the writer turned to English political history as an antidote to French radicalism. The argument, like

Zaki Fahmi's, was indebted to Montesquieu's description of British parliamentary traditions, as well as Edmund Burke's defense of the 'ancient constitution'. Burke of course regarded the 'levelers', such as the Jacobins of revolutionary France, as the greatest threat to political order. In this vein, the article continued by arguing that the British parliament evolved into a legislative body, yet the king maintained his rights as guardian of the state and constitutional customs. In this discussion, religious language was applied with terms such as tradition (*taqlid*) and community (*umma*) to describe the establishment of representative government in Britain. Likewise, representative government had only been attained through consultation (*shura*) among the classes (*hai'at*) and social groups (*jama'at*). The arguments indicated that monarchists adopted the language of cultural authenticity and an ideological position grounded in modern conservatism. Representation was thus a political function that belonged to the elites, comparable to Montesquieu's concept of 'political communities' or what Max Weber referred to as the 'political subjects' of the ruler.[84] The same point was made by Zaki Fahmi, who was writing at the same time that the *al-Ittihad* article was produced. Fahmi might have been the author of the essay, or else we can assume there was some intellectual collaboration or ideological alignment between Taha Husayn and Zaki Fahmi. Moreover, Diaedinne Saleh made similar arguments at the end of the interwar period. Hence, monarchist ideas were coherent and consistently articulated, marked by an accommodation of historic and Islamic political models, applied to modern constitutional theory. In monarchist ideology, representative government was premised on the idea that it was restricted to the male heads of social groups – the 'political subjects'. Monarchist thought offered a critique of modernity insofar as the breaking of traditional forms of authority, as had been accomplished by the revolution in France (in an analogy with the revolution of 1919), did not ensure political community or the common good.

Monarchist ideology in this form was represented as conforming to Egypt's 'traditions' or social values, implied by the use of religious terminology. Some of these ideas evoked Islamic reformist concepts, such as equating representation with *shura*. However, the tendency to make stark comparisons between good and evil suggested a fundamentalist orientation. Religious values were offered as a counter to the 'evils' of individualism and democracy. The insistence upon moral example was not unlike the rhetoric of the Wafd's electoral manifestos; thus, monarchists insisted that the key to political order was consensus through the proof of social and moral character. To draw out the analogy between Wafdist electoral practices and monarchist thinking, take for example Zaki Fahmi's biography of an Ittihadist candidate in the election of 1925, Hamid Pasha al-Shawarbi of Qalubiyya. As Fahmi recorded, Shawarbi was educated in the government schools, including the khedival law school, where he was versed in the obligations and virtues of patriotism (*wataniyya*). He was appointed to the position of secretary to a committee of surveillance in the Ministry of Interior, as well as to the Ministry of Justice and the Ministry of Education, and was afterwards appointed as a qadi in the *ahliyya* courts. In other words his training was typical of the effendiyya. Fahmi, however, underlined his moral, alongside his technical, training. He recorded in the biography that Shawarbi was entrusted with the care of a waqf belonging to the most powerful of the Shawarbis, Muhammad Pasha al-Shawarbi. In this position, he was responsible for the welfare of the poor of that family and by this proof of character was elected in 1925 by an overwhelming majority (*bi-aghlabiyya sahiqa*) as deputy for Qalyub. In this post he demonstrated his competency and therefore won the respect of the people and in recognition of this the king rewarded him with the status grade of pasha.[85] Although he was an effendi by training, the biography suggests that the politician was ultimately the patrician of a community, in this case the custodian of a religious endowment. In this role the notable distinguished himself by his qualities (*sifa*) and ethics (*akhlaq*), which established the reputation of the candidate and the trust of the community. The exemplary notable was responsible for the welfare of the lower classes, described in this biography as the 'working sons' of Egypt (*abna' al-kinana al-'amilin*, kinana having the meaning of the 'tribe' of the Egyptians and thus accentuating the primordial bonds of the nation). The deputy was specifically described as having been elected as a result of his service to the workers by distributing wealth through benevolent societies.[86] The description of the notable's social role fits the idea of a patron of a community, marked out by moral example.

The ideology, like the structure of the Ittihad party personnel, was not traditional, but traditionalist. The Itthad Party included members of both the conservative and radical wings of the Wafd. There were also members of the 1923 constitutional commission in the Ittihad membership. On the one side there were the great landowners, including Yusuf Qattawi, Sulayman Isma'il Abaza and Muhammad Fu'ad Pasha, while on the other side were the radicals, including Hasan Nash'at, 'Ali Mahir and Mahmud Abu Nasr. Mahir acted as party deputy leader and Nasr as party secretary. 'Ali Mahir stood as Ittihad candidate for the al-Wayli constituency in Cairo and his brother, Mustafa Mahir, stood against Zaghlul in Sayyida Zaynab. Therefore, each was at least in a position to perceive the need for an ideology that countered the Wafd's appeal. The Ittihad ideological message is recorded in one manifesto from the Abdin files, dated July 1925, in elections that followed the dissolution of the second parliament in March 1925. The content suggests that the monarchists represented the party as a moral community in antithesis to the politics of the effendiyya. The pamphlet, *'Nida' ila da'ira Mit Ya'ish'* (A call to the district of Mit Ya'ish) was signed by Hajj Muhammad Sulayman, a qadi in the *shari'a* courts.

> I call to the brothers (*ikhwan*) of the community by the knowledge that the people possess and the thanks of God as it was evident in the last elections to acknowledge the evil of the administration. I entreat the people by their trust (*amana*), by what sustains humanity, by the heavens, earth, and mountains, by a trust that calls forth the cause: to construct the future of Egypt which will be redeemed by our spirits and our acts. And as to whether the opponent is stronger than the Ittihad candidate, the opponent took the last election by the sword of the government alone, and he will regret this on the day of the election. As for myself, I will struggle toward the triumph of God alone.[87]

Establishing the distinction between the administration and the community, the evil and the good, the politician placed himself as first and foremost the leader of his local flock against the power of the state. The candidate went on to suggest that these elections would provide services for the people, noting that the last government had not achieved that result. Thus the ideological message declaimed the immoral and unjust methods of the Wafd at the same time as it promised that the Ittihadists would, in bringing just rule, distribute material rewards. In conclusion, the electors were reminded that although Zaghlul was respected by all the people, some of 'our opponents' used his name for lesser ends, but 'we must see their service to the nation with proofs, not with the clamour of tongues' (*ja'ja'a' al-lisan*). The clash of tongues fits the familiar reference to democratic anarchy, the factionalism of parties, underlining the point that the monarchists represented a cure to the ills of democratic, party politics and self-interested politicians.[88]

An eye witness report of a monarchist political rally in the provinces offers another perspective. The report was sent to the British Foreign Office by Neville M. Henderson, the Acting High Commissioner after the resignation of Allenby in June 1925. It was based on an interview with a reporter from *The Times*. Henderson sought an independent witness to verify reports of mass enthusiasm for the Ittihad Party. The correspondent reported that in a campaign through Kafr al-Shaykh the townsmen had cheered enthusiastically 'Long Live the King' (*Yahya al-Malik*). The political rally was attended by about 1,500 'stout country folk', which was taken to support the view that the monarchists were gaining ground in the provinces. Yet, 'the rally was nothing like the delirious enthusiasm which used invariably to mark the least Zaghlulist gathering'. The impression was that most Ittihadists supporters were moved by the 'idea that it would pay better and really last'. The violence that was endemic in electoral campaigns notwithstanding, the population of Kafr al-Shaykh came into the streets to voice their support for the king, reflecting a structure of politics in which the notables could be counted upon to mobilize their constituents. Another indicator of that conclusion was that the neighboring town remained totally quiet, suggesting that that town was securely held by a Wafdist notable. The king lacked the charisma of Zaghlul, but he did represent a patron to whom the conservative notables looked as a guarantor of their historical role as patricians of their local communities. The campaign speeches in Kafr al-Shaykh were made by Hilmi Isa Pasha, who said that the Ittihad Party had the benefit of the king's high guidance. Also in attendance was Sayyid Muhammad al-Biblawi, the *naqib al-ashraf* or head of a Sufi brotherhood. For this religious notable, the most important appeal was for national unity and the abolition of party feuds, a political virtue that he said could be found beneath the Ittihad banner.[89]

The overall impression is of a monarchist preference for the 'politics of the notables' in the sense of hierarchic order and moral community. The idea is represented in the traditionalism of the ideology and the way political society was represented in the electoral lists. Moreover, the monarchists were able to band together a body of support in the population with such ideas. *Al-Siyasa* admitted as much when it said that a large body of monarchist support was among conservative property holders, who 'deceived the simple minds of those who still live simply as laborers, promising them the best or defending them from evil'.[90] Something of the appeal of monarchist ideology is stated in a letter addressed to Ahmad Muhammad Hasanayn, who succeeded Nash'at as the king's principal political agent in 1926. The letter-writer described himself as a 'simple fellah' and complained of the tyranny of the party system and its 'ill effects on the nation, unprecedented in history'. It was thus necessary to liberate the 'people' (*sha'b*) from this tyranny and limit politics to the ruling house (*sahat al-qasr al-'amr*) so that all of the affairs were supervised by the elite of the nation (*yanzuru li-kull al-shu'un bi-'ayn al-qawmiyya*). Offering his opinion on the hypocrisy of political party rhetoric, the letter-writer went on to say that an individual did not have the right to restrict his thought to his personal preferences, but rather should direct it toward the benefit of the country. The letter concluded by begging pardon for this expression of opinion, as he was but a 'simple fellah' and not one of those 'people of the pen' or 'people of politics' (*ahl al-qalam* or *ahl al-siyasa*).

The letter underlined the way the middle stratum of notables viewed themselves as commoners (*sha'b*) in relation to the effendiyya and elite political society, yet also as the very bedrock of Egyptian society and cultural values. The status of the notables came from ascribed status and moral righteousness. The notable was accordingly the ideal political subject of the king.[91]

In short, the contest between the Wafd and the monarchists was one for political power, constitutionally defined and ideologically justified. The basic method to attain power for each party was through patronage over the rural and urban notability. The party membership lists provide a picture of the structure of social relations, particularly the social background of the parties and the importance of the social and administrative hierarchies. The social types of notable and effendi were the essential actors in moving the populace into political activity. The Ittihad electoral lists and manifestos can be contrasted to those of the Wafd, supporting a monarchist view of politics wherein the communities followed their social superiors, more often notables with 'traditionalist' credentials, rather than modernist. The functional role of the notable as shepherd of the flock, in this type of political model, was held to be the enduring or 'real' form of social relations and thus the foundation of political order. Hence, monarchist electoral lists and manifestos supported the idea of the elite classes, not the democratic majority, as representative of the social mass. These ideas were deeply engrained in Egyptian culture. So much so, that they had also been evident in the tactics, if not the rhetoric, of the Wafd Party. Such countervailing forces within the Wafd Party, as represented by the social roles and political attitudes of effendis and notables, radicals and conservatives, were important in the fracturing of the Wafdist parliament in 1924. The Wafd was particularly sensitive to cultural issues that had meaning within its base of support among the rural notables. Therefore, the collapse of the Wafd government should not be viewed solely as the result of British interference, the success of collaborators over nationalists, or rich landholders over the lower and middle stratum of society, but rather the consequence of deep cultural and ideological divisions within Egyptian political society.

CHAPTER 6

TRADITIONALISM

Under the colonial regime, reformers like Zaghlul reduced the ruler's powers of patronage over religious institutions. Likewise, during the First World War, liberal-minded statesmen like Yakan and Tharwat defended the principle of a constitutional monarch limited by a responsible ministry. These contests between the ruling dynasty and reformist politicians continued after 1919, with the king exploiting the constitutional reorganization of 1923 to reassert royal powers. The fall of the Wafd government in November 1924 enabled monarchists to divert the location of political power from ministry and parliament to the palace. Liberal nationalists were fully aware that these events threatened to determine the course of post-revolutionary politics and culture, as well as the scope of British neo-colonial control. By 1925 the ruler had established his powers of patronage, with influence over Islamic groups and institutions being a key part of the royalist programme. In 1926 Zaki Fahmi's *Safwat al-'Asr* initiated a royalist cultural campaign. With these events the revolution had apparently come full circle, from a modernizing, liberating cultural and political event, all the way to traditionalization and neo-colonialism.

One way to conceptualize this diversion from modern radicalism to 'tradition' is to compare the political history of the era with analysis of modern Egyptian culture of the same period. It has been argued by Albert Hourani, Israel Gershoni and James P. Jankowski that in the 1920s liberal nationalism was the dominant ideological trend.[1] The Egyptian-ness of the nation eclipsed its Islamic and Arab characteristics, just as modernist political discourse muted dynastic and Islamic ideology. The idea of a territorial, national community of citizens might have been dominant, but as Karl Mannheim has argued, any political society can be divided into rival cultural 'units'.[2] Each unit vies for dominance through its cultural work. Representations of Islam were advanced by monarchists to counter the democratic and liberal units. The monarchists imagined al-Azhar, the preeminent religious and educational institution, as a monolithic organization that could be mobilized behind the king. Of course, interpretations of the political agency of Islam were diverse. One scholar from al-Azhar, 'Ali 'Abd al-Raziq, defended the principle of liberal nationalism to counter the monarchist attempt to employ Islam as a political instrument, particularly over the issue of the caliphate as it surfaced in 1924. Another scholar at al-Azhar, Rashid Rida, rejected the king's bid to have the caliphate established in Egypt, after it was abolished with the formation of modern Turkey. According to Rida, the multi-cultural character of modern Egypt – its Westernization and foreign colonies – compared unfavourably with the 'pure, noble and independent Arabs' of Arabia.[3] Rida was a proponent of *salafiyya* ideology, which sought to restore the principles of an Islamic state founded by the Prophet Muhammad and his immediate successors, the first generation or 'ancestral' (*salaf*) Muslims. The monarchist Islamists tended more toward the practice of using Islam to legitimate the rule of a king. A prominent jurist at al-Azhar, Shaykh Muhammad Bakhit, represented the monarchist cultural unit by defending the medieval theory of the Islamic prince, rather than seeking a restored Arab caliphate.[4] As described in the preceding chapter, the feminist movement in Egypt also divided opinion at al-Azhar. Beth Baron's interpretation of the feminist trend in Egypt suggests that the prominence of 'secularist trends' in Egyptian feminism resulted in women becoming more ambivalent or even openly hostile to West-oriented ideologies. As a result, Egyptian feminism took a radical neo-traditional turn, with the adoption of Islamic terminology and elements of *shari'a* law. Many women thus chose a pragmatic 'bargain' with patriarchy, including re-veiling, rather than follow the liberal path.[5] Similarly, the secularism and liberal nationalism of mainstream Egyptian nationalism was also diverted, with many Egyptians coming to accept that cultural and political change must be accommodated with 'tradition'.

The weight of the past, social custom and culture, as well the investment of the elites in social structures meant that the course of post-1919 politics was tactical and provisional. Indeed, the Wafd Party's rise to power had involved a bargain with, firstly, the monarchy, secondly, the rural notables, and finally, as will be seen in the remaining pages, a post-revolutionary aristocratic elite. These contradictions within the Wafd opened the door to the development of conservative and traditionalist alternatives, equally provisional and contested among political groups and within cultural institutions, like al-Azhar. As it turned out, the course of events that brought the monarchists to power in 1925 diverted the Wafd Party from the radicalism of its core, effendi leadership. And although the authoritarianism and religious nationalism that characterized the Ittihad Party would not entirely dominate Egyptian politics in the interwar period, the subsequent alliances and coalitions of elite players in the various parties did represent a 'bargain' that discounted the radicalism of 1919 and directed politics towards elitism and conservatism.

Elitism and Religious Nationalism

While representing different ideological orientations, the monarchists and liberals developed similar conceptions of the relationship between the classes and the mass, political society and the majority of the population. For each, the 'people' constituted a politically disenfranchised mass, whose unfettered political engagement posed a menace to 'order' and 'progress'. The Liberal-Constitutional Party was the more articulate of the two parties, at least initially. For instance, the writ that declared the formation of the Ziwar ministry in November 1924 was phrased in evolutionary language typical of the liberals. It asserted the role of the 'elevated classes' to lead the nation toward modernity by a gradual development of its civil institutions:

> Nous esperons et souhaitons que les classes élevés de la population en se rendait compte que l'edifice de notre independence ne peut être construit en un jour mais par des années d'efforts et sur le fondement de notre progres civil, lequel seul nous donnera de plus en plus la force et le credit d'une nation civilisée. (We hope and wish that the upper classes of the population will realize that building our independence cannot be constructed in a day but only by years of effort and on the foundation of our civil progress, and only that effort will give us more and more the force and the credit as a civilized nation).[6]

Evolutionary theory not only distinguished the liberal nationalists from the radicals, but established a common political orientation, if not ideology, between liberals and monarchists. The idea of defining a political distance between the elevated classes and the mass became critical after the dissolution of the second elected parliament in March 1925. The parliament sat for only one day. Although the anti-Wafdist coalition- including the Ittihad Party, Liberal-Constitutional Party and independents- controlled about half the seats in the parliament, Zaghlul was able to win a vote for the presidency of the assembly of deputies, defeating the government's nominee, Tharwat Pasha. When Ziwar offered his resignation, the king dissolved parliament instead.[7]

The Ziwar ministry had already abolished the Wafd electoral law of 1924 and restored the 1923 law. However, the unruly nature of the parliament in March 1925 demonstrated to the conservatives that the electoral law did not provide the necessary framework to reduce the electorate to manageable dimensions and ensure the dominance of the 'elevated classes'. Therefore, in 1925 Ziwar's government campaigned to revise the electoral law of 1923 and implement a new one by royal decree in the absence of parliament. The campaign was led by liberals, including 'Abd al-'Aziz Fahmi, Muhammad 'Ali 'Aluba, Tawfiq Doss, as well as Ahmad Mahir and Hilmi Isa. The electoral commission drafted a law along the lines of the pre-war Belgian electoral system. The reform proposed a franchise of men over 25 years of age with those between 25 and 40 having to meet restrictive property qualifications.[8]

'Abd al-'Aziz Fahmi initially campaigned for electoral reform in a speech to the national bar at the court of appeal on 17 March 1925. In *al-Siyasa* Muhammad Husayn Haykal supported the proposal, arguing that 'Western democracy was "too rich" for Egyptian stomachs'.[9] Haykal showed the influence of Hippolyte Taine's naturalism when he said that the electoral law should be modified to conform to the 'nature of the Egyptian nation'. Haykal developed his understanding of naturalism during the war to establish the connection between the territory of Egypt and a specifically Egyptian mentality, which supported the ideology of territorial nationalism. According to Haykal, the 'natural environment' of the Nile Valley molded a homogenous 'race', characteristically calm, benevolent, obedient, which bred an unchanging political culture.[10] Alongside such imagining of a national essence, the idea of an unchanging social 'nature' was also paternalistic and elitist, as demonstrated by Charles D. Smith's analysis of Haykal's subsequent writings.[11] Equally in 1925 Haykal's journalistic writings applied naturalism to the issue of electoral reform. Against the arguments of radical democrats, Haykal argued that the electoral law should 'guarantee the representation of the vital elements of the Egyptian nation', which would 'enable the nation to enjoy its constitutional rights according to its physical system and nature'.[12] The term 'vital' opposed the elite minority to the majority, with the latter regarded as unsuited to modern representative politics. Naturalism, like evolutionism, supported the idea that politics should fit the actual 'nature' or evolution of Egyptian society, rather than impose foreign models.[13] To understand that 'nature', Haykal rephrased the question initially posed by colonialism: What was the evolutionary stage of the Egyptian social body and what constitutional system corresponded to that stage?[14] On 1 April 1925 'Abd al-'Aziz Fahmi made a similar observation in yet another speech to the national bar, when he said: 'I worked with the constitutional commission ... but practice has proved that the government is too big for the body.'[15]

For the liberals, the question was what constitutional formula approximated Egypt's corporate 'nature'. The Wafd Party journal, *al-Balagh*, replied that Fahmi's observation echoed the words of Reginald Wingate in response to the demand made by the Wafd (Fahmi was one of those initial members of the delegation) for self-government in 1918. Wingate's reply, according to the editorial, was 'that if an infant were given more food than necessary he would suffer from indigestion'.[16] The radical nationalist press thus highlighted the correspondence between colonialism and liberalism and hence asked if the 'vital powers' of the nation consisted of the educated class only. In this way the Wafd journal identified that colonial and liberal thinking were founded on a similar analysis of Egyptian social and political structures. The commentary of the Wafd editorial noted that the new electoral law would deny the vote to the agricultural and laboring classes, that is to say 90 percent of the population.[17] Indeed, it was a doctrine of colonial thinking that Egyptian political society consisted of only 10 percent of the Egyptian population.[18] To highlight the wide ideological distance between radical and liberal nationalists, the Wafd press framed its argument in socialist language, arguing that politics was not a means for the elite to establish its domination, but a struggle between classes. Society, in this argument, was not a product of nature, but of politics. The article continued with the claim that the electoral commission planned to restrict the vote to the narrowest possible 'social circle', eliminating representatives of the lower class completely with only those from a specific class eligible for the final stage of voting.[19] The electoral law would undermine the 'social system' reviving a system of 'caste distinctions' in these 'communistic times'.[20] The article continued with the claim that the 'aristocrats' were engaging in 'class warfare' by distinguishing in the 'text of the constitution' between the rich and the poor. But who, it was asked, were these 'aristocrats'? Fahmi was the son of a *ma'dhun shar'i* (a *qadi* authorized to write marriage contracts), 'Aluba was the son of a *katib* (clerk), and Doss the son of a bookseller in Asyut.[21] In other words, the 'aristocrats' were typical of the effendiyya, a social sector that had gained social mobility through the new educational system and bureaucracy. When Haykal and others theorized about the social system, whether in the language of naturalism or evolutionism, the subject was political. Likewise, when the radical nationalists employed the concept of aristocracy, it was not meant to describe a social estate with special privileges, but a type of political ideology or doctrine. The juxtaposition of aristocracy and democracy represented a political contest between ideological units with origins in the middle level notability, whose ideologues were mostly effendis.

Given the emergence of a liberal-monarchist coalition determined to limit the franchise, the Wafd Party embraced the liberal constitution of 1923 as a symbol of democracy and civil rights against the liberal 'aristocrats' and Ittihad 'autocrats'.[22] Differences between the three parties on domestic policy were less substantial, with the exception of cultural issues, particularly religion. A note composed in Abdin Palace in 1925 summarized the policies of the three parties. Each proposed nearly identical reforms of health, education and agricultural production, as well as reforming relations between capital and labor. The points of divergence were that the Liberal-Constitutional Party placed more emphasis upon the reform of the bureaucracy, indicating its preference for administrative 'order'. The Wafd Party programme was unique in calling for an improvement in the condition of women, particularly to safeguard the maternal role of child rearing. Emphasis upon maternity indicated the Wafd Party's concessions to patriarchy and conservative religious opinion. Yet, there was also a concern to involve women in the Wafd organization; thus in 1925 the Wafd Party supported the founding of a new women's journal, *al-Amal*, which declared the Wafd Party's commitment to female suffrage.[23] For the male leadership of the Wafd, this declaration was more symbolic than real. The Wafd Party remained indifferent to the issue of female suffrage through the 1920s and 1930s, underscoring the compromises that social custom or values placed upon the party leadership. The Ittihad programme mirrored the Liberal-Constitutional programme; however, it was unique for its call for the complete reform of the al-Azhar Mosque and University to prepare its graduates to occupy 'dignified' positions in the ministries of Justice and Education.[24]

The identification of the Ittihad Party with the *'ulama'* was intended to build a social and ideological basis for the party. On the first score, the king expanded his control over the Ministry of Awqaf after the

Wafd Party attempted to impose stricter state supervision in 1924. (The Wafd Party would try again after each successive election, for instance, in 1926 and 1928.) Monopoly over the distribution of public and private trusts (*waqf ahli* and *waqf khayri*) provided immense resources of patronage because the religious endowments comprised as much as one-tenth of Egypt's cultivable land. Control of the *awqaf* also had an impact upon the ability of the monarchists to represent the king as an agent of social morality because religious endowments included mosques and charitable societies, as well as urban and rural properties that could provide social services - such as employment, food and housing- as well as other benefits for the less advantaged in society. For instance, in 1925 the king was involved in setting up an asylum, a home for 'strays and waifs', and a workmen's dispensary in the working class district of Bulaq. The charitable societies later attracted Islamists, such as Hasan al-Banna of the Muslim Brotherhood. The Brotherhood recruited through the Young Men's Muslim Association, which had been founded through monarchist 'connections' (*wasta*) in the ministries of *Awqaf* and Education.[25] The term *wasta* suggests that the king built up a royal clientele in the bureaucracy through patronage over educational and religious institutions. Indicating the continuity of the monarchist group founded in 1925, Prince 'Umar Tusun, Hilmi Isa, Shaykh Muhammad Bakhit and Muhammad Zaki Ibrashi continued to defend the monarch's rights as patron of private *awqaf* through the 1940s.[26]

Royal patronage over appointments to al-Azhar resulted in the reorganization of al-Azhar's highest council so that the supervision of the school for *qadis* was restored to al-Azhar.[27] In a contest with the Ministry of Interior for a contract to supervise government schools in 1925, the award went to al-Azhar. Also, new schools were founded under royal patronage, normally in districts with candidates running for the Ittihad Party, which profited from such displays of royal largesse. Rules for state pensions were redrafted so that *'ulama'* serving in religious institutions were eligible, alongside government employees. Certainly, the king made good on his promises to the *'ulama'* in 1925 and subsequently by enhancing their status and social roles against the effendiyya. The cultural implications were shortly manifested when the *'ulama'* attempted to restrict the extension of effendiyya culture in the school system. The students at Dar al-'Ulum (a government teachers' college) typically wore the effendi attire of tarboosh and Western-type suit; in 1925 there was a debate about whether the hat should be worn instead of the tarboosh as a sign of the 'true' effendi. This caused a reaction, so that the students were warned that they would be expelled and their positions taken by students from al-Azhar if they did not adopt the turban and *jallabiyya*, the dress worn at al-Azhar. The king and Prince 'Umar Tusun supported the campaign against the tarboosh and the hat. As a result of these controversies, there was a *fatwa* issued at al-Azhar that 'bristled with warnings against assimilation to foreigners'.[28] The *fatwa* said that the hat was an improper headdress; that Muslim women must not marry non-Muslims; and that women must not be given equal rights to men in matters of inheritance. In this instance, monarchist domestic policy manifested itself as a type of cultural nationalism.

The king's campaign to establish his political party with a social and ideological basis had wider implications. Values, as they related to women, were rephrased in Islamic terms, establishing guidelines for post-revolutionary patriarchy. Principles, particularly as held by some members of the Wafd and Liberal-Constitutional parties, were also rephrased or reinterpreted. Take for instance liberal formulas in the constitution declaring that citizens enjoyed equal civil and political rights, as well as public duties and obligations, without regard to race, language or religion. This declaration could not be universally applied with regard to religion or gender in the face of the growing religious lobby. It should not be surprising, given the Wafd Party's ambivalent stand on social and cultural issues that it did not challenge the *fatwa*. Indeed Hasan Yassin, the leader of the Wafd Party's student executive, led the campaign to ban the wearing of hats in favor of the tarboosh at Dar al-'Ulum.[29] But the Wafd had difficulty keeping pace with the religious nationalists. The religious campaign of the palace emboldened Muslim activists to challenge the government on political as well as cultural issues; consequently in January 1926, students from al-Azhar signed a petition for the universal application of *shari'a* law in place of ahliyya law.[30]

The religious policy of the monarchists might be viewed as instrumental or purely tactical, founded on the idea of co-opting social groups attached to religious institutions or properties held as religious trusts. For sure, the *'ulama'* provided a base upon which the king could build social support; but this had an ideological impact also. The most obvious religious element in national political contests was the proposal to bring the caliphate to Cairo. The Wafd Party did not oppose the idea. However, Nash'at's influence over the *'ulama'* at the Ministry of Awqaf on this issue had constitutional implications. Thus when Shaykh Abu al-A'yan and the king's private imam and religious propagandist, Shaykh Muhammad 'Abd al-Latif al-Fahham, convened the Azhar Caliphate Committee, the Wafd attempted to halt its progress by supporting the Supreme Caliphate Committee, which was independently organized by Shaykh Abu al-Aza'im. That committee resolved that it was the duty of all Muslims to help install a caliph after the Ottoman caliphate had been abolished by the republican regime in Turkey.

Islam and the Constitutional Question

The king's religious policy posed a critical test to the alliance of the liberals and monarchists in the Ziwar government. While the Ittihad Party supported the king's caliphate campaign and the Azhar Caliphate Committee, the Liberal-Constitutional Party did not. The liberal position on religion and the state was articulated by 'Ali 'Abd al-Raziq in his critique of the Islamic caliphate, *Al-Islam wa usul al-hukm* (Islam and the Principles of Government), which appeared in the summer of 1925. 'Abd al-Raziq, a *qadi* in the *shari'a* courts, explicitly challenged the idea of an Islamic state and implicitly the king's Islamic policy by applying the logic of Taha Husayn's doctoral thesis, also published in 1925. Husayn's argument rejected the theory that religious solidarity was, alongside ethnicity, one of the surest bases upon which to build political community and legitimate authority. Husayn used historical analysis to show that the caliphate had been neither religious nor just. Following that lead, 'Abd al-Raziq took the example of Abu Bakr, the first caliph, who he said founded a state not on religious, but on ethnic bonds; (*'asabiyya*, Ibn Khaldun's term for group solidarity, was the term used by Raziq for this idea).³¹ The religious charisma of the caliphate was only a hollow justification for the absolute rule of an Arab prince. On the level of Egyptian politics, there was an implied lesson in the example of the monarchists exploiting religious issues to establish royal autocracy, which was manifest by the summer of 1925. Moreover, 'Abd al-Raziq denied Ibn Khaldun's assertion that the caliphate was founded upon the consensus or *ijma'* of the community when Raziq said that the caliphate had normally always been seized by force and denied that the selection of the caliph had been founded on the consensus or ijma' of the Muslim community or *umma*. This interpretation of Islamic history went against the interpretation adopted by the monarchists at al-Azhar. Even more provocative, 'Abd al-Raziq argued that the Prophet Muhammad had not intended to found an Islamic state and that Islam constituted a unity of faith and not of politics, just as the Prophet's message was spiritual and not political. As he said, 'If we were to collect all his [The Prophet Muhammad's] direct teachings on the question of government, we would get little more than a fraction of the principles of law and organizations needed for maintaining a state.'³²

In this way, 'Abd al-Raziq could use examples from Islamic history to argue for the effective separation of Islam from the political constitution. Unfortunately for 'Abd al-Raziq, his views tended to reiterate the Orientalist critique of Islamic civilization, namely that the imposition of the caliphate had justified despotism and that this accounted for the relative decline of Islamic civilization as compared to the West. The Orientalist perspective was typical of those Egyptians with a Western education. 'Abd al-Raziq had begun his education at al-Azhar, where he attained the degree of *'alim* (one of the *'ulama'*); he had also studied at the higher government schools, which had been brought together as the new Egyptian University in 1908. Later, he went to Oxford where his studies were cut short by the war and he returned to Egypt and took a post in the *shari'a* court system, as opposed to the *ahliyya* or national, secular courts. Before the war 'Ali 'Abd al-Raziq's family had been closely associated with the Umma Party, of which his brother, Hasan 'Abd al-Raziq, had been a founding member. After 1919, Hasan 'Abd al-Raziq joined Yakan's moderate group and died in the failed attempt to assassinate Yakan and Rushdi outside the offices of *al-Siyasa* in 1922. Therefore, it seems likely that 'Ali 'Abd al-Raziq's political message was founded upon a combination of Islamic reformism and liberalism as a likely partisan of the Liberal-Constitutional Party, even if he had not declared himself as such, which was not uncommon for those of liberal orientation. As the European Department at the Ministry of Interior reported, 'Ali 'Abd al-Raziq's education 'led him to discard accepted ideas on religious questions and seek for facts, by going back to the fountainheads, the Koran and the Traditions. In the mingling of civil and political authority, with the latter always predominant in Moslem countries throughout the ages, Shiekh Ali sees the principal reason for the failure of Mohammedan nations to advance as Christians have done.'[33]

The Orientalist critique of Islam, injected thus into political debates on the caliphate, created controversy. It provided the king with the opportunity to establish the Ittihad Party and the monarchy as defenders of 'tradition'. Relying on the support of the 'great mass of the illiterate population' on any religious question, the monarchists supported and probably encouraged the condemnation of 'Abd al-Raziq by a higher council at al-Azhar. This was the opinion of the Acting High Commissioner, Neville Henderson, who said that the monarchists were emboldened by the increasing support for the Ittihad Party in the electoral constituencies.[34] To score this point, the monarchist al-Azhar Caliphate Committee appealed to the Council of al-Azhar, which issued a *fatwa* on 14 August that compared 'Abd al-Raziq's arguments to those of the Kharijites, those who had seceded from the 'majority' Sunni community after the murder of Caliph 'Uthman beginning the period of party disunity in the Islamic *umma*.[35] The *fatwa*, like 'Abd al-Raziq's book, was loaded with a political message, implicitly comparing the *fitna* or civil war of Islamic history to the present state of party politics in Egypt. The *'ulama'* accused 'Abd al-Raziq of unorthodox views and expelled him from the *'ulama'*, which meant he was ousted from his post as *qadi* in the *shari'a* court of Alexandria. 'Abd al-Raziq appealed the ruling on the principle of 'absolute freedom of belief' guaranteed in the 1923 constitution.[36] But the council based its decision on the legal right of the higher council at al-Azhar to discipline any member of the *'ulama'*. Therefore, the council could declare that the constitutional right to freedom of opinion could not be applied against the religious authority of al-Azhar. In this way, controversy over the caliphate came to represent a debate on constitutional issues and a conflict of principles between liberal and religious nationalists, which manifested itself in a dispute between the Liberal-Constitutional and Ittihad ministers in the Ziwar government.

The controversy came to a head while Ziwar was on holiday. The Acting Prime Minister, Yahya Ibrahim, communicated the decision of the Council of al-Azhar to 'Abd al-'Aziz Fahmi, the Minister of Justice. Fahmi's interpretation of the al-Azhar regulations, which had been drafted by Fathi Zaghlul in 1911, indicated that the ruling of the *'ulama'* on Raziq's dismissal conflicted with the authority of the Minister of Justice. Fahmi claimed that employees of the *shari'a* and *ahliyya* courts were government officials and fell under the authority of the Ministry of Justice. Fahmi's opinion had political implications because he viewed the Ministry of Justice as the last bastion against royal 'absolutism'.[37] The issue was a continuation of the constitutional struggle between ministerial responsibility and the prerogatives of the ruler, in this case the question of authority over appointments to ministries. At a council meeting of the ministers, Fahmi refused to dismiss 'Abd al-Raziq and instead referred the issue to the Legal Department of the Ministry of Justice to determine if the constitution safeguarded citizens from a charge of 'false opinion'. Yahya Ibrahim protested that the legal department included Europeans, who were incompetent on religious issues. As he said:

> There are jurisdictions which concern certain classes of men, beside the jurisdiction of the Ulama, there is that which relates to the holder of a decoration, in case he commits an act unworthy of him he would be tried by a number of men holding the same decoration who could deprive him of it if they considered him unfit to hold it.[38]

Ibrahim went to Henderson at the British Residency and threatened to resign. Henderson cautioned him to preserve the coalition government. Ibrahim then visited the king. Although Fahmi had in the meantime agreed not to submit the issue to the Legal Department, Ibrahim's interview with the king resulted in the summary dismissal of Fahmi from the Ministry of Justice. 'Ali Mahir, a monarchist, was appointed in his place. The political principle that Ibrahim defended, backed by the king and the Ittihad Party leadership, was that the liberal declarations of the constitution did not supersede the historic role of religion in Egypt's political community. Shaykh Muhammad Shakar, a former vice chancellor of al-Azhar, who quit the Wafd Party for the Ittihad Party, stated the principle in the journal *al-Ittihad*.

> It was inadmissible that a decision of the Grand Ulama should be referred to Christian lawyers. In disapproving the verdict of the religious leaders of Islam, the State religion, the Minister of Justice attacked Islam and the Constitution. We are surprised the he did not ask the Contentieux [Legal Department] their opinion on Islam as the State religion.[39]

Joining the debate, *al-Siyasa* responded in an editorial arguing that Shakar should vent his anger at the 'Egyptian legislator who put aside the penalties provided by the Moslem Shariah and replaced them by our penal and Civil Codes taken from the French Law'.[40] On 8 September the Liberal-Constitutional Party met and declared the dismissal of Fahmi 'unconstitutional and not in accordance with political tradition'.[41] *Al-Siyasa* posed the rhetorical question: 'Why this sudden zeal for pure religion?'[42] The point was that Ittihad policy threatened to fundamentally alter the constitutional and legal framework of the Egyptian state. The political principles that divided liberals and monarchists included questions of ministerial responsibility and whether the civil code superseded the *shari'a* as the basis of national law. In 1923, the constitutional commission had debated these points without resolution. Fahmi and Makkabati had argued that the constitution should guard against the arbitrary power of the 'Oriental' ruler, particularly his power to dismiss 'his' ministers and elected representatives. At that time, Rushdi had replied that 'political traditions' in Europe had already established the limitations of the monarch's powers in relation to his ministers.[43] This assumption was less assured in 1925 because the king and his ministers had succeeded in bringing down one elected parliament and gone some distance toward establishing the dynast's historic autocratic powers. Clearly, the state's 'political tradition' was in dispute. For example, the Wafd Party petitioned the king against Ziwar's dissolution of the parliament in March, whereas the monarchist press asserted the king's constitutional 'right': 'On n'apprend pas a un roi son devoir' (We cannot deprive a king of his right).[44] On 8 September 1925 the Liberal-Constitutional Party denied that the divisions within the ministry had any religious significance, claiming that the members were all devout Muslims. But this simply reiterated the liberal principle of the separation of religious belief from politics and government. It was a view rejected by monarchists.

Some liberals stood on principle and resigned, including Tawfiq Doss, Muhammad 'Ali 'Aluba and Isma'il Sidqi. Nevertheless, even these liberals were confronted with a real dilemma. Thus, Doss observed that electoral success for the Liberal-Constitutional Party was only possible 'through the Unionists [Ittihad] with the prestige of the King's name behind them'. Yet, Doss could not remain in the ministry and break with liberal principle without 'a loss of public esteem and self respect'.[45] Even so, the pressure of public opinion against 'Abd al-Raziq was such that Doss quit the Liberal-Constitutional Party before the end of September, claiming that the religious issue had cost the party its popular support.[46] Indicating a widening ideological rift on the religious issue, the prominent liberal and religious scholar Shaykh Muhammad Bakhit resigned from the party to join the Ittihad Party. Critical of this flight from liberal principle before the religious campaign of the monarchists, *al-Siyasa* claimed that the constitution was inconsistent with a literal interpretation of Islamic law.[47] Bakhit, who succeeded Muhammad 'Abduh as grand mufti of Egypt in 1904, disagreed. In 1926 he published *Haqiqat al-Islam wa usul al-hukm* (True Islam and the Principles of Government), which argued that 'Abd al-Raziq had incorrectly distinguished between *shari'a* law and politics. Islamic law, Bakhit said, had not been intended as a spiritual truth only but as a law that established a political community. *Shari'a* law therefore required an executive authority to implement it and, after the Prophet, that duty was fulfilled by the caliphs. According to Bakhit, Islam rejected 'any authority the wielder of which is not charged with the execution of its [Islamic] edicts'.[48] Albert Hourani's analysis of this work suggests that what sounded like a defense of the 'great tradition' of Islam was in fact very much influenced by western ideas. In particular, Hourani noted the way Bakhit attempted to show that the caliph derived his authority from the consensus of the *umma*, rather than directly from God. In this, Bakhit did not depart from the principles of Islamic reformism, which equated the Islamic ideas of consultation (*shura*) and consensus (*ijma'*) with the idea of representative government. It was an assertion of the Islamic 'tradition', but not necessarily against the modern idea of representative institutions. On those principles the liberal constitution was not inconsistent with Islamic law or the caliphate. The issue was one of symbols. But Bakhit nevertheless rejected Raziq's thesis and reverted to Ibn Khaldun's theory that religious solidarity created consensus and community. Certainly this was one message that Bakhit wanted to assert, against those like Taha Husayn and 'Abd al-Raziq who would separate religion from politics. The monarchists successfully identified the Ittihad Party with this position. Those like Bakhit who split from the Liberal-Constitutional Party in September 1925 did so because the more radical liberals, such as Muhammad Husayn Haykal and 'Abd al-'Aziz Fahmi had denied or failed to appreciate the importance of Islam as a popular symbol and as a fundamental bond within Egyptian society. When Doss quit the party, he claimed that articles in *al-Siyasa* that denied that Islamic law could be reconciled with the constitution had damaged the party's public image and caused its split.[49]

The controversy enabled the Ittihad Party to more clearly establish an ideology that secured Islam as a symbol of the party. The Ittihadist leadership led a straightforward campaign on the religious issue in the run-up to elections. The secretary-general of the party, Mahmud Abu al-Nasr, made a speech on 11 November 1925 that condemned 'Abd al-Raziq's deceit (*kadhib*) and skeptical (*mutashakuk*) interpretation of Prophetic tradition (*hadith*), whereas the *fatwa* against 'Abd al-Raziq, he said, was founded on verifiable hadith. Nasr claimed that Islamic law could not, by definition, be unconstitutional. Rather, when 'Abd al-Raziq and 'Abd al-'Aziz Fahmi claimed that the Qur'an was full of inconsistencies and required interpretation, they plotted to create disturbances within the Islamic community. Nasr concluded, 'We should hold to religion first.' According to reports in the journal *al-Ittihad*, Nasr's speech received ecstatic chants of 'Brother, Brother, Brother!' His speech was followed by another from a lawyer in the *shari'a* courts in Alexandria that praised Nasr's words as an example of true patriotism (*al-wataniyya al-haqq*).[50] According to reports from Henderson, the language used by the monarchists defined the principles of ittihad in opposition to democratic party contests, with the monarchy as the key to political order. Ittihad meant that all parties must be agreed on the powers of the monarch in the constitution: 'Ittihad was a party of moderation and equilibrium, and a party of control if the consensus broke down.'[51]

The attempt to redefine the constitution along authoritarian lines rallied the remaining liberals and radical nationalists behind the constitution. But the king had already established himself as a powerbroker; thus criticisms of Ziwar's government carefully avoided any targeting of the king. After September 1925 the liberals concentrated their attacks on Nash'at, avoiding references to religion or monarch. In *al-Siyasa* 'Abd al-'Aziz Fahmi described the Ittihad political system as one based on rank (*mansib*), class or grade (*rutba*), and patronage or appointment. The organizers of this political system were described as profiteers (*naf'iyyin*). The only bond that held the governing system together was fear of revolt if autocratic restraints should be loosened.[52] The Wafd journal *al-Balagh* also carefully avoided criticizing the king, concentrating instead on making a case against the tyrannical rule of Nash'at, who was identified as the source of all evils. Nash'at's fall, it said, would mean more than the fall of a person, but of a system of authoritarian rule. It would mark the return to the principles of revolution, the people, and democracy (*thawra* 1919, *umma*, and *niyabiyya*). Nevertheless, *al-Balagh* did not fail to use republican rhetoric to pressure the monarchist government; thus it was said that it was not difficult to find historical examples comparable to the trials of the Egyptian people; indeed, in Britain and France patriots (*abna' al-bilad*) had struggled to attain democracy through revolution. Even if the present moment was not favourable to revolution in Egypt, the constitutionalists stood by the doctrine of natural right against the machinations of 'servile flatterers, sycophants, and the faithless'. The Ittihadists were such types, it reported, having concocted their party on a 'fairy tale' and sought thereby to instill a vestige of doubt in the minds of the 'loyal' (*ikhlas*).[53] *Al-Balagh* reminded its readers that the name ittihad was a poor cloak for the practice of exclusivity (*intiwa'*) and political rule by a clique ('*isaba*).[54]

In the Watani journal *al-Akhbar*, the Ittihad Party was described as having constructed autocracy (*hakim bi-amrihi*) on the rubble of democracy. In the present crisis, it said, the best weapon against autocracy was the constitution, which alone had established the rights of the individual (*fard*) and the authority of the people (*sha'b*). There were references to the Ittihad programme of rewriting the electoral law to weaken the legislative body, strengthen the executive (*tanfidhiyya*), and disenfranchise the people (*ahl*). The Watanist journal observed that the new editor of the monarchist journal, *La Liberté*, praised Mussolini. The article concluded, 'Truly they have lost their minds, their honour, their consciences, and their nationalism. For those who have lost these things how can they know the way to follow in life? Lost, they turn to a movement against the Egyptian nation.'[55]

The religious nationalism of the Ittihad Party broke the coalition of liberals and monarchists. It also revived the Wafd Party. All the opposition parties rallied around the 1923 constitution and the idea of a constitutional monarch in 1926. However, the episode also deepened ideological differences in Egyptian political society. The liberals were divided between those who had made the transition from Islamic reformism to liberalism and those who clung to 'tradition'. Hence, Bakhit held to the taboo regarding any religious question. Likewise, 'Ali Mahir's desperate attempts to moderate the monarchist position, the guardians of 'order and liberty', and win back the liberals committed to the coalition, failed. The divisions within liberal ranks indicated the ambivalence of elite politicians on the constitutional question. Ultimately, Nash'at's autocratic policies were too extreme. By threatening the constitution, he undermined the legitimate authority of the king. Yet, the liberals did not want a restoration of the Wafdist parliament of 1924. The fundamental constitutional question remained unresolved. This prompted Zaki Fahmi's prescription for rule by monarch and aristocracy.

The Elite of the Age

The question of the constitutional role of the monarchy was defended by Zaki Fahmi in 1926 in his *Safwat al-'Asr*. The context of his argument was clearly linked to the political debates and cultural controversies of the 1920s. Like Taha Husayn and 'Abd al-Raziq, Fahmi entered into the political debate on the proper interpretation of the Egyptian constitution. In the introduction to his work, Fahmi placed the king at the center of the constitutional regime by asserting that he had supported the writing of the 1923 constitution to establish cooperation between the government (*hukuma*) and the *umma*, establishing the principles of a responsible ministry while preserving the customs and traditions (*taqlid*) of the country. Fahmi claimed that the supporters of the monarchy, including Husayn Rushdi, had founded a constitution on consultative (*shuri*) and representative (*niyabi*) principles.[56] The language applied Islamic concepts (*shuri*) to Western forms of political representation (*niyabi*), indicating Fahmi's familiarity with Islamic reformism. Thus, the emphasis upon 'tradition' should not obscure the degree to which Fahmi crossed cultural boundaries, adopting some Western political ideas to fit within an overall Islamic and Middle Eastern framework. Although Zaki Fahmi supported the revolution, it was not the political revolution (*thawra*) of 'Abd al-Rahman al-Rafi'i and Mustafa Kamil, but rather the progressive (*ruqiy*) reformist plan or project of the Egyptian *nahda*, as exemplified by Muhammad 'Abduh and other reformers. He traced the way the Muhammad 'Ali dynasty turned to Western political models and administrative techniques and extolled the example of Muhammad 'Abduh and his followers, who chose the way of progress (*irtiqa'*) and education (*tahdhib*).[57] Yet, Fahmi's style and method were at odds with the dominant, liberal nationalist culture of literary Cairo, with its West-oriented literary formats.

Also in terms of content, Fahmi was somewhat removed from the Islamic reformist school insofar as his political thought did not rely on 'fundamental' Islamic concepts, but turned to medieval Islamic thought, particularly Ibn Khaldun, and modern Western conservatism. As noted in Chapter 2, Zaki Fahmi employed a 'mirrors for princes' or manuals for government literary form, which abounded after the fall of the classical caliphate between the tenth and thirteenth centuries.[58] Fahmi engaged in the debate on the caliphate by suggesting that rather than return to the classical era, Egyptians should look to the example of the medieval period. Another objective for Fahmi was to rehabilitate Ibn Khaldun's political thought, which had been critiqued by Taha Husayn.

Fahmi divided his work into three parts. The first part is a history of the Muhammad 'Ali dynasty, the second part is an interpretive history of constitutionalism, and the third part a collection of biographies of members of the elite. The purpose of the third part of the book was to identify the important political actors and their modes of social and political interaction. The analytical framework is thus one that views social relations in terms of personalities. One of the basic assumptions of this type of analysis is that, to paraphrase Zaghlul, political principles are inseparable from personality. It is important to see that a political theory premised on the idea of the strength of personality was attractive to notables, whose power was 'ascriptive', based on the customary deference accorded to members of the great families, most importantly the ruling family. The book therefore underscored the principle of deference and obedience in a specific language of status honours (known to Montesquieu as 'false honours') and family connections to the monarch. Inventing a royalist language was an integral part of the cultural campaign. Emphasis was placed upon status through titles and decorations. The title grades indicated the formality and ornamental cultural characteristics of the Egyptian regime between 1922 and 1952.

The civil list for the year 1936, for instance, described a system of grades beginning with the title of *riyasa* (first degree of honour) and following in hierarchic order through the *imtiyaz* (second degree of honour), degree of *bashawiyya* (pasha), and the degrees of *bikawiyya* (bey) of the first and second degree. The degrees established a pecking order in the elite structure of royal patronage. The degree of *riyasa* was available only to those who had held the office of prime minister, the degree of *imtiyaz* only to ministers; pasha was to be bestowed only on a *mudir, muhafiz* (rural and urban governor), or *a'yan* who had distinguished themselves by service to the country. The title bey was given to civil servants according to pay scale requirements. The list also included the grade *hadarat sahib al-dawla* (his highness lord of state) to be held only by ministers of the first rank; followed by similar epitaphs of excellence, including *hadara sahib al-mu'ala* to he held only by those holding the decoration of the Order of Muhammad 'Ali, presidents of the royal diwan, *mudirs*, and sirdars; *hadara sahib al-sa'ada* to be held by pashas; *hadara sahib al-'izza* to be held only by beys of the first degree. These restrictions did not apply to members of the royal family, who had access to them by right of heredity. The decorations also included the Order of Uthman, Isma'il and the Nile. Overall, the system dated from the year 1915, when the British Protectorate regime abolished the Ottoman system whereby the monarch was known as khedive, and instead created the sultanate, which was in its turn abolished with the declaration of Egyptian independence, constitutional government, and the monarchy in 1922. The civil list was first published in 1927, the year following the publication of Fahmi's book.[59]

To demonstrate that the king was the head of a modern, rather than patrimonial state, Zaki Fahmi said that the true 'men of politics' were distinguished by a proven record of bureaucratic service to the nation-state. The biographical treatments of the top level members of the elite, mostly pashas, were selective, not exhaustive. Most of those chosen were either relatives or clients of the king, but not exclusively so. Some of the king's clientele were those who had only been neutralized through political party contests and co-opted by the system of royal patronage. For example, the niece of Ahmad Lutfi al-Sayyid, a well-known liberal thinker, has said that the king pensioned off her father, Sa'id Lutfi al-Sayyid, to 'get at' her uncle Ahmad.[60] That Ahmad Lutfi al-Sayyid was also included in the biographies suggests that he had become one of the king's clients or had taken an independent course acceptable to the monarchists. The king thus neutralized important liberal opponents, at least in the short term, as Ahmad Lutfi might simply have been hedging his bets in 1925. (He took a position in the Fu'ad I University.) It is difficult to make strict categorizations according to ideological orientation because patronage could bring about unexpected alliances for purely tactical reasons; for example, the liberal intellectual TahaHusayn was the editor of the Ittihad journal, which propagated traditionalist arguments in favor of the monarchy, presumably a position taken by Taha Husayn for financial reasons or to block the Wafd's hegemony. It is notable that 'Abd al-'Aziz Fahmi was not included in the biographical dictionary, doubtless because of his implacable ideological aversion to royal autocracy. This is in accordance with the purpose of the *tabaqat* or 'prosopographical' literary form as a science that established the trustworthiness of witnesses and provided a model for social relations. 'Abd al-'Aziz Fahmi was one of those liberals who stood on principle and broke with the monarchists in 1925. Hence, although in one sense Zaki Fahmi's biographical dictionary simply listed those who were tied to the monarchy by royal patronage or family connection, it also described a political culture defined by the practice of *intisab*. This term implied patronage, describing the tendency in Ottoman political culture for state officials to seek the protection of important political households as a guard against the insecurities of appointments in the bureaucracy. Ehud Toledano examined this type of patronage in his study of nineteenth century Egypt, but such a political culture would have persisted to some degree into the twentieth century. *Intisab* is also very much like the political culture of Islamic societies in the medieval period described in Ibn Khaldun's *Muqaddima*. Nevertheless, the biographical dictionary speaks of nation, not household.[61]

The ruler took first place in the biographical dictionary with an account of the life and accomplishments of the king, who was referred to as *hadrat sahib al-jalala maulana al-malik al-mu'azzam Ahmad Fu'ad al-Awwal*. Fu'ad's biography was followed by a history of the Muhammad 'Ali dynasty, emphasizing its role in the construction of the modern Egyptian state. The dynastic history is followed by a description of the king's clientele among *dhawat*, *a'yan*, and *'ulama'*.

The elaborate hierarchy is summarized on the title page, which provides a ranking of the orders of the state, beginning with the king and princes of the royal house (*umara' al-bait al-malaki*), followed by lords of the state (*ashab al-dawla*) and prime ministers (*ru'asa' al-wizarat*), leaders of the coalition parties of 1925, ministers and deputy ministers, ambassadors, heroes of the revolution, governors, heads of departments, senators and deputies, the 'excellent' *'ulama'*, poets, journalists, doctors, *a'yan*, important merchants and 'all those of high standing and status among the noble sons of the Nile'. The list appears as a roll call in hierarchic order, prefiguring the parade of personalities that follows. The list also demonstrates the prestige and power of the state; therefore the deputies and senators follow in descending order after governors and heads of departments, whereas the provincial and urban notables come last, demonstrating an aristocratic power structure centered on the palace, the bureaucracy and the parliament, with the notability as the social base.[62]

Although carefully indicating hierarchy and order, Zaki Fahmi also recognized the accomplishments of the revolution; thus the biographies that make up the third section of the book began with Zaghlul, whose life epitomized the history of the national 'awakening' (*nahda*). His career was exemplary of the social integration of the *a'yan* into elite political society, if not equality with the *dhawat*. Born in 1860 into a family whose head held the post of *'umda* in the village of Ibyanh, Gharbiyya province, Zaghlul was educated in the village *kuttab* and then at al-Azhar. There he was profoundly influenced by al-Sayyid Jamal al-Din al-Afghani and his disciples, particularly al-Ustadh al-Imam al-Shaykh Muhammad 'Abduh. Zaghlul attended 'Abduh's lectures on divine unity (*risalat al-tawhid*); it was to this tuition that Fahmi credited Zaghlul's ability to perceive the way (*tariq*) – the way of moderation. But he was also, like Mustafa Kamil, adept in French and theories of patriotism and citizenship, which he learnt at the private French law school where he attained a license while employed in the Ministry of Interior. He was the first Egyptian to be appointed to the mixed courts. Zaghlul's political ascendance came with his marriage to the daughter of Prime Minister Mustafa Fahmi Pasha and his appointment to Fahmi's ministry on the advice of Lord Cromer, indicating the importance of family connection and patronage to secure political office. Zaki Fahmi reproduced a speech given by Zaghlul when Cromer 'elevated' him in 1907. It said that it was the party (*shi'a*) of 'Abduh that had chosen the way of education (*tahdhib*) and progress (*irtiqa'*). When he was elected to the legislative assembly in 1914, he began a new period in his life as leader of the opposition, demanding legislation that would establish the principles of freedom (*hurriyya*). But on this stage of Zaghlul's career Fahmi's language is more ambiguous, cautioning that freedom has two meanings and that the construction of authority (*amr*) was possible only with an understanding of the two meanings.[63]

While he was not explicit on the point, Fahmi implied that liberty was dangerous, leading as it might to democratic or social anarchy, as well as to individual freedoms. Liberty therefore had to be safeguarded by responsible consultative authority. Thus, alongside 'natural right' there was the conservative idea of the state as guarantor of liberty. To make this point Zaki Fahmi contrasted the exemplary patriotic leader, Zaghlul, with the exemplary prince, 'Umar Tusun, whose efforts to unite (*ittihad*) the parties followed immediately after Zaghlul's biography. The juxtaposition of Zaghlul's heroic efforts during the revolution with Tusun's Ittihad campaign underscored the special role played by the royal family in building of consensus and establishing legitimate authority. The Ittihad campaign was begun in December 1923 in a letter to *al-Ahram* signed by all the princes of the royal family and again in another letter published in *al-Akhbar* in December 1924. The first letter came in the midst of a bitter electoral campaign, the second after the fall of the Wafd government, but each claimed that Zaghlul had sacrificed the interests of the country for personal ends and that factional disputes were contrary to a 'true love of country'.[64] Tusun enjoined the leaders of the parties to 'forget past offenses and sink their personalities in the sole personality of the beloved nation'.[65] As the exemplary prince, Tusun was marked by willingness, so Fahmi implied, to submit self-interest to the common good. In his biography Tusun was described as having given gifts to charitable societies, such as the firmest bond group (*jam'iyyat al-'urwa al-wuthqa*), which used the phrase given by Afghani and 'Abduh to their political pamphlet published in Paris during their exile from Egypt). Tusun was credited with helping to organize the Wafd, which originally was designed to reconcile the various classes and personalities that competed among the 'brotherhood of Egyptians' (*misriyyin al-ikhwan al-shaqiqin*). The idea of community in this phrase, as in other references, had the sense of family, *shaqiq* meaning the blood tie of the full brother and sister, used in a figurative sense to define the nation as one organic family. The narrative underscores the point that the national family included all religious groups. Tusun was praised for his charitable donations to Islamic and Coptic groups, a policy designed to instill unity and social well-being within the national brotherhood. It is significant that Fahmi did not call for unconditional reverence of the prince; instead the prince must be seen to be fulfilling his political and social obligations, normally through charitable acts, one of the pillars of Islam. The biography recorded that Tusun was interested in agricultural reforms and the condition of 'his fellahin', improving the conditions and productive techniques on his family's estates (*da'ira*). This paternal concern for his tenants and sub-tenants was reciprocated, said Fahmi, by the love of the people for Tusun. And although Tusun was described as Ottoman in his breeding, he was nevertheless regarded as belonging for the most part to the Egyptian nation because of the concern he showed for the fellahin through philanthropy. Hence, Fahmi said that during the great national demonstrations of 1919 when a crowd assembled under the balconies of his palace, they cheered and shouted for him and would not disperse until Tusun appeared and greeted them. And that, said Fahmi, was their way with him on every public occasion and celebration. There is in Fahmi's description of relations between the prince and 'his peasants' a prescription for social order based on the patrimony of the great family estates in which the subjects recognized the authority and leadership qualities of the prince or notable. This description of the political relationship of the elite to the mass is typical of Fahmi's work because it stressed the moral element in the relationship and was applied equally to the class of princes, notables, and politicians in their relations with 'their' people. The reference to 1919 is remarkable because it described the demonstrations not as revolts against the great landholders but rather as a reaffirmation of the role of the notables in leading the people, even in revolutionary moments.[66]

The moral tone of the book's collection of biographies is established by the opposition of the virtuous prince to the Machiavellian politician. But the text also underlined a political philosophy founded on consensus and the king's role as ultimate arbiter. The sequence of biographies that followed upon Tusun's biography can be read as a chronology of events that led to the emergence of the king as the dominant figure in the political landscape. After Zaghlul and Tusun came the biography of 'Adli Yakan. Demonstrating the continuing importance of the household in Egyptian political society, *yakan* means son of the sister, 'Adli Yakan's father having been a nephew of Muhammad 'Ali. Yakan's origins were in a 'noble' Macedonian family associated with the dynasty from its inception. Educated in Istanbul from the age of eight and afterwards in France and in French and German schools in Egypt, Yakan married the daughter of a former prime-minister, Sharif Pasha, and secretary to another, Nubar Pasha. Beside this exceptional pedigree, Yakan served as a *mudir* in several provinces and as governor of Cairo, leading to his appointment as Minister of Interior. When the legislative assembly sat in 1914, he served as government deputy, whereas Zaghlul chose the opposition. Nevertheless, Yakan advised the government to support Zaghlul's proposed constitutional reforms.[67] Fahmi said that Yakan's political gravitas was such that he was able to 'crush' with a word of criticism or 'encourage' with a kind remark.[68] That he broke with Zaghlul in 1921 to join Tharwat and Rushdi in the official delegation is a fact ignored by Fahmi, doubtless because of the bitter factional conflict created thereby. The biography concludes by enumerating Yakan's virtues (*mazaya*) and honours: his appointment to the council of the Islamic Charitable Society (*majlis idara al-jam'iyya al-khayriyya al-islamiyya*), the Geographical Society, and to the senate on 4 March 1925. The last appointment marked his removal from political party contests.

The next figure in the sequence was Husayn Rushdi Pasha, serving a chronological purpose insofar as Rushdi chaired the constitutional commission that was established during the premiership of Tharwat that followed Yakan's ministry. Rushdi belonged to an 'old and respected' Albanian family that had come to Egypt with Muhammad 'Ali. His great grandfather served as a general (*qa'id 'amm*) in the army that expelled the British from Egypt at the battle of Sananiyya in 1807. His grandfather was also a *qa'id*. Rushdi was educated in Paris. Upon his return to Egypt, he was appointed a *mufattish* in the departments of finance and education and later in the mixed courts and appellate court. From 1908 he was involved in the reform of religious endowments, which cost him the favor of Khedive 'Abbas II. When war was declared and the khedive deposed, Rushdi was appointed prime minister after Muhammad Sa'id resigned. Rushdi countenanced martial law during the war to 'support the *umma* and the throne' and proved his patriotism during the revolution by supporting the Wafd. Fahmi pointed out that this support was not self-interested; rather it cost him politically when he resigned from the ministry in 1918. Like Yakan, Rushdi and his 'excellent' companions ('capitalists and engineers') collaborated with the British in the teeth of fierce resistance from the Wafd Party; nevertheless his efforts 'raised' Egypt in the estimation of other nations – the final proof of his patriotism. It seems from Zaki Fahmi's history of the negotiations with the British that Zaghlul, Yakan and Rushdi were regarded as equals. Zaki Fahmi supported the original Wafd coalition on the principle of equality between *dhawat* and *a'yan*, marking the transformation in the social composition of the elite, a revolutionary change in Egypt's political culture. Yet, Fahmi was equally concerned that the integration of notables did not radically alter the dynasty's hereditary role in politics. Therefore he concluded Rushdi's biography by describing the royal decree that set up the system of royal titles and decorations (*al-awsima wa al-nayashin*) accomplished under the Rushdi wartime ministry.[69]

Yahya Ibrahim followed Rushdi in the biographical section. He was initially educated in the administrative school established by Muhammad 'Ali and attended a student mission to France. Like the other *dhawat*, he had an exemplary record of government service. Yahya Ibrahim was a favorite of the king, with a long list of titles and decorations, including the *bashawiyya*, the Order of 'Uthman, the Order of the Nile, and in addition to these he was knighted by the British monarch. According to Fahmi, the most important service made by Ibrahim to the king (and the British) was the formation of a ministry after the fall of Tawfiq Nasim's government in 1923.

Fahmi said that Ibrahim's ministry was formed 'against the will of the people' (*jumhuriyya*). Yet, Ibrahim enabled the publication of a constitution 'that avoided prejudice and secured the king's powers of patronage' (*ri'aya*).⁷⁰

A theory of royal patronage runs through these descriptions of elite statesmen. The king distributed honors to sustain a cohesive ruling group over the mass of the royal subjects (*ra'iyya*). Political rule required technical and moral education of the prince (*brins*) and elite (*nukhba*).⁷¹ The theory is demonstrated, by Fahmi, in the course of the biographical list, which is abbreviated here to reflect Fahmi's portrait of the elite. It is supplemented with commentaries from the British Foreign Office file 'Leading Personalities in Egypt', which was produced in 1930, to draw a parallel between the political imagination of monarchist and colonial mindsets, particularly as these reified after the departure of Allenby from the summer of 1925. Colonial analysis after 1925 will be discussed in the following chapter.⁷²

Following upon Yahya Ibrahim, the biographical dictionary continued with portraits of other members of the old *dhawat* elite: Muhammad Sa'id Pasha, Yusef Sulayman- a Copt, who was a member of the original Wafd, but later turned to the king-; Ahmad dhu al-Fiqar of the Ittihad Party whose namesake from the era of Isma'il, 'Ali dhu al-Fiqar was described by Robert Hunter as having been practically 'raised in the laps of the viceroys' (the term viceroy synonymous with khedive);⁷³ Fiqar is followed by Muhammad Tawfiq Rafa'at Pasha, who is followed by Muhammad Fathallah Barakat Pasha, the leading Wafdist in the list after Zaghlul himself. Barakat is an example of the primordial bond in politics, being Zaghlul's nephew (*ibn shaqiqa*); moreover, it has been shown that by late 1924, Zaghlul had spoken of the importance of blood relatives in the formation of a secure political base because of the challenges he had suffered from factions within the Wafd Party. Zaghlul, it is recorded, could depend upon Fathallah Barakat for his 'loyalty and devotion' (*amana wa ikhlas*). Marqus Hanna Pasha, another Wafdist, followed Barakat, yet Hanna accepted an appointment to the senate in 1925, suggesting that the king neutralized one of the radical effendi ideologues. Hanna is followed by Mahmud Fakhri Pasha, a *dhawat* of Circassian origin who married the king's daughter, Princess Fawkiyya, and had previously been married to the daughter of the king's brother, Sultan Husayn, an indicator of the way the monarch knitted the royal family around him. Fakhri had held the position of governor of Cairo before holding a ministerial position between 1920 and 1923. In 1926 he was appointed diplomatic representative to France and, according to the British files on the elite, fitted the royalist paradigm of princely rule: 'He believes himself to be a master of the art of conciliation.'[74] 'Aziz 'Azt Pasha was also in the diplomatic corps, appointments to which relied solely upon royal patronage. The list continues with Sa'id dhu al-Fiqar, who was described in the Abdin Files as a highly trusted member of the king's cabinet, and had been involved in securing royal powers in the constitution;[75] al-Marham al-Fariq Rashid Husni Pasha was described as having associated with the royal family from the time of Isma'il; Ahmad Bey Muhammad Hasanayn, who succeeded Nash'at as president of the royal diwan and was to remain in that position for a decade; he was followed by a liberal, Rashwan Mahfuz Pasha, supporting the view that Fahmi's portrait of the elite praised the non-partisan union of parties; Salih Pasha 'Anan, minster of public works during the ministry of Ziwar; followed by 'one of the great personalities of Egypt' (*kibar wujaha' Misr*), doyen of the great Shawarbi family of Qalyubiyya, Muhammad Pasha al-Shawarbi; followed by Hamid Pasha al-Shawarbi and 'Umar Bey al-Shawarbi. Hamid al-Shawarbi stood as an Ittihad candidate in the elections. The dictionary continues with biographies of Qalini Fahmi Pasha, a Copt from Minya whose family was credited with assisting Muhammad Sultan Pasha and Nubar Pasha in the reform of the corvée after the British occupation; 'Umar Sultan Pasha, described as a great notable from the province of Minya (*kibar a'yan mudiriyyat al-Minya*), a descendent of the famous Muhammad Sultan who had established the family's political stake in Minya during the reign of Isma'il. These biographies indicate that Fahmi wanted to show the continuity of the royal family and its connection with those notables who had been recruited by the ruler to assist in the formation of the modern Egyptian state through the nineteenth and into the twentieth century. Sultan is followed by Husayn Pasha Wasif, an 'ancient' who had served in the legislative assembly before the war on the side of Zaghlul, but in 1922 acted as minister in the government of Tharwat; Muhammad Bey Sabri, a member of the Queen's family; Ahmad Bey Sadiq, a young man of good family and *mudir* of Girga; 'Abd al-Fatah Bey Raf'at, *mudir* of the state police; Husayn Bey Wahba Bash-Mufattish, inspector for the Ministry of Interior; Ahmad Lutfi Bey al-Sayyid, prominent liberal intellectual; Doctor 'Abd al-Hamid Bey Abu Hayf, director of the Arabic section of the law school after 1922; and, to conclude this sample from the highest grades of the monarchical regime, Afifi Bey Husayn al-Barbari, who had stood as a Wafdist in the first elections. Barbari is the 50th name in the list of 122 biographies of notables that follows upon those of the royal family (King Ahmad Fu'ad, Sultan Husayn Kamil, Muhammad 'Ali Pasha Kabir, Sa'id Pasha, Isma'il Pasha, Tawfiq Pasha, 'Abbas Hilmi Pasha II, Prince 'Umar Tusun, Prince Muhammad 'Ali and Prince Yusuf Kamil). The dictionary includes effendi tarboosh wearers and shaykhs in turban and *jallabiyya*. The shaykhs appear in a cluster of nine, including Muhammad 'Abduh. The 51st biography in the collection is the Coptic Patriarch (*ra'a*) Sum'an Bey Gabriel al-Qamis, who was also an *'umda* and was appointed to the senate with the grade of bey of the second degree. (Another four Coptic officials are included in the list.)

The general impression is that Fahmi's biographical dictionary contained all those who the king could count upon not to actively resist his authority, as well as those closest to him by family relation and clients who had proven loyal or accepted patronage. Political relations as envisaged by Fahmi were primarily those of blood relationships, the most potent form of group solidarity, as described by Ibn Khaldun. But there was also the bond of clientelism, cemented by 'false honors'. The biographical treatments also included representatives of important families who could be expected to have an interest in bureaucratic or political influence. The inclusion of Wafdists might seem contradictory, as the Wafd Party was not reconciled to monarchism, yet by 1925 Zaghlul had been forced to make bargains with his rivals, both liberals and monarchists. The compromises made by Wafdists did not establish ideological consensus, but did bring about a greater degree of parity between the parties and leading personalities. Therefore, there was less room for political action according to ideological preference.

Compromise was imposed upon liberals, radicals, and monarchists alike. In this way, Fahmi's portrait of politics resembled the elite model described by Max Weber, Louis Namier, Louis Joseph Cantori, John Waterbury and Malcolm Yapp. For instance, Zaghlul's nephew Fathallah Barakat accepted appointment to the coalition ministry in 1926, acting perhaps as Zaghlul's proxy in a government that denied Zaghlul a ministerial position. Likewise, the names that Zaki Fahmi put at the top of the hierarchical arrangement of personalities were those the king had neutralized, or shortly would, by appointments and honors, such as Yakan, Rushdi and Tharwat, or those who had been loyal to the king, such as Yahya Ibrahim, Tawfiq Nasim and Muhammad Sa'id. Together these men led the governments from the creation of the legislative assembly in 1913 until the first elections held in 1923 and 1924. The biographical dictionary included all the prime ministers of the period, and, at the administrative level prominent officials identified with the king's clientele in all the ministries and departments.

To conclude, Zaki Fahmi's description of the elite confronted the unresolved question: under what arrangement could the classes, communities and parties find consensus, what political settlement would stick, and what would be the glue, legal contract or monarchic patronage. The liberal constitution of 1923 had not resolved the question because it retained the statute laws of the khedival regime and its symbols. The liberal position was premised on the idea of a gradual evolution toward a West-oriented modernity, but that view did not satisfy radical or conservative visions. Moreover, the elections had brought new social groups into the political process malleable to political persuasion from the left and the right. The new political framework had seen the king, firstly, ally with the Wafd, and, secondly, initiate a monarchist campaign that was both political and cultural. Published in 1926, Zaki's Fahmi's book was part of that campaign. Its portrait of society was highly ideological; it offered a political model based on the idea of royal patronage as the regulating principle over and above political factions and cultural divisions. Fahmi's political theory represented the king and notables as the guardians of social order by their virtues, particularly duty to the state, charity and philanthropy toward the masses, and, finally, respect for 'tradition'.

In Fahmi's estimation, the ethic of personal example was uniquely suited to the princes and notables, who inspired the lower orders by their moral example. Indeed, there is some concession to the democratic spirit of the times in imagining the middle stratum of notables also demonstrating their moral character through the electoral process. But the virtues thus extolled were pre-modern. Fahmi sanctified the traditional aristocratic 'right' to lead, with the lower orders represented as essentially obedient and subservient to the elevated classes. Fahmi's political theory was thus founded on the idea of social and moral cohesion inherent in hierarchical and deferential social relations between the prince and his subjects, the lords and 'their' local communities. That the middle level notables and effendis were included in the status hierarchy alongside the *dhawat* and pashas, just as they were candidates for royal patronage, might suggest that the consolidation of the post-revolutionary aristocracy was as much a consequence of the royalist cultural campaign as it was conditioned by the elite structure of Egyptian political society.[76]

CHAPTER 7

NEO-COLONIALISM

British policy underwent a critical period of reanalysis in the interwar years, even if the outcome was only a new form of old imperial methods. Allenby adopted the Milner recommendation for concessions and treaty negotiations in 1921, to the dismay of many in British political society. A remark by the Foreign Secretary, Austen Chamberlain, to one of the dismissed members of Allenby's staff, Archibald Kerr, gives some indication of the attitudes of members of the British cabinet. As Chamberlain said: 'There was a moment last year [1924] when we here [the British cabinet] thought that you in Cairo were not playing the game.'[1] The rules of the game involved perpetuating British power through the old Cromerian methods of collaboration and indirect rule. Whereas Winston Churchill would have reduced politics to a palace coterie with British support, Foreign Office policy involved the British in a complicated arrangement of Egyptian political personalities whose acts were tortuous to predict or control, yet followed a pattern similar to Waterbury's theory of segmented cliques interested in protecting their power bases by access to state patronage.[2]

Allenby's policy had been premised on the idea that it was impossible to administer Egypt in the face of immense popular demonstrations against British rule and military occupation. Allenby was therefore ready to countenance a withdrawal of troops from Cairo and Alexandria to strategic sites along the Suez Canal; meanwhile, as a consequence of the 1922 declaration, which was pushed through only at Allenby's insistence, many British officials were removed from posts in the Egyptian administration. However, the chiefs of staff of the British military establishment were determined to retain bases in Cairo and Alexandria.[3] Moreover, the British cabinet regarded Egypt as an integral part of the British Empire, with political influence in Cairo a key component in overall strategic thinking.[4] Recognizing the limits of imperial reform, Allenby's staff in Cairo and the Foreign Office in London developed a line of argument that showed that Egypt had always been an autonomous, self-governing province of the Ottoman Empire and that the Protectorate regime had been an expediency measure only. The key to British influence in Egypt was to find acceptable terms for a treaty between Britain and Egypt and normalize international relations between the two sovereign countries.

One of those officials that departed Egypt with Allenby, Maurice Amos, gave lectures in England on the constitutional history of Egypt to educate the British public on Egypt's relations with Britain. His lectures involved a critique of some of the accepted doctrines of British imperial thinking. As he said, 'I always used to think as a young man whenever I heard the fellahin mentioned that I saw the cloven hoof of the Tory.'[5] On the one hand Amos thus pointed to the conservatism of British colonial ideology, founded as it was on the idea of an aristocratic obligation to govern primitive peoples. Pure theory, the idea of a British mandate over the fellahin was nothing more than a justification for perpetual British military occupation. Another dimension of colonial doctrine, according to Amos, was that the British had a duty to instruct the Egyptians in the principles of good government. As Amos said, many Egyptians had fully accepted that logic and avidly learnt the principles; therefore they had come to expect that the British should support the setting up of a modern type of representative political system in Egypt, self-governing and independent. The incurable perception that Egypt could not govern itself was a theory propagated by the 'Tory' imperialistic establishment. But on the contrary, as Amos argued, Egypt had a long-standing constitutional history of self-government under an Egyptian dynasty ruling with ministerial advice. After the Dufferin Dispatch of 1883, the British had, in theory, acted only as advisers to the ministers. Egyptian ministers were of course compelled to accept the advice of British Foreign Office staff and appointees to advisory positions in the Egyptian ministries. However, the Egyptian constitutional system, dating from before the British occupation, remained intact and operative. Thus rather than conforming to colonialism and its dogmas of tutelage or mandate to safeguard subject populations, the relationships between Egypt and Britain were a normal matter of international law. The Protectorate had been the anomaly, not the norm. It was therefore necessary to restore Egyptian autonomy and, with the collapse of the Ottoman Empire, normalize relations through an international treaty. These facts were laid out in the Milner Report and adopted as policy by Allenby in Egypt.

Allenby's policy was not posed as revolutionary change, but a reversion to the policies of Cromer and the pre-Protectorate status quo. Basic observations on Egyptian politics and society established by Cromer were reiterated by Amos: 90 percent of the population was illiterate and beyond the pale of political participation; political society was restricted to the 10 percent of those educated in Western-type government or private schools; Egypt's elder statesmen were largely foreign in culture, Turkish Muslims or Syrian Christians; however, the rural notables represented a powerful and wealthy indigenous class, with strong religious and social bonds with the mass of the illiterate population.[6] Officials like Amos had come to recognize that the nationalist demands of the educated Egyptians were a legitimate expression of national opinion; moreover, the political culture of the effendiyya was entirely modern. Whereas Lord Cromer, Lord Kitchener and Sir Reginald Wingate had steadfastly denied this fact, Amos said that the educated Egyptians were representative of the entirety of Egyptian society, having close ties with the lower orders in society through the press, the café and family bonds.[7]

This type of analysis, developed in the teeth of massive protests by the Egyptians, led to the new policy of concessions and treaty negotiations. The officials in Cairo did not entirely abandon the idea of imperial or colonial duty to the Egyptians; it was expressed in the belief that the British needed to direct Egyptian politics along a moderate course between the extremes of revolutionary disorder and absolutist rule. Thus, a new form of colonialism took shape premised on the idea of normalizing relations between Britain and Egypt through a treaty or some form of settlement that safeguarded imperial interests, whilst at the same time shaping Egyptian political culture and forging links with influential leaders of Egyptian political society. British policy in this form met the interests and values of a significant sector of the Egyptian elite, as well as at least offering the possibility that Egypt would continue to serve as the British intelligence centre and military base in the Middle East. Although Churchill rejected this policy on principle and Allenby's successor, Lord Lloyd, obstructed treaty negotiations, Milner and Allenby had indeed changed the playing field, if not the rules of the game.[8]

The Rules of the Game

The rules of the game involved respecting the interests and ambitions of the great notables, who in recompense would enable the British to influence decisions affecting British strategic interests. The arrangement was not new. It had been evident in Cromer's policies; however, the wartime regime had degraded British status and enhanced the power of the notables. Moreover after 1919 British officials were less confident of the application of force; thus, colonial relationships became more political, less a matter of paternalistic supervision by British agents. This was apparent in Amos' rejection of the 'Tory' or aristocratic mode of imperial rule.[9]

The practice of British influence was apparent in the reports of Neville M. Henderson, who served as Acting High Commissioner after the departure of Allenby in June 1925 until Lloyd's arrival in October. Henderson's analysis accentuated the interests of the pashas and beys within the limited arena of Cairo's royal court and political clubs. The code of behaviour in this context depended upon establishing contacts and associates with access to power and thereby maintaining a stake in political brokering. The code was broken when one chose an independent course, as did Zaghlul, at the expense of socializing with one's peers. Muhammad Saʻid, for instance, accused Zaghlul of betraying all those with whom he had ever formed a political alliance.[10] British officials, including Henderson, liked to observe that the king and Zaghlul were old adversaries at the gaming tables of the Muhammad ʻAli Club. The 'gentleman's club' is a suitable metaphor for the social world of elite political society, intimate and relatively confined, restrictive in its rules of admittance and, more so, in its standard of conduct. Politics was a game of shifting allegiances among friends and rivals for relative, but not absolute, advantage. The politician was forced to engage in constant wagering of political capital to maintain political stakes. Masters of this style of politics were Sidqi, Yakan, Tharwat and Nasim, none of whom would take a political party card. Tharwat thus refused to publicly declare allegiance to the Liberal-Constitutional Party, although he effectively led the liberals from 1921 to 1923 and 1927 to 1928. In this type of political arena, the king imagined himself arbiter and appeared to have won the game when Zaghlul fell after the murder of the Sirdar. However, the liberals, whom the king loathed on grounds of personal dislike and political principle, could not be forced from the political arena because Yakan, Tharwat and Sidqi were required to win the confidence of Egyptian bureaucratic officials and British observers at the High Commission.

It is notable that Sidqi is mentioned in Zaki Fahmi's book, but denied a biographical treatment. This is not necessarily partisanship, but the moral language Fahmi used could hardly be applied to the 'strong man', the Machiavellian manipulator and coercer. Nor could an independent figure like Sidqi be reconciled to the monarchist idea of consensus, consultation and party coalition. He was, however, essential to the neo-colonial arrangement. In the estimation of Henderson and John Murray, who commented on Henderson's reports, Sidqi was an invaluable political asset, although utterly shameless in his private and public life. In the first instance, his seduction of Yahya Ibrahim's daughter cost him his seat in Rushdi's ministry in 1915, which meant that he was irreconcilable with the king's favorite, Ibrahim. In the second instance, he was renowned for his unprincipled political maneuvering.[11] The king compared Sidqi to Tharwat. The two were on the surface apparently friends, but Tharwat was an obstacle to Sidqi's ambitions to become prime minister. Sidqi therefore pressed for Tharwat to be absorbed into the senate, and the king complied. The king also neutralized in this way Yakan, Rushdi, Yusef Qattawi and Sulayman Abaza. But the king criticized Sidqi for taking an independent card and in doing so identified one of the typical tactics of elitist politics: maintaining autonomy of movement so as to be able to form strategic alliances for immediate advantage. Henderson, to whom the king made these observations, advised the king that Sidqi was useful in the Ministry of Interior for his firm hand.[12] The British relied upon Sidqi's authoritarian command of the bureaucracy, yet Henderson was equally aware of the dangers and uncertainties that attended too great a reliance on one personality. 'I have the impression that once he [Sidqi] has crushed Saad [Zaghlul] he would like to put on the mantle as the saviour of his country from the British. He is a strong man as well as the brain [in the administration] and I shall do what I can to prevent his throwing in his hand. I have the highest admiration for his intelligence but I distrust him for his arrière-pensées' (ulterior motives).'[13]

Liberals, like Sidqi, typified a mode of politics based on personal autonomy and strategic, short term alliances. Thus, Henderson described Muhammad Mahmud as 'egregious' when he pulled a faction of liberals away from the coalition liberal-monarchist government during the Raziq controversy. Mahmud helped forge the opposition bloc with the Wafd and thus won the king's lasting enmity. Meanwhile, the less ambitious liberals like Tawfiq Doss and Muhammad 'Ali 'nailed their colours' to the fence, biding their time until a safe gap allowed them to make it to one side or the other of the political divide. The faction led by Muhammad Mahmud in 1925 was designed only to block the monarchist surge, rather than support for the Wafd. The point was aptly expressed in the liberal journal, *al-Siyasa*: 'Constitutional principles in their least favourable manifestations are yet preferable to the most just absolute government. No dark intrigue, no favouritism can exist where the constitution reigns and is respected.'[14] Any alliance with the Wafd was purely tactical; ideological differences were clearly stated.

From the king's point of view, according to Henderson's reports, politics was intrigue and the king's power had to be constantly negotiated.

The same could be said of British influence. Henderson noted that Ziwar was loyal but weak, seeking rather than providing comfort for the royal household. He was therefore dominated by Sidqi. 'Adli Yakan was also loyal to the dynasty, but weak, dominated by Tharwat and Sidqi. The king valued the support of Ibrahim, and to a lesser extent Nasim. However, he was 'violently abusive' of Mahmud, whom he described as the curse of the Liberal-Constitutional Party, frustrating the king's ambition to marshal the liberals into line.[15] After the dissolution of the coalition government of 1925, Mahmud designed to put himself at the head of the liberals by forging links with the weakened Wafd, but this move was resisted by the liberal Ghazali Abaza who said, 'They speak of union between ourselves and the Wafd, we will unite when they restore to us our murdered friends.'[16] Thus, to ideological differences and personal rivalries was added the blood feud. The reference was probably to the botched assassination attempt on Yakan and Rushdi; however, violence was endemic throughout these years, particularly during election campaigns. Any number of incidents perpetuated the civil conflict. In a similar instance of the 'primordial' sentiment in politics, Ibrahim would not reconcile himself to Sidqi's continued presence in the liberal-monarchist government because of their 'ancient' feud. Nor could he be persuaded to desist in his hatred for Sidqi, even when Henderson objected that Ibrahim's hatred for Zaghlul made it more binding upon him to ally with the liberals to win the coming electoral campaign against the Wafd.[17] But the situation was even more complicated, observed Henderson, because 'Abd al-'Aziz Fahmi, who was 'known as a nepotist himself', had aroused Ibrahim's 'violent resentment owing to his [Fahmi's] refusal to promote unduly' Ibrahim's son.[18] In short, the primordial motives of hatred, revenge and material reward were isolated by Henderson as the determining factors in political relations. Constitutional factors were, according to him, negligible.

As a guide, Henderson suggested that observers could rely on the disorganization of the liberals and the subservience of loyal, yet weak, monarchists. There was the exception of those of near equal status to the king, such as Prince 'Umar Tusun and Yusuf Kamal, who wielded immense influence in Lower and Upper Egypt, respectively. Both were distrusted because they stood as possible contenders to the throne. The king could, however, count upon the support of Muhammad Sa'id and Tawfiq Nasim; the latter in particular was motivated by his 'deep grudge' against Tharwat. Nasim was described in a Foreign Office report as an example of Ottoman political culture. He was entirely 'unscrupulous'.[19]

Henderson's analysis highlighted subtexts in political contests, ignoring the ideological differences that were the most obvious cause of the split in the liberal-monarchist coalition during Henderson's tenure as high commissioner. Betraying his own ideological propensities, Henderson steadfastly represented Egyptian political behaviour as conforming to the golden rule that personal ambitions, animosities, suspicions, feuds and hatreds determined the result in the elite political arena. Personalities, cliques and factions in the clubs of Cairo were the essential ingredients of politics. In these intimate settings, moral sanctions were particularly telling; the obligation to honor pledges was matched by the duty to avenge wrongs. Alongside these motives, there was naked self-interest, the desire for material rewards for oneself and one's clients. Henderson's analysis thus contrasted with that of Amos and others belonging to Allenby's staff between 1919 and 1925, which had pointed to the social and cultural dimensions shaping the various political parties. But Henderson's analysis reflected the temper of political society after November 1924. By 1926 Zaghlul had himself come to accept the logic of an elite political world, exclusive of lower class groups, youth, and women. Perhaps a kind cynicism enveloped Egyptian political society after the collapse of the first Wafd government in 1924. The outcome was not inevitable; not the consequence of Egyptian social structures, but the result of an ideological struggle between the Wafd and its rivals.

The Course toward Elitism

Allenby had imagined that the multi-party electoral process would moderate Egyptian politics. To some degree, the threat posed by the king to the Wafd Party in early 1924 had achieved that result. Therefore, Allenby had informal talks on treaty negotiations with Zaghlul in the spring of 1924. After the assassination of Stack, Allenby returned to the policy of setting up a political party that would defeat the Wafd in elections. In one of his last reports he divided the political landscape between autocratic, aristocratic and democratic 'forces'.[20] Again, his assumption was that a moderate Egyptian government would negotiate a treaty with the British government. However, the position of the British government was more complex. For Churchill and Lloyd, the point was to manipulate treaty negotiations in such a way as to establish a 'veiled protectorate'.[21] For the Foreign Office staff, a negotiated treaty with an elected Egyptian government was the objective.[22] As a result of these policy conflicts, negotiations stalled.[23]

The outcome tended to serve the purpose of the 'Tory' imperialists. The new British High Commissioner, George Ambrose Lloyd, reverted to the pre-Milner Mission logic that the Egyptians were incapable of producing a government that could negotiate a treaty according to the doctrine that the Egyptians had not arrived at political modernity. In a speech to the Colonial Institute before his departure for Egypt, Lloyd asserted that there was a need to combine 'traditional authority' and 'ordered progress'.[24] After taking up his duties in Cairo in October 1925, Lloyd observed that politics in Egypt involved a straightforward 'fight between autocracy and demagogy'.[25] Neither option was acceptable. Lloyd claimed that his governorship in India enabled him to appreciate 'fully what the initiation of constitutional government in an Oriental government meant'. For him, it meant 'anarchy'. Thus he said that British influence 'would be thrown on the side of order against the forces of anarchy'. Although Lloyd preferred to assert British power by force, he adjusted his attitudes somewhat by making the monarchy the main instrument of British influence. As Lloyd said, although the autocratic policy of the Ittihad government had brought odium on the king, 'we do not wish to be precluded from supporting [the king] in a proper measure.[26]

Lloyd forced the king to remove Nash'at from his political post in December 1925, cognizant of the fact that Nash'at had probably been involved in the assassination of Stack and that his policies had brought about the dissolution of the liberal-monarchist coalition government. Although the king expressed some exasperation with the decision to weaken the monarchist grip on the administration, he was philosophically in agreement with Lloyd's assessment of Egyptian politics. He was reported to have commented that the 'West could never understand the East' and that without the controlling hand of the palace the 'country would go to ruin'.[27] Lloyd advised the king to replace Nash'at with Yakan. The idea was to shore up 'traditional authority' with 'men of greater influence'; however Yakan preferred a more independent posture. As a result, Lloyd recommended that the royal cabinet be headed by Ahmad Muhammad Hasanayn Bey, who he described as a 'more reliable channel of communication with His Majesty'.[28]

Lloyd accounted for the new spirit of cooperation between the Wafd and Liberal-Constitutional Party by noting that Zaghlul was chastened by the momentous events of 1924.[29] The assassination of Stack had cost the Wafd nearly half its parliamentary seats and complicated the political arena by creating the monarchist party. These developments provided new opportunities for British agents. *Al-Ahram* admitted as much in an editorial commentary that warned (apparently in reference to Lloyd's arrival) that the British should not imagine that they could manipulate the party divisions to their advantage because the politicians were bound by their sacred pledges to national unity.[30] However, the events of 1924 and 1925 had brought about significant changes in Egyptian politics. This was reflected in Wafdist tactics. To ensure the participation of liberals and Watanists in a coalition against the Ziwar ministry in the autumn of 1925, Zaghlul pursued a moderate policy. The Wafd was careful to follow legalistic, constitutional principle; thus the declaration convening the dissolved parliament in November 1925 was justified according to article 96 of the constitution. Such tactics indicated that the balance of power in political society had shifted somewhat away from the monarchy: 134 parliamentarians met at the Continental Hotel on 21 November. During the proceedings, resolutions were made condemning the dissolution of parliament and Ziwar's rule by decree law. Zaghlul was elected president of the lower house, with Muhammad Mahmud acting as vice-president. Tharwat and Sidqi also showed their support for the coalition.[31]

The liberals were the primary beneficiaries of the shifts from left to right, evident in their allying first with the monarchists and secondly with the Wafd. The liberals were of course motivated by their distaste for the autocratic politics of the monarchists and Zaghlul's 'demagoguery', and thus the idea of a middle course between democracy and autocracy was their prime concern. In the context of the flowering of royal autocracy in 1925, this meant reconciliation with Zaghlul. The willingness of Zaghlul to also overcome his animosity toward the 'dissentients' of 1921 indicated a fundamental change in political attitudes in 1926.

Zaghlul and Yakan were reunited at a tea party on 28 December 1925. On 7 February 1926 Zaghlul returned Tharwat's visit. The 'last hatchet' was buried with the visit of Sidqi to Zaghlul on 15 February, when Hamid al-Basil and Mahmud were also present, bringing together three of the four that had been exiled to Malta in 1919. Thus, the well-known names of Zaghlul, Yakan, Tharwat and Sidqi were ranged against Ziwar's government. On that day a national congress was held in the garden of the palace belonging to Muhammad Mahmud. Centre stage was given to Zaghlul, who was received by Yakan, Tharwat and Mahmud. A petition was framed asserting that any government voted into office on the basis of Ziwar's electoral law (written by the liberals) would be illegal and would bring about the collapse of Egypt's constitutional system. The monarchists, represented by Ziwar and 'Ali Mahir, conceded to the demands of the congress and fixed dates for elections in May.

This might be viewed as a triumph for Zaghlul and the Wafd. However, by adopting the role of 'judicious' statesman rather than uncompromising revolutionary hero, Zaghlul had brought the revolutionary years full circle.[32] To mark the new style of politics, Zaghlul had the more radical cells of the Wafd, such as the students'. committee, removed from his own residence at *bait al-umma*. On 19 February, the final day of the congress, Zaghlul called for a union of all the parties. The accord brought together Yakan, Tharwat, 'Abd al-'Aziz Fahmi, and Sidqi alongside radical effendis like Mustafa al-Nahhas and Najib al-Gharabali.

It was the ideological differences between Zaghlul and the king, as well as the fissure between the left and right within the Wafd Party, that had shattered the government of 1924. Likewise, the fundamental divergence on the question of the utility of religion in politics had broken the liberal-monarchist government of 1925. In each case the British had reasserted their role as powerbrokers and weakened the autocratic and democratic forces, equally despised by the liberals and British agents.

The *Zu'ama'*

The elitist dynamics of politics is evident in the files of the king's secret intelligence service, which reported on the political negotiations that preceded the elections of 1926.[33] In these reports political society is referred to as the *zu'ama'*, literally the 'leaders', with the meaning of a political arena dominated by the bosses. Party politics was restricted to a relatively small group of men, thus the coalition of Wafd and Liberal-Constitutional parties called for a coordination of party activities to ensure that the respective leaderships would all have access to an uncontested nomination (*tazkiyya*, which was of course a valuable commodity). The police files recorded Zaghlul's ambitions to dominate the political stage; however, in the long-term the norms of the *zu'ama'* as a corporate group would seem to have been imposed even upon the great national leader.

Although Zaghlul needed to accommodate the liberals to build an effective opposition to the king, he favoured Wafdists in selections for certain nominations in the electoral constituencies. This resulted in protests from liberals, demanding that Zaghlul share the parliamentary seats that he carried like so many tickets in his hand. Liberals and others had to beg his favour to win a nomination for themselves or important clients. Zaghlul exerted his personal influence over the committee formed for the allocation of constituencies, giving the liberals only 20 of 47 requested seats. Zaghlul further frustrated the liberals by denying 16 liberals a nomination in constituencies to which they had been elected in the last parliament.[34] In one instance, reports showed that the liberals begged Zaghlul to allow a liberal candidate, 'Ali Bey Ibrahim, to have the Wafd's blessing in his contest with 'Abd al-Rahmam Fahmi in Bab Sha'riyya. Zaghlul rejected both candidates and supervised the candidacy of a 'bey' instead. The word 'bey' was used by Zaghlul as if the type and the status carried by the title counted for more than the candidate in question, which supports the view that politics had taken a hierarchical arrangement wherein the party bosses controlled the distribution of political rewards.[35]

But the coalition with the liberals also led to a reorganization of the Wafd Party. A report made by the king's secret service reported on a meeting between Zaghlul and 'Abd al-Rahman Fahmi, a 'dedicated' Wafdist previously involved in the militant wing of the Wafd and in labour politics. Once praised as the archetypal political activist, Zaghlul alienated Fahmi by refusing to endorse his candidature. When Fahmi called upon Zaghlul at home to protest, Zaghlul accused Fahmi of supplying Nash'at with information on the Wafd organization. The argument reflected the enduring damage inflicted by the monarchists on the Wafd Party. Fahmi accused Zaghlul of betraying him and then left angrily. To avenge himself, Fahmi put forward his nomination in the Cairo district of Bab Sha'riyya against a Wafdist candidate. Zaghlul denounced this betrayal and said to his secretary, 'We will produce a shilling for his silence.' The comment was a straightforward admission of a type of politics where political power was purchased, rather than won by election. Also, the episode suggested that Zaghlul sought to distance himself from the more radical effendis. Trade union organizations suffered, as did the student groups. Hasan Yassin, the leader of the student committee, was denied direct access to Zaghlul.[36]

The behavior of the liberals was particularly revealing. Their candidates maneuvered for short-term individual advantage, rather than party or coalition interests. There was the reported case of the endorsement of candidatures in the Sharqiyya district of al-Taliya, where the Wafd candidate Ibrahim Radwan Bey stood against Uthman Abaza, who was the president of the Ittihad Party in Sharqiyya. Shamsi reported to Zaghlul that the liberals had nominated Muhammad Bey Sadiq Abaza as the liberal candidate in this district. Muhammad Bey was the nephew of Uthman and was persuaded by Uthman to 'deliver himself to the [Ittihad] government'. For this service, Muhammad Bey was given a seat in Abu Kabir, where he was assured a candidacy. It is therefore hardly surprising that the police reported that Zaghlul vented his 'hatred' for the liberals. For their part, the liberals lived in dread of Zaghlul's betrayal (*jadr*), which experience showed them would not be long in coming anyway. When Zaghlul's wrath fell on them, exclusion from government office and the ruin of their local power bases was assured. Electioneering thus meant placating Zaghlul, seeking reconciliation, and, as the elections approached, the liberals were all quite abject before him. An informer to the police, Muhammad Bey Ahmad Abud, reported a conversation between Yakan, Tharwat and Sidqi at the Muhammad 'Ali Club. Tharwat discussed the nomination of a liberal candidate, 'Abd al-Fataj Pasha, saying that he had thanked Zaghlul personally for the '*tazkiyya*' of this candidate while at the same time honouring Zaghlul with the compliment that victory in the elections could only be credited to his fame. Abud said that Tharwat had related this story so that Abud could repeat it and thus increase Tharwat's personal prestige by currying favour with Zaghlul. In a similar instance, Sidqi asked his elector-delegates to be sure to praise Zaghlul as the leader of the nation, *za'im al-umma*, when going to the polls.[37]

The liberals accepted whatever constituencies Zaghlul granted them, just as there was little recourse for 'Abd al-'Aziz Fahmi and Tawfiq Doss when Zaghlul refused them candidatures. Fahmi resigned as president of the Liberal-Constitutional Party. The liberals stood as candidates in 43 seats, but a number of independents stood against them. The Ittihad fielded 100 candidates. The lists of candidates published on 18 April showed that 43 of 154 Wafdists were unopposed, whereas all 43 liberals were opposed, as were 7 out of 9 Watanists. Two of the 100 Ittihadists were unopposed; however, one of these was 'said to be in Sarwat's pocket and ready to declare himself Liberal'. The Wafd was destined to dominate the assembly; however, the power of the Wafd was not overwhelming. While final results showed that unanimous election made up altogether one-fifth of the elected deputies in the assembly this result was based on deals struck among the political leadership (*zu'ama*') and the notables in their localities. Acting as intermediaries between *zu'ama*' and the constituencies, the notables in 1926 chose in large measure to hedge their bets. Altogether, 102 candidates stood as independents, awaiting the final outcome before declaring their allegiance. As Henderson liked to put it, they nailed their colors to the fence. After the final stage of voting, the results showed 144 seats in the parliament declared for the Wafd Party, 28 liberal, 7 Ittihad, and 5 Watani. The relative autonomy of the notables meant there was room for maneuver. In sum, a strategic shift in the attitude of the liberals in mid-1925 had an impact on the notables, leading to a major switch in the balance of power between the Wafd and the monarchists. The power of the Wafd was not absolute, nor was that of the king. This political framework suited British strategy, as developed by Lloyd.

Lloyd relished the course of events after the elections were completed. Given that politics in Egypt involved a delicate balance of power among the zu'ama', a measured application of British influence could tip the government from the Wafd to the liberals or palace as conditions warranted. The shifting coalitions also fitted the analytical model of elite politics, shaped by factions and primordial sentiments. Thus after the events of 1924, a chastened Zaghlul no longer sought to impose a radical interpretation of the constitution. Instead, he negotiated between political factions. For certain, his goal was to be the ultimate political arbiter, but even this ambition was frustrated by his cohorts, according to Lloyd. Negotiations were undertaken by his peers to deprive him of the premiership, evident upon his reception at a fête at the Continental Hotel after the final round of elections in 1926. The audience applauded Zaghlul. But when he took the stage he tested the ground by suggesting to his audience that perhaps his age disqualified him from taking the highest office in the land. Tumultuous applause left little doubt that his peers preferred a nonpartisan government. Zaghlul surrendered the stage to Yakan.[38]

The subsequent history involved similar judicious bargains. Yakan managed to lead a coalition from June 1926 until April 1927. Upon his resignation, he was succeeded by Tharwat, who led a ministry from April 1927 until March 1928. Muhammad Mahmud succeeded him, followed by Yakan in October 1929, who supervised the elections that brought the Wafd to power in December 1929. The government of Nahhas lasted just over six months, replaced by the Sdiqi regime from 1931–1934, which involved another overhaul of the constitution and electoral law.

The elite thus showed a high degree of corporate unity. It had many heads, but one corporate structure, known as the *zu'ama*. The *zu'ama* were motivated by access to the rewards of office; nevertheless this hardly meant that ideological differences were nullified by material interests. Indeed, the Sidqi regime was authoritarian and its ideology founded on the idea of corporate unity, which was viewed as necessary to preserve the community and resolve the ideological discord attending the democratic experiment. The corporate idea was articulated in a speech in the assembly of deputies during Sidqi's tenure as prime minister. The paramount idea was that the *zu'ama* was a corporate body defined by the proper qualities of leadership (*shim al-zu'ama'*). The speaker recalled that in 1920 Yakan and Zaghlul were bound together as friends. Zaghlul, however, cut the bonds that held the *zu'ama* together by making speeches to the crowd (*jamahir*). He exploited ignorance and thus, 'by his speech', Zaghlul unloosed his party of followers (*ansar*) upon the nation. Zaghlul's factionalism was contrasted with Sidqi's principle of corporate unity (*ittihad*). Whereas the nation was a single rank (*umma muwahhad saff*, a phrase suggesting the organic philosophy of Italian fascism of a fasces or 'bundle of rods'), Zaghlul divided it into groups. The nation, accordingly, needed one party to lead it toward prosperity (*falah*, a word having the meaning of a prosperous tilling of the soil). It was according to the pact of national coalition or cooperation (*ishtirak*, the word applied to socialism) that Sidqi joined the official Wafd in 1921; however, the Wafd policy of ruin resulted in the collapse of this coalition and the downfall of Yakan, the most distinguished of the *zu'ama'*. What was required in the political situation was to build instead of ruining, to combat rancor with trust (*ikhlas*). This had been the policy of Sidqi and Tharwat after the fall of Yakan in 1921 – to create a monarchy that possessed supremacy (*dhat siyada*). The Wafd refused to cooperate with this government and, while a constitutional committee of thirty patriots drafted a law that would provide for the political participation of the people, the Wafd's resistance taught the people to doubt these exemplary men of the *zu'ama'*. 'But if the constitution is reactionary why do they now support it? Or are they lying? But I have mastered the uncertainty – that they are liars yesterday as they are today. These people have forged the chain of destruction (*silsil al-hadm*) and promise to kill and burn to the end because they fail to appreciate the direction of reform or the raising up of prosperity.' And so, the Wafdists came to the 1923 elections without trust in the constitution, but only as a weapon in their *jihad* against England. Zaghlul's reply to the speech from the throne in 1924 rejected the most modern principles of government, but, said the speaker, if we separate words from actions we can see that the Wafd is a party without principles, corrupting the uses of money, title, and rank, just as dignity, honor, and nobility are destroyed. The elected deputies exploited the constitution as a means to construct a false majority (*aghlabiyya mulaffaqa*) by purchasing consciences with seats and stealing away free will by a promise. When the parliament was convened where were those who fired the first shot in the Egyptian revolution: Tharwat, Sidqi, Ibrahim, Rushdi, and Yakan? Where were those who took the hand of Egypt and raised it up from its fall? Where were those who created an Egyptian monarchy with supremacy?[39]

Although the speech unmistakably used the language of European fascism to condemn the democrats, it also had recourse to Islamic terminology favoured by reformers and traditionalists. Thus, the speaker reminded his listeners that the purpose of a parliament is consultation (*shura*) and according to this principle the senator Hadara Sahib Ahmad Zaki Abu al-Sa'ada Pasha set forth a social law. Nahhas resisted it whilst the deputies occupied themselves with the question of negotiations with England. The speaker said that whereas most deputies could not stand up to Zaghlul, the leadership of Nahhas posed a greater danger because of his weakness. The deputies applied pressure upon him, hence the problem with democracy, that deputies without morals made 'predatory' attacks upon legitimate leadership, as represented by Yakan and Tharwat. Zaghlul had himself praised Yakan and Tharwat in a speech given on 13 November 1926. Sidqi was also a distinguished statesman. But most of the Wafdists and liberals lacked the character to govern, the custom of obligation and the practice of leadership (*shim al-zu'ama'*). Without the patient concern of the king, there would have been civil war (*al-harb al-ahliyya*).[40]

This speech sums up the monarchist critique of democracy. It presaged Sidqi's condemnation of the liberal experiment in 1939. The language of the speech was similar to that used by Zaki Fahmi. It underlined the deeply conservative response to democracy, party politics, and the populist politics of the Wafd. Although delivered by a partisan of the *Sha'b* Party, the point was a more general defense of social and political order. There was thus a tendency to draw a stark contrast between good and evil, order and disorder. The language was moral and religious in tone, although the purpose was political. There is the familiar concern to protect honor, status, and a hierarchy of notables, aristocracy and monarchy; alongside that, an emphasis upon organic social cohesion against the dangers of the disbanded fragmentation of the demos. Mainstream colonial culture was also ideologically bound to the idea of an Egypt that resembled all the certainties of a pre-modern world – fixed by the dependable values of propriety, trust, patronage, and government by the responsible few.

CHAPTER 8

CONCLUSION

This book considered three conventional interpretations of Egyptian politics in the interwar period: 1) that Egyptian politics should be understood as essentially elitist, 2) that monarchy and aristocracy were the consequence and product of colonial interference, and 3) that liberal, territorial nationalism characterized the political culture of the era. To sum up, a discussion of these three themes follows:

Elitism

The Weberian theory of the patrimonial state says that relations between 'political subjects' and ruler were based on the same moral sanctions that guided the patriarch in his relations with his household. The 'traditional' state was thus bound together by a moral economy: the moral claims available to the subjects of 'traditional' authority meant that the ruler was 'very much dependent upon the good will of those from whom he derives revenues'.[1] This type of politics is not autocratic because the ruler does not have overwhelming power in relation to his 'political subjects', which is to say the rural notables or urban patricians of a pre-modern society. Rather, Weber viewed the elite as a corporate body, with the basic regulating principle being the 'minimization' of power differences within the elite group to ensure equality and solidarity among 'members of their own ruling layer'.[2] Political relations according to this model recall the observation that a political society might exhibit many heads but its elite structure remained constant. Hence, Malcolm Yapp's analysis of the 'years of the notables' in Egypt showed that the appearance of political instability cloaked the reality of ministerial continuity. The 32 Egyptian cabinets that formed between 1922 and 1952 held office on average for less than a year, but the men that held office were few in number and drawn from a tightly bounded political elite.[3]

The theory of an elite society, resembling a multi-headed hydra, is attractive, but exclusive of other motives. In the Abdin files the political elite is sometimes described as something like an organic body, the *zu'ama'*, which indeed had the meaning of a political leadership with a corporate identity. There was not one paramount leader, certainly not the king, who was constantly subject to the implied threat of a coup d'état or revolution. In 1919 the Wafd was a caucus of men roughly agreed on a basic platform of national independence and liberal modernism. After the British authorities rejected the Wafd's pleas and exiled the Wafd leadership, Zaghlul attained paramount status as the national leader (*za'im al-umma*) with a broad base of support. Many members of Egyptian political society viewed Zaghlul's preeminence as a threat to their own hereditary authority, not to mention a perversion of the customary codes of the *zu'ama'*. Thus, the *zu'ama'* split. Prominent members of Egyptian political society formed a party led by 'Adli Yakan, Husayn Rushdi and 'Abd al-Khaliq Tharwat, to check Zaghlul's ambition to dominate political society. The group was given an ideological identity as the Liberal-Constitutional Party when 'Abd al-'Aziz Fahmi and Muhammad Husayn Haykal supported Yakan in his contest with Zaghlul. Fahmi and Haykal were adept in modern political and social theory; however, the content of the public speeches of many 'liberals' reflected the codes of the *zu'ama'*, rather than liberalism or secularism. Nevertheless, the commitment to fundamental principles of responsible government defined the liberal position, motivated as it was to avoid the extremes of despotism and democratic anarchy.

CONCLUSION 185

Elite political society was divided along political party lines by 1922. Moreover, the elections meant that the parties had to reach diverse constituencies among the middle and lower stratum of society. Zaghlul's domination of the political landscape was not absolute. The liberals posed a real threat, with significant social influence through the landholding notability. As a result, the first elections saw the Wafd form an alliance with the king. Only the king had enough gravitas in political society to separate significant sectors of the rural notables and conservative-minded effendis from the Liberal-Constitutional Party and, subsequently, from the Wafd organization. It was the efforts of the king's agents in this regard that established the political saliency of the monarchy, which was not a colonial plot, but a result of party contests and ideological differences. The most dramatic contest was the king's challenge to the ascendancy of the Wafd Party after the elections of 1923. Once elected, Zaghlul's stature as *za'im al-umma* declined. In keeping with the idea of elite social structure, it could be argued that the *zu'ama'* needed to check Zaghlul's personal power and impose upon him the constraints of group membership; all factions within the *zu'ama'* asserted their 'right' to have access to the spoils of political office. However, the terminology of *zu'ama'* is ill-suited to describe the expansion of political society that came with the electoral process. The claims upon Zaghlul were diverse, including radicalized factions in the parliament, regional blocs, feminist organizations, and ultra-nationalists. By failing to meet the political expectations of these diverse groups in terms of rights, liberties, geopolitical gains and the undying demand for the spoils of office, Zaghlul appeared more as demagogic leader of a faction or mob rather than the paramount figure within the elite. Indeed to tighten his grip on power, Zaghlul attempted to concentrate power and authority among his closest supporters, mostly effendis, who had constituencies in student groups, labour unions and regional fiefdoms. But these tactics deepened ideological divisions by threatening to include new groups in the political process. The opening to the monarchists was obvious. The king's men actively engaged in separating a conservative sector of the Wafd's social base among the notability and the 'ulama', as well as other constituencies, to construct a viable political opposition to the Wafd.

Central to these contests was the idea of mobilizing social constituencies outside of the *zu'ama'*. The monarchy was not only the product of the maneuvers of elite segments; it involved political and ideological struggles also, firstly with the Liberals and secondly with the Wafd. After the opening salvos in 1922 and 1924, the monarchy engaged in a cultural campaign to fix the monarchy and Islam as the symbols of an independent Egyptian nation-state. To do so, the king relied upon cultural issues that moved diverse communities of Egyptians outside the elite. The writings of 'Abd al-Raziq and Zaki Fahmi were indicative of the shift toward cultural topics in politics. However hesitant, each book engaged with the issue of the politicization of cultural issues that came with the electoral process and party politics. It is hard to entirely reconcile these features of interwar politics with the elite model of politics.

Equally qualified, yet clearly evident, was a change in British analysis of the political situation. The more influential colonial officials in Cairo rejected the old colonial doctrine that Egypt was divided between Turkish elite and Egyptian mass, with the latter essentially apolitical and accustomed to bowing to authority. Allenby's band of officials asserted instead that political society was divided between parties, radical and moderate, and social sectors: rural landholders and the educated and older bureaucrats and professionals versus the religious establishment, students, and a younger generation of bureaucrats and professionals.[4] The key social sector was the 'middle class' or effendiyya, whose origins in village society enabled them to access vertical associations of family, clan, and sect, while at the same time forming cohorts in schools, professions, and bureaucracy. The effendiyya had ties to the urban and provincial notables, who in turn communicated with lower class groups through community associations like the mosque, café, and the extended family.[5] While recognizing in this way that the Egyptians had forged a national political community – an idea anathema to the old colonial logic – Allenby's staff predicted that the majority of notables would separate from the radical leadership and fall in line with the Liberal-Constitutional Party, which formed in 1922 under British sponsorship. The point was to find a 'middle way' between despotism and democracy, which was an idea

Conclusion

dear to the secular liberals and moderate Islamic reformists. The subsequent development of conservatism and elitism was a consequence of these political and cultural preferences, not necessarily a function of elite social structures.

Colonial Interference

The counter-revolutionary course of politics after 1919 has been described by revisionist social scientists as an outcome determined by Egyptian social structure. This argument was a significant advance on the conventional view that the elitism of the era was largely a consequence of British interference or the impact of the European colonies in Egypt. The revisionist argument concluded that the new social formation of the effendiyya was integrated into the old ruling class, which in turn resulted in compromises on liberalism or what was described as the traditionalization or indigenization of nationalist ideology. That process was evident in Wafdist electoral rhetoric. Likewise, analysis of social structures distinguished between the urban radicals and rural notables, concluding that the social origin of the effendi in the class of rural notables resulted in the political dominance of the rural sector. This also had an impact upon political culture and ideology.

Rather than colonial interference or elite social structures, this book has considered the degree to which colonial ideology melded with indigenous cultural values, particularly the aristocratic codes of the notables. Indeed, social scientific analysis of elite social structures was not unlike colonial and liberal, Egyptian political analysis, which was also the foundation of a conservative political ideology that justified the establishment of an authoritarian regime. These ideas were evident in debates over the design of the constitution and electoral laws in the 1920s. The period also witnessed a three-way constitutional contest between the nationalists, the liberals, and the monarchists, which played itself out as an ideological conflict between democrats and autocrats. The liberal-nationalists of the Wafd and Liberal-Constitutional Party attempted to place the crown above the political fray, in keeping with the British parliamentary example where the king ruled but did not govern. Diaeddine Saleh showed that the Wafd won the first contest when Zaghlul was able to impose ministerial authority over the king's prerogative to appoint members of the senate. However, the liberal-monarchist coalition government of Ziwar reestablished the 'khedival system' in 1925 when a decree dispensed with the requirement for ministerial countersignature. As was observed by a royalist publicist in 1925, 'The salvation of the country is in the union of the people and the throne.'[6] The authoritarian vision thus imagined the king as the embodiment of the nation: the king applied himself to the order of the interior administration, social well-being and democracy through the education of the people in the principles of political maturity. The 'khedival regime' was, according to this vision, suited to Egypt's social and moral evolution. Monarchists relied to a large degree on colonial and Egyptian liberal ideology. It was evolutionary and developmental; indeed developmental ideologies continued to justify authoritarian government in Egypt throughout the twentieth century and into the twenty-first.

The monarchy emerged as a political and cultural power in the interwar years. In cultural works, the monarchy represented itself as inceptor of the modern Egyptian nation-state. Indeed, the monarch had the support of a bureaucratic cadre, as well as aristocratic families, significant sectors of the landed rural elites, and much of the religious establishment. It placed religion at the centre of political debates, where it has remained. The combination of a monarchist social base and ideological coherence, as represented by a new status honour aristocracy and religious symbols of 'tradition', crushed the 'hopes of 1919'.[7] Authoritarian and patriarchal, the language of the monarchy owed much to the paternalistic ideology of British colonialism.

As a result of the autocratic style of politics from the late 1920s, opposition was stifled, suppressed, forced underground into subversive and anti-establishment types of political activism. The politics of dissent of the 1930s and 1940s meant that the popular imagination came to conceive of the ruling elites as an 'ancien régime' or a neo-colonial instrument of divide and rule strategies. According to this point of view, the combination of aristocracy and colonialism strengthened Egypt's ruling dynasty while weakening the Wafd. The British contributed to the formation of the Liberal-Constitutional Party, the

Ittihad Party, and the *Sha'b* Party for this purpose. Such arguments have been made in national histories according to which the 'revolution of 1919' was suppressed by the alliance of colonial power with parties that represented large landholding interests and the ruling dynasty. While these images capture the disappointments of a generation animated by the revolutionary enthusiasm of 1919, British power was not so overwhelming. The British exploited ideological differences and social divisions that already existed within Egyptian political society. The British did not invent or even control these forces. Also, it has been argued that political parties were vehicles for the political interests of elite politicians, without a basis in ideological politics. Accordingly, the Wafd did not represent a revolutionary political programme; rather, its character as an elite organization immobilized it as a force for radical change. Indeed, it is worth considering how a nationalist organization that championed lower class groups, women, and youth between 1919 and 1924 was co-opted to an elite type of politics. Rather than determined by the elite structure of Egyptian political society or colonial interference, this cooptation was shaped by political party rivalries and ideological contests. These conclusions question the assumption that there was ideological consensus within Egyptian political society in the 1920s. Rather than consensus, debates upon Egypt's political identity intensified. Indeed much of the rivalry of the Wafd-led parliaments and the monarchy in the interwar years revolved around fundamental issues of what the symbols and bases of political authority should be in modern, post-colonial Egypt.

Liberal Nationalism

As noted, the questioning of British colonial doctrine resulted in the acceptance of certain nationalist principles into the colonial dialogue. In 1923 a 'liberal constitution' and democratic, electoral system were established. However, the monarchy was made hereditary and the king secured the power to prorogue parliament; as well, the liberal electoral law was premised on an elitist political landscape wherein the rural notable dominated. Liberalism after 1922 was marked by such strains and compromises. Thus, Nadav Safran spoke of a 'crisis of orientation' in Egyptian liberal nationalism during the interwar period, pointing in particular to the concessions made by liberal nationalists to social custom or religion. The leading liberal ideologue after 1922 was Muhammad Husayn Haykal. While Charles D. Smith disagreed with Safran's characterization of liberal nationalists in 'crisis' and thus denied the theory of reversion to a religious type of identity, he did show that liberals like Haykal were deeply concerned with the engagement of the lower classes in politics. This is apparent in Haykal's journalism, books and memoirs. Rather like Muhammad 'Abduh, Haykal used religious concepts and narratives to support a basically liberal or modernist ideological orientation. Nevertheless, the insistence upon 'liberalism without democracy' betrays the unease occasioned by the national revolt of 1919 and the liberal constitution of 1923.[8] The elitism of the liberals pointed to the difficulty of defining Egypt's political community in terms of Western-inspired liberal democracy or at least it points to the same sort of tensions experienced in Western political cultures during a period of democratization. The problem is evident in the ideological and party political contests wherein nationalism was the dominant theme, always anti-British, sometimes republican and anti-monarchist. However, within the dominant framework of the nation-state there were divergent views on the role of religion, youth, women, and labour in politics, in short different definitions of the 'people' and the 'nation'.

The monarchist cultural policy found a platform because the king's agents wished to exploit religious sentiment and social divisions to foster support for authoritarian, monarchical rule and defeat the Wafd. However, the new policy was also driven by a deep fear of the corrosive impact of Western democracy and other foreign cultural influences upon Egyptian society and politics. Rather than colonial invention or a manifestation of reactionary sectors in society, the cultural policies and politics of the monarchists should be understood as a dimension of Egypt's modern political culture. One characteristic of the Wafd was to make a charismatic figure the centre of a national cult, which accounts for Zaghlul's extraordinary political power. Another feature of Wafd politics was the way it rested upon the communal groupings of village, urban quarter and lineage group. To mobilize in these milieus, nationalist ideology made reference to customary social bonds, including patriarchal, familial, moral and religious ideas. Nationalist ideology was not exclusively religious, as it was sometimes represented in colonial analysis. Nationalists redefined the concept of Egyptian community according to the new ethic of patriotism and national politics; nevertheless, socio-cultural values were the basis of most localized political groupings. Therefore it was always necessary to fit the nationalist ethic within social and cultural conventions, localized, most often with a strong religious current. It was thus not surprising to see the monarchists quickly learn from the Wafd's success in this regard and turn to religious themes to mobilize the 'people', conceived as *umma*, not *sha'b*.

Whereas the national idea was dominant in the Wafd's ideology, the idea of the Islamic prince supported by elites was overarching in monarchist ideology. Certainly some of the most celebrated literary and artistic figures of the 1920s and 1930s articulated the liberal idea of an Egyptian territorial nation. However, most liberals failed to enter the field of electoral, ideological politics. For those who did, Islam was an irresistible symbol of the Egyptian national identity. The liberal orientation of the Wafd leadership meant that it was susceptible to the religious policy of the monarchists, which found fissures in the Wafd Party on questions of women, religion, and class. In short, the monarchists highlighted cultural issues that had meaning to the Egyptian population, but were difficult to reconcile to a liberal vision of political community. The monarchist experiment was significant because it challenged some of the basic assumptions of liberal democracy espoused in theory by the leadership of the Wafd and Liberal-Constitutional Party. The monarchist position was more than a strategic bid for power, but expressed a very modern concern with the negative consequences of rapid political or cultural change. The monarchy was represented as a restraining mechanism or regulating principle. Zaki Fahmi used the language of Ibn Khaldun to defend the idea of a 'traditional' political community against the democratic alternative. In this he was not unlike European sociologists, such as

Emile Durkheim, who turned to Ibn Khaldun because his theory of social cohesion was remarkably modern in its concern for social order in a situation where change threatened 'civilization'.

Egyptian liberalism was indebted to British colonial thinking. It distanced itself from the majority of the population, viewed as another society living in another time. Likewise colonial doctrines, in spite of the insights of Maurice Amos, persisted in viewing Egyptian political motives as essentially primordial, not political, driven by lineage, clan, religious, or personal animosities. Lords dominated 'their' communities. This logic was reflected in the structure of the constitutional and electoral landscape constructed by the liberals, with British collaboration. The imagining of the political landscape in this manner was an attempt to impose an elitist structure upon Egyptian political life. Accordingly, the politics of the notables was supposed to be directed along a predictable course of landholders' self-interest and material benefit. However, the ideological ferment of the era fractured this design and questioned the assumption that Egyptian political society was a corporate body with shared interests and values. Rather than building consensus, the revolution of 1919, the constitutional debates that followed, and the subsequent elections intensified debates upon Egypt's political identity. It is this disputation that defines the liberal era – the inability to find consensus on the modern political constitution. Egyptians failed to agree on even the most basic principles of their national identity, such as a clear definition of Egypt's territorial borders, civil and political rights, and the supremacy of civil law over religious law.

NOTES

Chapter 1 Introduction

1. Zaki Fahmi, *Safwat al-'Asr* (Cairo: Matba'at al-I'timad, 1926) and Diaeddine Saleh, *Les Pouvoirs du Roi dans la constitution Egyptienne* (Paris: Librairie Generale des Droits et de Jurisprudence, 1939).
2. Albert Hourani, *Arabic Thought in the Liberal Age* (London: Oxford University Press, 2nd ed., 1983).
3. 'Abd al-Rahman al- Rafi'i, *Thawra sana 1919: Tarikh misr al-qaumi min sana 1914 ila sana 1921* (Cairo: Maktaba al-nahda al-misriyya, 1946) and *Fi a'qab al-thawra al-misriyya*, 3 vols. (Cairo: Maktaba al-nahda al-misriyya, 1947–1951). See Yoav Di-Capua, '"Jabarti of the Twentieth Century": The National Epic of 'Abd al-Rahman al-Rafi'i and other Egyptian Histories', *International Journal of Middle East Studies* 36 (2004): 429–50. For royalist histories see Gabriel Hanotaux, *Histoire de la nation Egyptienne* (Cairo, published under the auspices of King Fuad, 1931) and Joseph Cattaoui Pasha, *Coup d'Oeil sur la chronologie de la nation Egyptienne* (Paris: Libraire Plon, 1931) and Georges Douin, *Histoire de regne du Khedive Ismail*, 3 vols. (Rome: Institute Poligrafico, 1933–1941) and Etienne Combe, Jacques Bainville and Edouard Griault, *Précis de l'histoire d'Egypte*, 3 vols. (Cairo: L'Institute Francais, 1933).
4. White Ibrahim, *La Nouvelle Constitution de l'Egypte* (Paris: Librairie de Jurisprudence Ancienne et Moderne, 1926).
5. Ahmed Abdesslem, *Ibn Khaldun et ses lecteurs* (Paris: Presses Universitaires de France, 1983), p. 59, fn. 3. Abdesslem observed that this statement inverted the Orientalist formula that Ibn Khaldun was the Montesquieu of the Orient. Tahtawi's view made more sense chronologically. The European

'discovery' of Ibn Khaldun is undoubtedly over emphasized; it seems likely that after his death in Cairo in 1406, he would have had some lasting influence upon Arab letters, but this is not asserted by Abdesslem for want of evidence. See pp. 41–58 for a discussion of Ibn Khaldun's influence upon positivism and sociology.
6. Karl Mannheim, *Ideology and Utopia: An Introduction to the Sociology of Knowledge* (New York: Harcourt, Brace and Co., 1936).
7. V. Y. Mudimbe, *Parables and fables: Exegesis, Textuality, and Politics in Central Africa* (Madison: University of Wisconsin Press, 1991) and Edward W. Said, *Orientalism* (London: Routledge, 1978).
8. Earl of Cromer, *Modern Egypt* 2 vols. (London: Macmillan, 1908) and *Abbas II* (London: Macmillan, 1915).
9. Jacques Berque, *Egypt: Imperialism and Revolution* (London: Faber and Faber, 1972).
10. Foreign Office (FO) 371/6295 4919/260/16, 16 April 1921, 'Alternative Proposals for Future Government of Egypt', Memorandum by Amos and Patterson, with commentary by Allenby.
11. FO371/7730 652/1/16, Cabinet, 16 January 1922, 'The Egyptian Question' and FO371/7730 767/1/16, 20 January 1922, Lord Allenby to Curzon. See also Maurice Amos, *England and Egypt* (Nottingham: Cust Foundation Lecture, 1929).
12. Wm. Roger Louis, *In the Name of God Go! Leo Amery and the British Empire in the Age of Churchill* (New York: Norton, 1992), p. 131.
13. Middle East Centre Archives (MECA), Oxford, GB 165-0295, Gordon Waterfield, Box 5, Letters of Gerald Delany to Waterfield. On Churchill's entanglement in the Egyptian scene during the aftermath of the First World War, see John Darwin, *Britain, Egypt and the Middle East: Imperial Policy in the Aftermath of War* (Oxford: Oxford University Press, 1982).
14. FO371/6301 8245/260/16, Imperial Conference, 6 July 1921. See in particular the comments of the Colonial Secretary, Winston Churchill, on the idea of a veiled protectorate.
15. See the correspondence between Lloyd and Austen Chamberlain, Churchill College Archives, George Ambrose Lloyd, GLLD, Files 13/3 and 13/4A and 13/4B.
16. FO371/10889 143/32/16 and FO371/6301 2794/431/16.
17. FO371/8963 9507/10/16, Scott to Curzon, 14 Sept. 1923, Situation in Egypt, Audience with the King upon Zaghlul's return to Egypt.
18. Saleh, *Les Pouvoirs du roi*, pp. 19–30 and 180.
19. Afaf al-Lutfi al-Sayyid Marsot, *Egypt's Liberal Experiment 1922–1936* (Berkeley: University of California, 1977) and Marius Deeb, *Party Politics in Egypt: The*

Wafd and its Rivals 1919–1939 (London: Ithaca Press, 1979) and Janice J. Terry, *The Wafd, 1919–1952: Cornerstone of Egyptian Political Power* (London: Third World Centre for Research and Publishing, 1982) and Israel Gershoni and James P. Jankowski, *Egypt, Islam and the Arabs: The Search for Egyptian Nationhood, 1900–1930* (New York: Oxford University Press, 1986).
20. Robert Springborg, *The Ties that Bind: Political Association and Policy Making in Egypt* (Ann Arbor: PhD University of Michigan, 1974), p. 6.
21. Leonard Binder, *In a Moment of Enthusiasm: Political Power and the Second Stratum* (Chicago: University of Chicago Press, 1978). Binder applied the term 'second stratum' to the notables. See also Barrington Moore, *The Social Origins of Dictatorship and Democracy: Lord and Peasant in the Making of the Modern World* (Boston: Beacon Press, 1966).
22. Louis Joseph Cantori, *The Organizational Basis of an Elite Political Party: The Egyptian Wafd* (Chicago: PhD University of Chicago, 1966).
23. Nathan J. Brown, *Peasant Politics in Modern Egypt: The Struggle against the State* (New Haven: Yale University Press, 1990).
24. Karl Marx, *The Eighteenth Brumaire of Louis Bonaparte*, as cited by Binder, *Moment of Enthusiasm*, p. 19.
25. Reinhard Schulze, *Die Rebellion der Agyptischen Fallahin 1919 – A conflict between an agrarian-oriental society and a colonial state in Egypt 1820–1919 (English translation)* (Berlin: Baalbek, 1981).
26. Albert Hourani, 'Ottoman Reform and the Politics of the Notables', in William R. Chambers and Richard L. Polk, eds., *Beginnings of Modernization in the Middle East: The Nineteenth Century* (Chicago: University of Chicago Press, 1968).
27. Philip Khoury, *Urban Notables and Arab Nationalism: The Politics of Damascus 1860–1920* (Cambridge: Cambridge University Press, 1983).

Chapter 2 Historical Context

1. Gabriel Baer, *Studies in the Social History of Modern Egypt* (Chicago: University of Chicago Press, 1969) and Robert F. Hunter, *Egypt under the Khedives: From Household Government to Modern Bureaucracy* (Pittsburg: University of Pittsburg Press, 1984).
2. FO141 620/5603/6 'Accesssion of Sultan Ahmad Fuad', *Journal Officiel* no. 86, 10 Oct. 1917 and FO141 620/5603/21, *Journal Officiel* no. 88, 15 Oct. 1917.
3. FO141 620/5603/29.
4. Cantori, *The Egyptian Wafd*, p. 155.
5. Cantori seemed to find the republican language significant, although his thesis was that elite social structures moderated the Wafd's politics; see

pp. 247 and 311–313. See also Ahmad Shafiq, *Hawliyat Misr al-siyasiyya*, vol. 2 (Cairo: Matba'at shafiq basha, 1926).
6. Sawsan al-Messiri, 'The Changing Role of the *Futuwwa* in the Social Structure of Cairo', in Ernest Gellner and John Waterbury, eds., *Patrons and Clients in Mediterranean Societies* (London: Duckworth, 1977).
7. Thomas Russell Pasha, *Egyptian Service 1902–1946* (London: John Murray, 1949), pp. 190–206.
8. Margot Badran, *Feminists, Islam, and Nation: Gender and the Making of Modern Egypt* (Princeton: Princeton University Press, 1995), p. 75 and 'Epilogue' in Huda Sha'rawi, *Harem Years: The Memoirs of an Egyptian Feminist (1879– 1924)*, trans., ed., Margot Badran (London: Virago, 1986).
9. Joel Beinin and Zackary Lockman, *Workers on the Nile* (Princeton: Princeton University Press, 1987).
10. Ellis Goldberg, 'Peasants in Revolt: Egypt 1919', *International Journal of Middle East Studies*, 24 (1992): 261–80 and Brown, *Peasant Politics*.
11. Muhammad Husayn Haykal, *Mudhakkirat fi al-siyasa al-misriyya*, vol. 1 (Cairo:Maktab al-nahda al-misriyya, 1951–53), pp. 89–92.
12. FO371/4978 5168/6/16, 17 May 1920, Report of Lord Milner's Special Mission to Egypt.
13. FO371/4978 5168/6/16.
14. FO371/6301 8245/260/16, Imperial Conference, 6 July 1921. Churchill referred to his 'shock' in August 1920 when an outline of Milner's recommendations was leaked to the press.
15. FO371/4978 1047/6/16, H. M. Anthony to Lord Curzon, 'Reception of Lord Milner's Mission' and FO371/4978 5168/6/16, 17 May 1920, Report of Lord Milner's Special Mission to Egypt.
16. FO371/6296 6037/260/16, Secret Intelligence Service, 25 May 1921, 'Zaghlul and Adli': The first to leave Zaghlul in 1920 were Isma'il Sidqi, Mustafa Abu Nasr, the latter described as a leading lawyer in the religious courts, and Husayn Wasif, a rich proprietor and former governor of the Suez Canal, followed by Muhammad 'Ali, Ahmad Lutfi al-Sayyid, Muhammad Mahmud, Hamid al-Basil, 'Abd al-'Aziz Fahmi and Hafiz Afifi.
17. In 1921 Wafd manifestos referred to the moderate politicians involved in negotiations with the British as infidels (*murtaddin*) or heretics (*munshaqqin*), Cantori, p. 319 and *Parliamentary Papers*, vol. 42, no. 24, Egypt no. 3 (1921), Military Court of Inquiry into the Alexandria Riots, May 1921, p. 240. Although the use of religious terminology in this context is significant, the terms should probably be understood in the nationalist sense of traitors to the cause.
18. Rafi'i, *Thawra sana 1919*, vol. 2, p. 166.

19. FO371/6301 8049/260/16, 13 July 1921, Protest issued by Egyptian lawyers against official delegation made reference to Churchill's intervention and FO371/6301 8137/260/16, 1 July 1921, protest from British Chamber of Commerce in Egypt, with the claim that Churchill's statement was unfounded, given the many years of cooperation between British and Egyptians before and after the military occupation.
20. FO371/6301 8245/260/16, Statement of Lord Curzon, Imperial Conference, 6 July 1921. These discussions on the impact of the Milner Report and the proposed treaty included Lloyd George, Winston Churchill, Arthur Meighan (Canada), William Hughes (Australia), William Massey (New Zealand) and Jan Smuts (South Africa). The discussion resulted in the modification of the previous Milner treaty proposals to protect the geopolitical security interests of the empire.
21. FO371/7741 830/61/16, Report of Public Security Dept. and FO371/8973 651/351/16, Situation Report, 7 January-15 January 1923. There were 14 Britons killed by assassins in 1922.
22. FO371/7741 61/61/16, Allenby to Curzon, 24 December 1921, Report of Public Security Department, references to attacks on soldiers, speeches encouraging demonstrations, and divisions between 'Zaghlulists' and 'Dissentients'.
23. FO371/6301 8283/260/16, 30 June 1921, 'Situation in Egypt', Keown Boyd (Oriental Secretary) wrote the report; he quoted Adli Yakan.
24. FO371/8972 306/306/16, 4 January 1923, Foreign Office Minute, by John Murray, 'Memorandum on the Political Situation in Egypt'.
25. FO/371/4979 10456/6/16, Scott to Curzon, 25 August 1920.
26. FO/371/4979 7828/6/16, Allenby to Curzon, 3 July 1920.
27. FO371/10022 9549/22/16, Kerr to Chamberlain, 3 Nov. 1924, 'The Power of the King'.
28. FO370/7733 3947/1/16, 11 April 1922, Secret Intelligence Service (SIS), 'King Fuad, seconded by Sarwat Pasha, is becoming despotic and talks of governing with the whip'.
29. FO371/8961 3397/10/16, Allenby to FO, 24 Mar 1922, Egyptian Situation.
30. FO371/8972 306/306/16, 'Memorandum of the Political Situation in Egypt', 4 January 1923, Appendix B, Part 2, October 15 1922, (original FO file E11477/1/16), 'Remarks by Sarwat Pasha'.
31. Egyptian National Archives (ENA), Majlis al-Wuzara', Box 1/3/B, 29 July 1922. Press reports from *La Liberté*.
32. FO371/8960 1958/10/16, Allenby to Curzon, 8 February 1923, Enclosure 1.
33. FO371/4978 5168/6/16, 17 May 1920, Report of Lord Milner's Special Mission to Egypt. Foreign Office personnel identified 'elimination

of Egyptians from the Sudan' as one of the passages that should be excised from the published document as 'sensitive' to Egyptian political opinion.
34. Elie Kedourie, *The Chatham House Version and Other Middle Eastern Studies* (London: Wiedenfeld and Nicolson, 1970), p. 175 and Muhammad Khalil Subha, *Tarikh al-hayat al-niyabiyya fi Misr*, vol. 5 (Cairo: 1939), p. 459.
35. FO371/8973 1409/351/16 Allenby to Curzon, Situation Report, 28 January to 5 February 1923.
36. FO371/8973 4591/351/16, Allenby to Curzon, Situation Report, 28 April to 7 May, 'The Constitution'. Those journals sponsored by the monarchists and Wafdists denied that there was any conflict between the 'throne' and the 'people'.
37. FO371/8961 4589/10/16, Allenby to Curzon, 23 April 1922, 'Egyptian Constitution'.
38. FO371/8961 3397/10/16, Allenby to Curzon, 24 Mar. 1922, 'Egyptian Situation'.
39. FO371/10020/3102/22/16 Allenby, 29 March 1924, refers to outbursts in the parliament over the issue of the Sudan.
40. Badran, *Feminists, Islam, and Nation*, pp. 80–81.
41. FO371/10044 10208/368/16, 'Political Developments in Egypt prior to the Murder of Sir Lee Stack'.
42. FO371/10889 143/32/16.
43. FO371/8961 3397/10/16, Allenby to Curzon, 24 March 1922, Egyptian Situation, 'Note of Sir Maurice Amos'.
44. FO371/10887 2337/29/16. The report, made two years after the assassination, claimed that Shafiq Mansur was 'screaming in his cell' that Nash'at was behind the assassination. One of those hanged for the assassination of Stack in 1926 was Mahmud Isma'il, a friend of Nash'at's. See FO371/11582 637/25/16.
45. ENA, Abdin Files, 'Review of Parties', Hizb al-Ittihad, Box 218. A letter dated January 1925.
46. FO371/10887 1257/29/16.
47. FO371/10886 85/29/16 and FO371/10886 86/29/16.
48. FO141/819 17628/1 and FO371/10887 1257/29/16.
49. At first count, the Wafd held 54 percent of the chamber of deputies.
50. FO371/10887 783/29/16.
51. FO371/10887 2664/29/16. See also Charles Adams, *Islam and Modernism: A Study of the Modern Reform Movement Inaugurated by Muhammad 'Abduh* (London: Oxford University Press, 1933), p. 266.

NOTES

52. FO371/10888 2746/29/16 and 2748/29/16 and 2825/29/16, Reports of Henderson to Chamberlain.
53. FO371/10087 1734/29/16, Allenby to Chamberlain, 22 June 1925.
54. FO371/10889 3265/29/16, Speech to Royal Colonial Institute, October 1925 and Baron George Ambrose Lloyd, *Egypt Since Cromer*, vol. 1 (London: Macmillan, 1933), p. 149.
55. FO371/10889 3458/29/16 and 3469/29/16 and 3605/29/16.
56. FO371/10889 3265, Press Reports, *al-Ahram*.
57. On the connection of these men to the Wafd and conversion to monarchism, see FO371/8963 5343/85/16 and FO371/8968 7510/85/16 and FO371/7744 4554/189/16.
58. FO371/10889 3402/29/16, Convention of parliamentarians at Continental Hotel, 21 Nov. 1925 and FO371/10889 3628/29/16, Zaghlul's speech on associations law, 28 October 1925.
59. The liberals took 13 percent of the seats in the assembly of deputies.
60. Lloyd, *Egypt since Cromer*, vol. 2, p. 167.
61. FO371/10888 1898/29/16, Henderson to Chamberlain and FO371/10888 2147/29/16, John Murray, Foreign Office Minute, where the king was described as a firm believer in the divide and rule theory.
62. Lloyd Papers, Churchill College, GLLD 13/3, Letters from Sir Austen Chamberlain to Lord Lloyd, 19 and 28 March 1928.
63. P.J. Vatikiotis, *The History of Egypt* (London: Weidenfeld and Nicolson, 1980).
64. Malak Badrawi, *Ismail Sidqi, 1875–1950: Pragmatism and Vision in Twentieth Century Egypt* (Richmond, Surrey: Curzon Press, 1996).
65. Gordon Waterfield, *Professional Diplomat: Sir Percy Loraine of Kirkharle* (London: John Murray, 1973).
66. Malcolm Yapp, ed., *Politics and Diplomacy in Egypt: The Diaries of Sir Miles Lampson 1935–1937* (Oxford: Oxford University Press, 1997), pp. 23–4.
67. Yapp, *Politics and Diplomacy*, pp. 36 and 39.
68. Ibid., pp. 30–5.
69. Anthony Eden, *Facing the Dictators: The Memoirs of Anthony Eden, Earl of Avon* (Boston: Houghton-Mifflin, 1962).
70. James P. Jankowski, *Egypt's Young Rebels: 'Young Egypt', 1932–1952* (New Haven: Stanford University Press, 1975) and Brynjar Lia, *The Society of the Muslim Brothers in Egypt: The Rise of an Islamic Mass Movement 1928–1942* (Reading: Ithaca, 1998).
71. Saleh, *Les Pouvoirs du roi*, pp. 272–83.
72. Charles Tripp, *Ali Mahir Pasha and the Palace in Egyptian Politics 1936–1942: Seeking Mass Enthusiasm for Autocracy* (London: PhD dissertation University of London, 1984).

Chapter 3 Democracy, Autocracy, Aristocracy

1. Abd al-Rahman al- Rafi'i, *Thawra sana 1919: Tarikh misr al-qaumi min sana 1914 ila sana 1921* (Cairo: Maktaba al-nahda al-misriyya, 1946), p. 263.
2. Charles Wendell, *The Evolution of the Egyptian National Image: From its Origins to Ahmad Lutfi al-Sayyid* (LA: University of California, 1972), pp. 295–314.
3. Israel Gershoni and James P. Jankowski, *Egypt, Islam and the Arabs: The Search for Egyptian Nationhood, 1900–1930* (New York: Oxford University Press, 1986), p. 86.
4. 'Abd al-Rahman al-Rafi'i, *Mustafa Kamil ba'ith al-haraka al-wataniyya* (Cairo: 1939), pp. 104–105 and 195.
5. Albert Hourani, *Arabic Thought in the Liberal Age* (Cambridge: Cambridge University Press, 2nd ed. 1983) and Taha Husayn, *The Future of Culture in Egypt*, trans. Sidney Glazer (Washington: American Council of Learned Societies, 1954), originally published in 1938.
6. 'Ali Mubarak, *al-Tawfiqiyya al-jadida li-Misr al-Qahira wa mudiniha wa biladiha al-qadima wa al-shahira* (Cairo: al-Matba'a al-kubra al-amiriyya, 1886–1889).
7. Sami Zubaida, *Islam, the People, and the State* (London: I.B.Tauris, 3rd ed. 2009), p. 10.
8. Quentin Skinner, *The Foundations of Modern Political Thought* (Cambridge: Cambridge University Press, 1978).
9. There is a more detailed examination of these themes, with specific page references, in the third section of this chapter and in Chapters 7 and 8.
10. Ibrahim, *La Nouvelle constitution*, pp. 38–9 and 45.
11. Ibrahim, *La Police judiciaire*, p. 35.
12. Saleh, *Les Pouvoirs du roi*, pp. 1–4.
13. Ibid., p. 4.
14. Ibid., pp. 4–12.
15. Ibid., pp. 51–2.
16. Ibid., p. 53; for Saleh's treatment of the caliphal state, see pp. 47–54.
17. Ibid., p. 57.
18. Ibid., pp. 57–9.
19. Ibid., pp. 53–4.
20. Ibid., p.73.
21. Ibid., p. 57.
22. Gabriel Baer, *A History of Landownership in Modern Egypt* (Oxford: Oxford University Press, 1962), pp. 8–16 and 58.
23. Saleh, pp.18–25.
24. Ibid., p. 72.

25. Ibid., p. 165.
26. On the political consequences of land redistribution see Brown, *Peasant Politics*, pp. 15 and 24–25; Kenneth M. Cuno, 'The Origins of Private Ownership of Land in Egypt: A Reappraisal' and Roger Owen, 'Egypt and Europe: from French Expedition to British Occupation', in Albert Hourani, Philip Khoury and Mary C. Wilson, *The Modern Middle East: A Reader* (London: I.B.Tauris, 1993).
27. Saleh, pp. 80–85.
28. Ibid., p. 85.
29. Ibid., pp. 91–3.
30. Ibid., p. 96.
31. Ibid., p. 97.
32. Ibid., pp. 106 and 124.
33. The prominent republican nationalist historian writing in this period was Mohamed Sabry, an associate of Sa'd Zaghlul. Sabry dealt with Isma'il's reign in his published dissertation, *La genèse de l'esprit national égyptien, 1863–1882* (Paris: Librairie Picart, 1924).
34. Saleh, p. 72.
35. Ibrahim, *La Police Judiciaire*, pp. 31–2.
36. FO78/3564, 26 April 1883, Lord Dufferin's Scheme for Reorganisation.
37. Lord Cromer, *Modern Egypt*, vol. 2, p. 481.
38. Ibrahim, *La Police*, p. 31.
39. Ibid., p. 35.
40. Ibrahim, *La Nouvelle Constitution*, p. 14.
41. Ibid., p. 27.
42. Ibid., p. 69.
43. Ibid., p. 85.
44. Saleh, p. 180.
45. Ibid., p. 199.
46. Ibid., p. 206.
47. Ibid., p. 215.
48. Ibid.
49. Ibid., p. 219. The final version conformed to the Belgian constitution, which was modeled on the unwritten British constitution.
50. Ibid., p. 221.
51. Ibid., p. 223.
52. Ibid., p. 231.
53. Ibid., p. 233.
54. Ibid., pp. 249 and 261.
55. Fahmi, *Safwat al-'Asr*, p. 19. For the history of nineteenth century, see pp. 49–63.

56. Cromer, *Modern Egypt*, vol. 1, p. 107.
57. Hunter, *Egypt Under the Khedives*, pp. 219–20, citing 'Abd al-Rahman al-Rafi'i, *Asr Isma'il*, vol. 2, pp. 137–8 and 200–207.
58. Saleh, p. 97. See Georges Douin, *Histoire de regne du Khedive Ismail*, 3 vols (Rome: Institute Poligrafico, 1933–1941) and Angelo Sammarco, *Histoire de l'Egypte moderne*, vol. 3, pp. 123, 230. For the republican perspective see also Mohamed Sabry, *L'empire egyptien sous Ismail*, pp. 109–110 and 207–55. These works are discussed by Yoav Di-Capua, *Gatekeepers of the Arab Past: Historians and History Writing in Twentieth-Century Egypt* (Berkeley: University of California Press, 2009), pp. 147–79.
59. Fahmi, pp. 45–55 and 59–63.
60. Annelien de Dijn, *French Political Thought from Montesquieu to Tocqueville: Liberty in a Levelled Society?* (New York: Cambridge University Press, 2008).
61. Anouar Abdel-Malek, *La Formation de l'ideologie dans la renaissance nationale de l'Egypte 1805–1892* (Paris: Doctoral dissertation, University of Paris, 1969), p. 222.
62. Fahmi, pp. 14–15
63. Gabriel Hanotaux, *Histoire de la Nation Egyptienne* (Cairo: published under the auspices of Fu'ad, 1931) and Joseph Cattaoui Pasha, *Coup d'Oeil sur la Chronologie de la Nation Egyptienne* (Paris: Librairie Plon, 1931) and Georges Douin, *Histoire de Regne du Khedive Isma'il*, 3 vols. (Rome: Institute Poligrafico, 1933–1941) and Etienne Combe, Jacques Bainville and Edouard Griault, *Précis de l'Histoire d'Egypte* 3 vols. (Cairo: L'Institut Francais, 1933).
64. Donald M. Reid, 'The Egyptian Geographical Society: From Foreign Layman's Society to Indigenous Professional Association,' *Poetics Today*, 14/3 (1993): 539–72.
65. Reid, 'The Egyptian Geographical Society', p. 555.
66. Hourani, 'Ottoman Reform and the Politics of the Notables', in Polk and Chambers, eds., *Beginnings of Modernization in the Middle East*. For chronicles written in the modern period see 'Abd al-Rahman al-Jabarti, *'Ajai 'b al-Athar fi al-Tarajim was al-Akhbar* (Cairo: 1870–1871, 1882, 1904–1905) and 'Ali Mubarak, *Al-Khitat al-Tawfiqiyya al-Jadida li Misr wa al-Qahira* (Cairo: 1887–1889) and Mahmud Fahmi, *Al-Bahr al-Zakhir*, as cited by Bernard Lewis and P.M. Holt, eds., *Historians of the Middle East* (London: Oxford University Press, 1962), p. 410.
67. Hourani, 'Politics of the Notables', p. 43.
68. A.K.S. Lambton, *Theory and Practice in Medieval Persian Government* (London: Variorum Reprints, 1980) pp. 419–42.
69. Hourani, *Arabic Thought*, p. 12.

NOTES 203

70. 'Abd al-Rahman Ibn Khaldun, *The Muqaddimah: An Introduction to History*, trans. Franz Rosenthal, ed. N.J. Dawood (London: Routledge and Keegan Paul, 1967).
71. Quentin Skinner, *Foundations of Modern Political Thought*, vol. 1, *The Renaissance* (Cambridge: Cambridge University Press, 1978), pp. 128–38 and 180–185.
72. Nikki R. Keddie, *Sayyid Jamal al-Din 'al-Afghani': A Political Biography* (Berkeley and Los Angeles: University of California Press, 1972), pp. 102–110.
73. On Ibn Taymiyya see, Hourani, *Arabic Thought*, p. 21 and Henri Laoust, *Essai sur les doctrines socials et politique de Taki-b-Din b. Taymiyya* (Cairo: 1939).
74. Ibn Khaldun, *The Muqaddimah*, p. x.
75. Fahmi, pp. 133–4, where the description of Zaghlul's character exemplifies his approach.
76. H.A.R. Gibb and H. Bowen, *Islamic Society and the West*, vol. 1, part 2, (London and New York: Oxford University Press, 1950), p. 182.
77. Saleh, pp. 195–221.
78. Fahmi, p. 15.
79. Ibid., pp. 133–4.
80. Ibid., p. 116.
81. Ibid., pp. 114–116.
82. Ibid., pp. 139 and 152.
83. Ibid., pp. 133–34.
84. Ira M. Lapidus, 'The Golden Age: The Political Concepts of Islam', *The ANNALS of the American Academy of Political and Social Science*, 524/1 (1992): 13–25.
85. Naguib Mahfouz, *Fountain and Tomb* (Washington DC: Three Continents Press, 1988), pp. 24–33.
86. Schulze, *Die Rebellion der ägyptischen Fallahin*.

Chapter 4 Effendis and Notables: The Elections

1. *La Bourse Egyptienne*, 16 January 1924.
2. 'In the popular urban discourse of Egypt and Iraq, the *effendiyya* were the educated or semieducated in general, that is, graduates of secondary or primary schools who adopted *ifranji* (Western) dress, engaged in modern political discourse, read newspapers, and, for the most part, worked or sought to work as teachers or state bureaucrats.' Michael Eppel, 'Note about the Term *Effendiyya* in the History of the Middle East', *International Journal of Middle East Studies*, 41 (2009): 535–39.

3. Khaled Fahmy, *All the Pashas Men: The Performance of the Egyptian Army during the Reign of Mehmed Ali Pasa* (Ph.D dissertation: Oxford, 1993).
4. Timothy Mitchell, *Colonising Egypt* (Cambridge: Cambridge University Press, 1988), p. 14.
5. Michael Ezekiel Gasper, *The Power of Representation: Publics, Peasants, and Islam in Egypt* (Stanford: Stanford University Press, 2009).
6. Nathan Brown, 'Peasant and Notables in Egyptian Politics', *Middle Eastern Studies*, 26/2 (1990): 145–60.
7. Afaf Lutfi al-Sayyid, 'Review of Gabriel Baer's Egyptian Guilds in Modern Times', *Middle Eastern Studies*, 2 (1966): 275.
8. Gabriel Baer, *Studies in the Social History of Modern Egypt* (Chicago: University of Chicago Press, 1969) and Edward William Lane, *Manners and Customs of the Modern Egyptians* (The Hague and London: East-West Publications, 1978), p. 36, where he explains: 'The Turks often apply this term ["fallāh"] to the Egyptians in general in an abusive sense, as meaning the "boors," or the "clowns".'
9. Alasdair MacIntyre, *After Virtue: A Study in Moral Theory* (London: Duckworth, 2nd ed., 1985), p. 28, who employed Max Weber's typology.
10. The ideal type is a standard Weberian concept. See H.H. Gerth and C. Wright Mills, eds., *From Max Weber: Essays in Sociology* (London: Routledge, 1948).
11. Ferdinand Tonnies, *Community and Civil Society*, ed. José Harris (Cambridge: Cambridge University Press, 2001).
12. FO371/8963 85/85/16, Scott to Curzon, 20 Sept. 1923. The file includes the commentary of Professor Azmi in a conversation with *The Times* on 28 December 1924 when he said that the revolution had brought the 'fellahin' and Egyptians of 'urban ancestry' into national politics. The political 'fellah' included all those with origins in the middle stratum of society and, as a result of social changes over the previous couple of generations, the term 'fellah' had come to refer to both urban effendis and rural shaykhs as distinct from the old 'Turkish' (*dhawat*) ruling elite.
13. Robert Springborg, *Family, Power and Politics in Egypt: Sayed Bey Marei – His Clan, Clients, and Cohorts* (Philadelphia: University of Pennsylvania Press, 1982), pp. xv-xxvii and 54–60.
14. Max Weber, *Economy and Society: An Outline of Interpretive Sociology*, eds. Guenther Ross and Claus Wittich (New York: Bedminister Press, 1968), vol. 2, pp. 598 and 1010–12 and 1020.
15. Roger Owen, 'Explaining Arab Politics', *Political Studies*, 26/4 (1976): 507–12.
16. Sami Zubaida, *Islam, the People, and the State* (London: I.B.Tauris, 3rd ed., 1988), pp. 129–40.

17. Roger Owen, *State, Politics and Power in the Making of the Modern Middle East* (London: Routledge, 1992).
18. Haykal, *Mudhakkirat*, pp. 89–92.
19. Charles D. Smith, *Islam and the Search for Social Order in Modern Egypt* (Albany: New York University Press, 1983).
20. Jacob Landau, *Parliaments and Parties in Egypt* (Tel Aviv: Israel Publishing House, 1953), p. 9 and Binder, *In a Moment of Enthusiasm*, p. 125 and Baer, *Studies in the Social History*, p. 55.
21. Hamied Ansari, *Egypt: Stalled Society* (Albany: State University of New York Press, 1986), p. 63.
22. FO78/3568, 26 April 1883, 'Lord Dufferin's Scheme for Reorganisation'.
23. FO371/8972 306/306/16, Memorandum of the Political Situation in Egypt, 4 January 1923, Appendix B.
24. FO371/8973 4591/351/16, 'The Electoral Law'.
25. FO371/8963 10383/10/16, Ernest Scott, 14 October 1923.
26. The last sentence in this paragraph paraphrases the British historian Sir Lewis Namier, as cited by Howard R. Penniman and Austin Ranny, eds., *Democracy at the Polls A Comparative Study of Competitive National Elections* (Washington: American Enterprise Institute, 1981), p. 183. Namier's analysis of British electoral politics concluded that family connection and patronage were determining factors; Sir Lewis Namier, *The Structure of Politics at the Accession of George III* (London: Macmillan and Co., 1929). This book reflects a dimension of British political culture in the interwar era, wherein family and patronage trumped political party and social class in any explanation of the political process. Malcolm Yapp has argued that Namier's analysis provided the 'best model' for Egyptian politics in the period between 1922 and 1952; Yapp, *The Near East*, p. 55.
27. Binder, *In a Moment of Enthusiasm*, p. 45. See the Egyptian official journal, *Al-Waqa'i al-Misriyya*, nos. 89, 106, 110, 112, which appeared between September and November, 1923. See also discussion of electoral politics in Allenby, FO371/8973 4591/351/16 and FO371/8973 5168/351/16. Lord Lloyd also gives a history of electoral reform until 1926 in FO371/10889 3696/29/16. The total number of seats in the assembly of deputies was 214, inclusive of the three frontier districts. For an analysis of a landlord dominated electoral system in modern Egypt, see Roger Owen, 'Socio-economic Change and Political Mobilization: The Case of Egypt', in Ghassan Salamé (ed.), *Democracy without Democrats: The Renewal of Politics in the Muslim World* (London: I.B.Tauris, 1994).
28. FO371/4973 5168/351/16, General Situation Report, 12 to 22 May 1923.
29. FO371/4973 5168/351/16.

30. *Egyptian Gazette*, 29 Sept. 1923.
31. FO371/8973 6291/351/16, Allenby to Curzon, Situation Report, 10–18 June 1923, 'The Forthcoming Elections': The provinces accounted for 11,259,973 and the urban districts 1,155,219 of the total population based on figures from the 1917 census. Total registration of voters was 2,726,768, with the urban districts accounting for 269,237 of that number and the provinces 2,457,531. The electorate comprised 22.5 percent of the entire Egyptian population. For the breakdown of percentages by province and governorate see FO371/8963 10383/10/16, Scott to Curzon, 14 October 1923 and FO371/8974 10235/351/15, Scott to Curzon, 5 October 1923. In Cairo, the total number of voters was approximately 137,000 divided into 4,564 groups of thirty. In the case of about 873 of these groups, no votes were recorded at all, i.e., over 19 percent; in Alexandria, 23 percent. In Cairo, reports indicate that pressure was certainly used, amounting on occasion to intimidation by partisans, especially by emissaries of the Wafd's 'Students' Electioneering Committee'.
32. FO371/8963 9507/10/16, Scott to Curzon, 14 Sept. 1923, 'Situation in Egypt'.
33. FO371/7744 3712/189/16, Secret Intelligence Service (SIS), 6 April 1922, Political Situation in Egypt.
34. FO371/10022 9303/22/16 and *Egyptian Gazette*, 8 January 1924 and 12 January 1924.
35. Heyworth-Dunne, p. 8, who says that the cooperatives were begun in 1909 by a 'ruling prince and a bey of a high ruling family'. Beinin and Lockman, *Workers on the Nile*, p. 62, credit 'Umar Bey Lutfi, brother of Ahmad Bey Lutfi al-Sayyid, with the creation of the cooperatives.
36. Cantori, *Egyptian Wafd*, p. 255 and *Egyptian Gazette*, 18 Oct. 1923.
37. FO371/7744 3712/189/16, SIS, 6 April 1922, Political Situation in Egypt.
38. FO371/7733 4236/1/16, Ernest Scott, Acting High Commissioner, 11 April 1922.
39. FO371/8961 2512/10/16.
40. FO371/8972 306/306/16, Memorandum of the Political Situation in Egypt, 4 January 1923, Appendix B, 30 Sept. 1922 (E 10769, Allenby to Curzon, 9 Oct).
41. FO371/8972 306/306/16.
42. FO371/7741 3803/61/16.
43. FO371/8972 306/306/16, Appendix B, 2, 15 October 1922 (E11477/1/16).
44. FO371/8960 2512/10/16, Murray, FO Minute, 6 Mar. 1923.
45. FO371/8973 1409/351/16, Situation Report, 28 January to 5 February 1923.

NOTES 207

46. FO371/8960 2512/10/16, Murray, FO Minute, 6 March 1923, 'Memorandum by Mr. Murray', based on interviews with British officials of longstanding service just returned to England.
47. FO371/8960 2512/10/16, Murray, FO Minute, 6 Mar. 1923.
48. FO371/8968 7510/85/16, SIS, 18 July, Egyptian Elections.
49. FO371/ 8963 9694/10/16, Scott to Curzon, 13 Sept. 1923.
50. *Egyptian Gazette*, 9 Oct. 1923.
51. *Egyptian Gazette*, 6 Oct. 1923.
52. FO371/8973 5774/351/16, Allenby to Curzon, Report on General Situation, 27 May-4 June.
53. *Egyptian Gazette*, 9 Oct. 1923.
54. FO371/8963 10431/10/16, Furness to Murray, 14 Oct., Situation in Egypt.
55. FO371/8960 2512/10/16.
56. Ibid.
57. FO371/7741 4241/61/16.
58. *Egyptian Gazette*, 20 Oct. 1923.
59. FO/371 8963 10383/10/16, 'Zaghloul Pasha's Electoral Campaign'.
60. *La Bourse Egyptienne*, 8 January 1924 and *Egyptian Gazette*, 18 January 1924.
61. Egyptian National Archives (ENA), Abdin Files, Box 216, dossier, 'Saad Zaghloul Pacha et le Wafd'.
62. *Egyptian Gazette*, 15 Nov. 1923.
63. *La Liberté*, as cited by FO371/8973 5168/351/16, editorial by Leon Castro; at this juncture this journal supported the Wafd Party. After 1924 it openly switched to a monarchist position.
64. FO371/14637 140/140/16, P. Lorraine to A. Henderson, 14 January 1930, 'Leading Personalities in Egypt'.
65. ENA, Abdin Files, Box 220, Report of a party meeting, n.d., but that the file includes a list for the Sha'b Party suggest that the date is 1931.
66. FO371/10019 22/22/16.
67. *Egyptian Gazette*, 11 January 1924 and FO371/8973 5774/351/16, Allenby to Curzon.
68. FO371/8974 11318/351/16, Allenby to Curzon, 31 Oct. to 13 Nov., Situation Report.
69. FO371/8974 10949/351/16.
70. FO371/10019 22/22/16, Alleny to Curzon, 23 Dec. 1923, Speech of Tawfiq Bey Doss.
71. FO371/8974 10949/351/16, Scott to Curzon, 3 Nov. 1923.
72. *Egyptian Gazette*, 18 Sept. 1923.
73. FO371/8974 11318/351/16, Allenby to FO, 31 October-13 November, Situation Report.

74. FO371/8973 7105/35/16, Allenby to Curzon, 30 June to 9 July 1923 and FO371/10020 1727/22/16.
75. *Egyptian Gazette*, 9 Nov. 1923.
76. Zaki Fahmi, *Safwat al-'Asr*, p. 419.
77. FO371/8974 10619/351/16, Scott to FO, 19 Oct. 1923, Situation Report.
78. FO371/8974 10619/351/16.
79. FO371/8974 10949/351/16, Scott to Curzon, 3 Nov. 1923.
80. FO371/8974 10949/351/16.
81. FO371/8963 11706/10/16, Allenby to Curzon, 30 Nov. 1923.
82. FO371/8963 11706/10/16.
83. Ibid.
84. *Egyptian Gazette*, 11 Dec. 1923.
85. ENA, Abdin Files, Box 216, 'Confidential Cairo City Police, 19 April 1926, Special Branch, High Command of the Police', addressed to Hadara Sahib al-Ma'ali Sa'id Dhuwa al-Fiqar Pasha, who was described as a 'highly trusted member of the King's Cabinet'.
86. ENA, Abdin Files, Box 219. The note was attached to a document dated 16 January 1925.
87. The works of 'Abd al-Rahman al-Rafi'i use such terms throughout; however a specific reference where Rafi'i shows that Zaghlul also used these types of terms can be found in Rafi'i, *Thawra sana 1919*, vol. 2, p. 166.
88. George Rude, *The Crowd in History 1730–1848* (London: John Wiley and Sons, 1964), pp. 7–9.
89. Eric Hobsbawm, *Primitive Rebels: Studies in Archaic Social Movements in the Nineteenth and Twentieth Centuries* (London: Norton, 1959), pp. 1–12 and Regis Debray, 'Marxism and the National Question', *New Left Review*, 105 (1977). Cantori, *The Egyptian Wafd*, investigates this process specific to Egypt, referring to it as a 'pragmatic policy of political agitation' that 'indigenized the imported ideology of liberal nationalism', p. 220.
90. Sawsan El-Messiri, *Ibn al-Balad: A Concept of Egyptian Identity* (Leiden: E.J. Brill, 1978).
91. Cantori, *The Egyptian Wafd*, p. 420, where he observed that Zaghlul would have acquired the symbolic authority of the notable in each locality.
92. ENA, Abdin Files, Box 216, Al-Ahzab, Hizb al-Wafd 1919–1947, Wafd Manifesto.
93. Schulze, *Die Rebellion der ägyptischen Fallahin 1919*.
94. Haykal, *Mukhakkirat*, vol. 1, pp. 89–92, records the mingling of diverse status classes in his memoirs.
95. *Al-Ahram*, 9 January 1924.
96. Ibid., 10 January 1924.
97. Rafi'i, *Fi a 'qab al-thawra al-misriyya*, p. 130.

NOTES 209

98. FO371/10020 883/22/16., Kerr to Curzon, 28 January 1924, citing an article in *al-Mahrussa*. See *Hans Wehr Dictionary* for a definition of *tazkiyya* in the classical sense and for its place in early modern Egyptian law see Norman Anderson 'Law Reform in Egypt 1850–1950' in P.M. Holt, ed., *Political and Social Change in Modern Egypt* (London: Oxford University Press, 1968).
99. FO371/10020 655/22/16.
100. *La Bourse Egyptienne*, 8 January 1924.

Chapter 5 Radicals and Conservatives: The Parliament

1. Hourani, 'Ottoman Reform and the Politics of the Notables', in Chambers and Polk, eds., *Beginnings of Modernisation in the Middle East*.
2. John Waterbury, *The Commander of the Faithful* (London: Weidenfeld and Nicholson, 1970), p. 70.
3. Cantori, *The Egyptian Wafd*, p. 395.
4. Taha Husayn, *The Days* (Cairo: American University in Cairo Press, 1997), pp. 400–02. Originally published as *al-Ayyam* between 1929 and 1939.
5. Vatikiotis, *Egypt*, p. 280.
6. Berque, *Egypt*, pp. 375–376.
7. Ibid., p. 378.
8. FO371/10887 850/29/16.
9. Binder, *In a Moment of Enthusiasm*, p. 128.
10. FO371/10020 891/22/16, New Ministry, 28 January 1924.
11. *Egyptian Gazette*, 14 January 1924.
12. ENA, Majlis al-Wuzara', Box 5/b and *Journal Officiel*, 29 January 1924.
13. FO371/10020 2853/22/16, Allenby to MacDonald, 22 Mar. 1924.
14. ENA, Various Subjects 1922–1957 Box 1.
15. Ibid.
16. FO371/10020 3102/22/16, Allenby to MacDonald, 29 March 1924, includes analysis of Zaghlul's reply to the speech from the throne. See also FO371/10022 9971/22/16.
17. FO371/8974 7888/351/16, Scott to FO, Egypt Situation Report, issued by the European Department, Ministry of Interior. The laws were passed to ensure the government would continue to have repressive powers after abolition of martial law in 1923.
18. FO371/10020/3102/22/16, Allenby to MacDonald, 29 March 1924.
19. Binder, *Moment of Enthusiasm*, pp. 248 and 300.
20. FO371/10020 3532/22/16, Allenby to MacDonald, 12 April 1924. *Kashkul* was described as the most popular Egyptian journal, with double the circulation of any daily because it appealed to the 'illiterates'. Allenby's

commentary on the events in the assembly of deputies can be found in FO371/10020 2853/22/16, Allenby to MacDonald, 22 March 1924.
21. FO371/8973 6291/351/16, Allenby to Curzon, 10–18 June 1923, Situation Report, Egyptian Delegation to Feminist Congress in Rome.
22. FO371/8973 5774/351/16, Allenby to Curzon, 27 May – 4 June 1923, Situation Report.
23. FO371/ 8973 7434/351/16, Allenby to Curzon, 8 July.
24. FO371/8974 7888/351/16, Scott to Curzon, Situation Report, European Department, Ministry of Interior.
25. FO371/8974 7888/351/16.
26. Badran, *Feminists, Islam, and Nation*, pp. 80–81.
27. *Egyptian Gazette*, 15 Nov. 1923.
28. FO371/10021 5253/22/16. The editor was Sulayman Bey Fawzi. He was arrested 7 June 1924.
29. FO371/10020 3532/22/16, Allenby to MacDonald, 12 April 1924.
30. *L'Information*, 11 February 1924.
31. FO371/10040 3651/368/16, Allenby to MacDonald, 22 April 1924.
32. It appears that Foreign Office officials believed that Allenby was advocating a policy of withdrawal; however, the evidence suggests that Allenby's position was near that subsequently adopted by Eden and Lampson in 1936. Yet, in 1924 Allenby was regarded by some British officials as taking too conciliatory a line with the nationalists. See FO371/10040 3563/368/16, Minutes of Murray, Oliphant and Ingram, 22 April 1924. On the aims of the War Office to increase Britain's military presence in the Nile Valley, see FO371/10040 3785/368/16, Cabinet, 16 April 1924.
33. FO371/10020 1114/22/16, Kerr to MacDonald, 4 February 1924.
34. FO371/10021 4598/22/16.
35. FO371/10020 3595/22/16.
36. FO371/10020 3595/22/16 and FO371/10020 3697/22/16.
37. FO371/10020 3534/22/16, Enclosure 1, No. 1, Patterson to Allenby, Cairo, 2 April 1924.
38. Hasan Nafi was also present at the political rally. In the words of historians of the Egyptian working class, Fahmi and Hasan Nafi, a lawyer acting as the counselor (*mustashar*) of the syndicate, represented the 'developing relationship between the bourgeois nationalism of the Wafd and the emerging working class labour organizations', Beinin and Lockman, *Workers on the Nile*, pp. 127 and 157–58.
39. *Al-Ahram*, 5 July 1924.
40. FO371/10021 6081/22/16, Allenby to MacDonald, 14 July 1924.
41. FO371/10021 6081/22/16.

NOTES   211

42. FO371/10022 11524/22/16, Press Reports.
43. FO371/10021 6249/22/16, Allenby to MacDonald, 21 July 1924.
44. *L'Information*, 11 February 1925.
45. ENA, Majlis al-Wuzara', Box 6.
46. Benedict Anderson, *Imagined Communities: Reflections on the Origin and Spread of Nationalism* (London: Verso, 1983), pp. 9–12.
47. FO371/10020 9971/22/16, Allenby, 9 Nov. 1924.
48. FO371/10022 9745/22/16, Allenby to MacDonald, 2 Nov. 1924.
49. *La Liberté*, 3 Nov. 1924.
50. FO371/10022 9971/22/16.
51. FO371/10022 9132/22/16.
52. FO371/10022 9971/22/16, Allenby, 17 Nov. 1924.
53. FO371/10021 5233/22/16, Allenby to MacDonald, 8 June 1924.
54. FO371/10022 11294/22/16, Allenby to Chamberlain, 3 Dec. 1924.
55. FO371/10022 10023/22/16, Allenby to Chamberlain, 24 Nov. 1924.
56. FO371/10022 10023/22/16.
57. FO371/10044 10208/368/16, 'Political Developments in Egypt Prior to the murder of Sir Lee Stack'.
58. FO371/10044 10340/368/16, 'Situation in Egypt'.
59. FO371/10044 10208/368/16.
60. FO371/10046 11296/368/16, Allenby to Chamberlain, 15 Dec. 1924.
61. FO371/11582 637/25/16.
62. FO371/10044 10327/368/16, Lord Cecil to Secretary of State and FO371/10044 10195/368/16.
63. FO371/10046 11086/368/16.
64. FO371/10087 372/29/16.
65. FO371/10022 11614/22/16, Henderson to Chamberlain, 6 Dec. 1924.
66. FO371/10887 335/29/16, Egyptian Press, 2 February 1925.
67. FO141/819/17628/1, Allenby to MacDonald, 9 January 1925.
68. FO141/819/17628/1.
69. ENA, Abdin Files, Review of Parties, Hizb al-Ittihad Box 218. Letter dated January 1925, indicates the cultural and ideological divisions. See also FO371/10887 1257/29/16.
70. FO371/10886 86/29/16.
71. FO371/10886 128/29/16.
72. *Manchester Guardian*, 12 January 1925.
73. FO371/10886 128/29/16.
74. FO371/10887 1336/29/16, Review of Elections.
75. FO371/10887 376/29/16, Allenby to Chamberlain, 5 February, 1925.
76. *Egyptian Gazette*, 3 April 1925.

77. FO371/10022 9971/22/16.
78. ENA, Abdin Files, Box 218, telegraph addressed to Nash'at Pasha, 'ra'is al-diwan al-maliki', 12 July 1925.
79. ENA, Abdin Files, Box 218, telegraph, 12 July 1925.
80. ENA, Abdin Files, Box 219, note attached to a document dated 16 January 1925. Boxes 218 and 219 contain the party lists of the Ittihad Party. The practice of selling constituencies was the subject of a political scandal later in the year. See FO371/10889 3402/29/16.
81. FO371/10888 2939/29/16.
82. ENA, Abdin Files, Box 218, 'Dossier al-hukuma al-malakiyya al-misriyya' (Report of the royal government of Egypt), contains a telegram from Beheira addressed to the 'master of ceremonies', which includes a membership list. Religious or traditionalist titles outnumber effendiyya or modernist titles two to one.
83. ENA, Abdin Files, Box 219, Review of Parties, Hizb al-Ittihad: *Al-Ittihad*, 16 January 1925. That the editor of the journal was Taha Husayn underscores the liberal aversion to the Wafd in the early 1920s and the quest for alternatives to its populism. Oddly, a liberal intellectual might have been one of the first to articulate a conservative ideology. For the alignment of liberals and monarchists, see ENA, Abdin Files, Box 600, 1925, containing a file regarding a celebration in honour of *al-Muqtataf*, attended by Taha Husayn, Shawqi Bey, Rashid Rida, Ahmad Lutfi al-Sayyid, 'Abbas Mahmud al-Aqqad, Mustafa 'Abd al-Raziq, Ibrahim al-Mazini and Charles Stambouli, a list inclusive of liberals, salafists and conservative monarchists (Stambouli).
84. Weber, *Economy and Society*, vol. 2, pp. 1010–1012 and 1020.
85. Fahmi, p. 297.
86. Ibid., p. 345.
87. ENA, Abdin Files, Box 218. The manifesto appeared in a telegraph to the king, dated 12 July 1925 and addressed to Nash'at, *ra'is al-diwan al-maliki* (head of the royal cabinet).
88. ENA, Abdin Files, Box 218, telegraph, 12 July 1925.
89. FO371/10888 1898/29/16 and 2674/29/16.
90. *Al-Siyasa*, 12 Dec. 1925.
91. ENA, Abdin Files, Box 219, letter, unsigned, residence Giza, undated, but the context suggests the letter was written between 1926 and 1931.

Chapter 6 Traditionalism

1. Albert Hourani, *Arabic Thought in the Liberal Age*, 2nd ed. (Cambridge: Cambridge University Press, 1983), passim; for Hourani, liberal nationalism in Egypt reflected the cultural dominance of Europe in the liberal age

(1798–1939). Israel Gershoni and James P. Jankowski, *Egypt, Islam and the Arabs: The Search for Nationhood 1900–1930* (New York: Oxford University Press, 1986), p. 271. Gershoni and Jankowski underscore the shift of cultural and political orientations from the Ottoman Empire and Islam to the Egyptian nation after 1919.
2. Karl Mannheim, *Ideology and Utopia: An Introduction to the Sociology of Knowledge* (New York: Harcourt, Brace and Co., 1936), pp. 237–80.
3. FO371/10022 8837/22/16 and 8650/22/16, Press Reports, Rashid Rida supported the claims of Ibn Saud in articles in *al-Muqattam*. The Wafd Party aligned itself with the *salafiyya* because of its antipathy to the palace in articles in *al-Balagh*. The Wafd also supported the claims of Ibn Saud to the caliphate because of his hostility toward the monarchists.
4. See arguments in this chapter.
5. Beth Baron, *The Women Awakening in Egypt: Culture, Society, and the Press* (New Haven: Yale University Press, 1997), p. 114.
6. FO371/10886 38/29/16.
7. FO371/10887 1257/29/16, where Sidqi was reported to have said that the Wafd and Ittihad government controlled about 90 seats each. Berque, *Egypt*, p. 393, recorded that the Wafd had 60 percent of the vote.
8. FO371/10889 3628/29/16, Lloyd to Chamberlain, 14 Dec. 1925.
9. *Egyptian Gazette*, 1 April 1925.
10. Gershoni and Jankowski, *Egypt, Islam and the Arab*, pp. 35–9.
11. Charles D. Smith, 'The "Crisis of Orientation": The Shift of Egyptian Intellectuals to Islamic Subjects in the 1930s', *International Journal of Middle East Studies*, 4 (1973): 382–410.
12. *Egyptian Gazette*, 1 April 1925.
13. As demonstrated in Chapter 3, these arguments were made in 1939 by Diaeddine Saleh and thus constituted a pillar of conservative ideology.
14. The colonial argument according to evolutionary logic and specific to Egypt was articulated in FO78/3568, 26 April 1883, 'Lord Dufferin's Scheme for the Reorganisation' and FO371/4978 5168/6/16, February 1920, 'Report of the Special Mission to Egypt'. A classic colonial literary text on the subject can be found in Alfred Milner, *England in Egypt* (London: Edward Arnold, 1893).
15. *Egyptian Gazette*, 1 April 1925.
16. Ibid.
17. Ibid.
18. The doctrine of the ten percent was a colonial commonplace, but can be found in Maurice Amos, "The Constitutional History of Egypt", *Publications of the Grotius Society,* 14 (1929): 131–35 or Lord Milner, 'Report of the Special Mission to Egypt'.

19. *Egyptian Gazette*, 2 April 1925.
20. FO371/10087 1142/29/16, Allenby to Chamberlain, 20 April 1925, 'Review of Press'.
21. *Egyptian Gazette*, 1 April 1925.
22. FO371/10087 1142/29/16.
23. Badran, *Feminists*, p. 207.
24. ENA, Abdin Files, Box 219, 'Note'.
25. ENA, Abdin Files, Box 207 and FO/371/10888 2674/29/16.
26. Gabriel Baer, *Studies in the Social History of Modern Egypt* (Chicago: University of Chicago Press, 1969), pp. 83–8.
27. FO371/8974 9277/351/16. The school of *qadis* was created for students from Azhar to take courses required for positions as court clerks and judges; the school was initially set up in 1907 to staff the *ahliyya* courts, which were set up in the mid-nineteenth century to try criminal cases. The Muslim courts were responsible only for civil cases and cases of murder. There was an attempt by 'Ali Mubarak to create a special section for *qadis* at Dar al-'Ulum, which failed. The school for *qadis* was the outcome of a commission looking into the Muslim courts set up by Muhammad 'Abduh, who noted that the *qadis* were selected without regard to 'personality, character or conduct'. Subsequently, Zaghlul nominated Atif Barakat as the first principal of the school (1908–1921). From 1919 the school was described in this British report as the 'storm centre of school-strikes' and a lever of 'terrorism', reaching even into the elementary schools. The school for *qadis*, however, weakened the authority of al-Azhar, which had previously appointed judges from its graduate amongst the 'ulama'. In 1911 al-Azhar succeeded in having the power to appoint the principal of the school transferred from the Ministry of Education to al-Azhar; in 1916 it won the right to have half of the available judicial posts available for graduates of al-Azhar; thus the recent reforms were the culmination of a contest between government officials and religious authorities, with the latter regaining ground.
28. FO371/11582 908/25/16, Lloyd to Chamberlain, 19 April 1926. The fatwa was issued 28 March 1926.
29. FO371/11582 693/25/16, Lloyd to Chamberlain, 13 March 1926.
30. FO371/11582 637/25/16, Lloyd to Chamberlain, 23 February 1926.
31. Leonard Binder, *Islamic Liberalism: A Critique of Development Ideologies* (London: University of Chicago Press, 1988), pp. 131–36. Binder shows the degree to which Raziq's thesis is a dialogue with the thought of Ibn Khaldun.
32. Jamal Mohammed Ahmed, *The Intellectual Origins of Egyptian Nationalism* (London: Oxford University Press, 1960), p. 118.

NOTES 215

33. FO371/10888 2825/29/16, 28 Sept. 1925, Report of European Department, Egyptian Ministry of Interior.
34. FO371/10887 2664/29/16, Henderson to Chamberlain, 11 Sept. 1925.
35. Adams, *Islam and Modernism*, p. 266.
36. FO371/10888 2825/29/16.
37. FO371/10889 3342/29/16, Henderson to Chamberlain, 16 Nov. 1925.
38. FO371/10888 2990/29/16.
39. FO371/10888 2748/29/16, Henderson to Chamberlain, 21 Sept. 1925.
40. FO371/10888 2825/2916.
41. FO371/10888 2746/29/16, Henderson to Chamberlain, 12 Sept. 1925.
42. FO371/10888 2825/2916.
43. Saleh, *Les Pouvoirs*, pp. 215–21.
44. FO371/10887 1484/29/16, *Journal du Caire*.
45. FO371/10888 2746/29/16.
46. FO371/10888 3142/29/16.
47. FO371/10888 2919/29/16, Henderson to Chamberlain, 5 Oct. 1925.
48. Bakhit as cited by Hourani, *Arabic Thought*, p. 190.
49. FO371/10888 2836/29/16, Henderson to Chamberlain, 28 Sept. 1925.
50. *Al-Ittihad*, 11 Nov. 1925.
51. FO371/10888/2168/29/16, Henderson to Chamberlain, 27 July 1925.
52. ENA, Abdin Files, Box 222, *al-Siyasa*, 14 Dec.1925.
53. ENA, Abdin Box 222, *al-Balagh*, 23 Oct. 1925.
54. ENA, Abdin Box 219, *al-Balagh*, 7 February 1926.
55. ENA, Abdin Box 219, *al-Akbar*, 20 Dec. 1925.
56. Fahmi, pp. 14–15.
57. Ibid. pp. 133–34
58. Hourani, *Arabic Thought*, p. 12.
59. ENA, Abdin Files Box 28 and ENA, Council of Ministers Files, Various Subjects, 1922–1957, Box 1, Civil List.
60. Nancy Elizabeth Gallagher, ed., *Approaches to the History of the Middle East: Interviews with Leading Middle East Historians* (Reading: Ithaca Press, 1994), p. 91.
61. Ehud Toledano, *State and Society in Mid-Nineteenth Century Egypt* (Cambridge: Cambridge University Press, 1990), p. 102 and Ibn Khaldun, *The Muqaddimah*.
62. Fahmi, title page.
63. Ibid., pp. 134–38. Cantori argued that marriage of Egyptian notables to dhawat was the significant indicator of social integration in this period.
64. FO371/10019 194/22/16 and *Egyptian Gazette*, 25 Dec. 1924.
65. Fahmi, p. 158.

66. Ibid., pp. 75–81.
67. Ibid., pp. 163–65.
68. Ibid., p. 171.
69. Ibid.
70. Ibid., pp. 175–176.
71. Ibid., p. 4.
72. FO371/14637 140/140/16, P. Lorraine to A. Henderson, 14 January 1930, 'Leading Personalities in Egypt'.
73. Hunter, *Egypt Under the Khedives*, p. 223.
74. FO371/14637 14663.
75. ENA, Abdin Files, Box 216, 'Confidential City Police, April 1926, Special Branch'.
76. Anthony Pagden, ed., *The Languages of Political Theory in Early Modern Europe* (Cambridge: Cambridge University Press, 1987). On the distinction between the paternalism of utilitarianism against the 'pre-modern' notion of command and obedience by moral example, see Kathryn Tidrick, *Empire and the English Character* (London: I.B. Tauris, 1992).

Chapter 7 Neo-Colonialism

1. MECA, GB165-0115, Sir Robert Allason Furness, Box 3/1, Letter, Kerr to Furness, 8 December 25.
2. Waterbury, *Commander of the Faithful*, p. 70.
3. FO371/10040 3785/368/16, Cabinet, 16 April 1924. The file shows that the War Office intended to increase Britain's military presence in the Nile Valley.
4. J.A. Spender, *The Changing East* (London: Cassell, 1926), Spender was privy to the tenor of discussion during treaty negotiations between Curzon and the Wafd in 1920. See pp. 74–5 and FO371/6301 8245/260/16, Statement of Lord Curzon, Imperial Conference, 6 July 1921.
5. Sir Maurice Amos, 'The Constitutional History of Egypt for the Last Forty Years', *The Grotius Society*, vol. 14, (1929), p. 153.
6. Sir Maurice Amos, *England and Egypt* (University College Nottingham: Cust Foundation Lecture, 1929).
7. FO 371/6295 4919/260/16, 16 April 1921, 'Alternative Proposals for Future Government of Egypt', Memorandum by Amos.
8. Lloyd Papers, Churchill College, GLLD 13/3, Letters from Sir Austen Chamberlain to Lord Lloyd, 19 and 28 March 1928, censuring Lloyd's obstruction of treaty negotiations. The letters include reports showing that Lloyd had declared himself in favour of the use of 'force' in British relations

NOTES

with Egyptians, rejecting the 1922 declaration and the 1923 constitution as unworkable.

9. Lloyd Papers, Churchill College, GLLD 13/3, Letters from Sir Austen Chamberlain to Lord Lloyd, 28 Dec 1926, shows Chamberlain's preference for the methods of Cromer against Lloyd's desire to assert British imperial will.
10. FO371/7741 1039/61/16.
11. FO371/10888 2147/29/16.
12. FO371/10888 1898/29/16.
13. FO371/10888 2007/26/16.
14. FO371/10888 2666/29/16 and FO371/10888 2674/29/16, *al-Siyasa*, as cited by Henderson.
15. FO371/10888 1898/29/16.
16. FO371/10888 2825/29/16.
17. FO371/10888 2746/29/16.
18. Ibid.
19. FO371/8972 306/306/16.
20. FO371/10087 1734/29/16, Allenby to Chamberlain, 22 June 1925.
21. FO371/6301 8245/260/16.
22. Lloyd Papers, Churchill College, GLLD 13/3, Letters from Sir Austen Chamberlain to Lord Lloyd, 28 Dec. 1926.
23. Lloyd Papers, Churchill College, GLLD 13/3, Letters from Sir Austen Chamberlain to Lord Lloyd, 25 April 1928.
24. Lloyd, *Egypt since Cromer*, vol. 2, pp. 147–149.
25. Lloyd, vol. 2, p. 332.
26. FO371/10889 3265/29/16.
27. FO371/10889 3697/29/16.
28. FO371/10889 3458/29/16 and FO371/10889 3469/29/16 and FO371/10889 3605/29/16.
29. Lloyd Papers, Churchill College GLLD 13/3, Letters from Sir Austen Chamberlain to Lloyd, 21 April 1925 and Lloyd, *Egypt since Cromer*, vol. 2, p. 159.
30. FO371/10889 3265/29/16.
31. FO371/11582 692/25/16.
32. The term 'judicious' was used by the translators of Naguib Mahfouz's *Palace of Desire* (London: Doubleday, 1991), p. 309, wherein Mahfouz described the new style of politics emerging with Zaghlul's overtures to the liberals and Watanists in 1926. Indeed, this sea change in Egyptian politics is a central theme in Mahfouz's 'Cairo Trilogy'; thus after the first volume, *Palace Walk*, climaxed with the martyrdom of the revolutionary hero, Fahmy, the second

volume, *Palace of Desire*, depicted the infatuation of Fahmy's brother, Kamal, with the daughter of an aristocratic family.
33. ENA, Abdin Box 216, 'Confidential Special Branch, from high commander of the police addressed to Sahib al-ma'ali Sa'id dhu al-Fiqr Pasha, kabir al-amma' bi-diwan Sahib Jalalaha al-malik, 19 April 1926.
34. FO371/11581 515/25/16.
35. ENA, Abdin 216, Confidential Special Branch, 19 April 1926.
36. Ibid.
37. Ibid.
38. Lloyd, *Egypt since Cromer*, vol. 2, p. 167 and FO371/11581 1078/25/16 and Lloyd Papers, Churchill College GLLD 13/3, letter, Chamberlain to Lloyd, 16 June 1926, where Chamberlain argued that Zaghlul should be allowed the premiership, thus crediting the political outcome as founded upon colonial strategies is unfounded.
39. ENA, Abdin Files Box 223, Hizb al-Sha'b, 1931/2/19 – 1934/1/29, document, undated, untitled.
40. Ibid.

Chapter 8 Conclusion

1. Weber, *Economy and Society*, vol. 3, pp. 1010–20.
2. Ibid., p. 949.
3. Malcolm Yapp, *The Near East since the First World War* (London: Longman, 1991), p. 55.
4. FO371/7730 767/1/16 and FO371/8961 3397/10/16.
5. FO371/6295 4919/26016 and FO371/6301 8245/260/16.
6. Leon Castro, editor of *La Liberté*, as cited by Saleh, p. 261.
7. Berque, *Egypt*, pp. 312–24 and 363–402.
8. Abdeslam M. Maghraoui, *Liberalism without Democracy: Nationhood and Citizenship in Egypt, 1922–1936, Politics, History, and Culture* (Durham, N.C.: Duke University Press, 2006).

SELECT BIBLIOGRAPHY

Primary Sources

Several series of files at the Egyptian National Archives (Dar al-Watha'iq), Cairo, were consulted in the writing of this book. The Abdin Files are records produced by the Egyptian royal house including confidential reports of the royal cabinet and the royal intelligence service. Also the ENA holds the files of the Egyptian Council of Ministers (Majlis al-Wuzara') and files dealing with the political parties of the era, including documents, memorandum, letters, and the electoral lists. The archival record indicates that there was great interest in the elections of 1923, 1925 and 1926, suggesting that Egyptians were very much aware of having been engaged in an important cultural and political project.

The Egyptian National Library (Dar al-Kutub) holds periodicals, journals, and newspapers of the era, including the government's official journal. In addition, the library of the Jesuit College of Sainte Famille, Cairo, has an important collection of works in French and Arabic. In London the National Archives hold the files of the Foreign Office (FO), which was responsible for Egypt during the period of the British military occupation. These FO files provide a more systematic survey of the political events of the era. Files at the Middle East Centre at St. Antony's College, Oxford, and Churchill College, Cambridge, were also consulted in the writing of this book.

Secondary Sources

Abdel-Malek, Anouar, *Ideologie et renaissance national: l'Egypte moderne*, Paris: Edition Anthropos, 1969.

Abdesselem, Ahmed, *Ibn Khaldun et ses lecteurs*, Paris: Presses Universitaires de France, 1960.

Adams, Charles C., *Islam and Modernism: A Study of the Modern Reform Movement Inaugurated by Muhammad 'Abduh*, London: Oxford University Press, 1933.

Ahmad, Leila, *Women and Gender in Islam*, New Haven: Yale University Press, 1992.

Ahmed, Jamal Mohammed, *The Intellectual Origins of Egyptian Nationalism*, London: Oxford University Press, 1960.

Allan, Roger, *A Period of Time, Part One, A Study of Muhammad al-Muwaylihi's Hadith Isa Ibn Hisham*, Oxford: St. Anthony's Middle East Monographs, no. 27, 1992.

Amos, Maurice, 'The Constitutional History of Egypt for the Last Forty Years', *Publications of the Grotius Society*, vol. 14, 1929.

Amos, Maurice, *England and Egypt*, University College Nottingham: Cust Foundation Lecture, 1929.

Anderson, Benedict, *Imagined Communities: Reflections on the Origin and Spread of Nationalism*, London: Verso, 1983.

Anderson, J.N.D., 'Law Reform in Egypt', *Political and Social Change in Modern Egypt*, P.M. Holt, ed., London: University of Oxford Press, 1968.

Ansari, Hamied, *Egypt: The Stalled Society*, Albany: State University of New York Press, 1986.

Badran, Margot, *Feminists, Islam and Nation: Gender and the Making of Modern Egypt*, Princeton: Princeton University Press, 1995.

Baer, Gabriel, *A History of Landownership in Modern Egypt*, London: Oxford University Press, 1962

———, *Studies in the Social History of Modern Egypt*, London: Oxford University Press, 1969.

Baron, Beth, *The Women's Awakening in Egypt: Culture, Society and the Press*, New Haven: Yale University Press, 1997.

———, 'Unveiling in Early Twentieth Century Egypt: Practical and Symbolic Considerations', *Middle Eastern Studies*, 25 (1989).

Beinin, Joel and Zackary Lockman, *Workers on the Nile: Nationalism, Communism, Islam, and the Egyptian Working Class: 1882–1954*, Princeton: Princeton University Press, 1987.

Berger, Morroe, *Bureaucracy and Society: A Study of the Higher Civil Service*, Princeton: Princeton University Press, 1957.

Berque, Jacques, *Egypt: Imperialism and Revolution*, London: Faber, 1972.

Binder, Leonard, *Islamic Liberalism: A Critique of Development Ideologies*, London: University of Chicago Press, 1988.

———, *In a Moment of Enthusiasm: Political Power and the Second Stratum*, Chicago: University of Chicago Press, 1978.
Brown, Nathan J., *Peasant Politics in Modern Egypt: the struggle against the state*, New Haven: Yale University Press, 1990.
———, 'Peasants and Notables in Egyptian Politics', *Middle Eastern Studies*, 26/2, 1990.
Burke, Edmund, *Reflections on the Revolution in France*, London: Macmillan, 1892.
Butovsky, A., 'The Language of the Egyptian monarchy', *Harvard Middle Eastern and Islamic Review*, 1, 1994.
Cantori, Louis Joseph, *The Organizational Basis of an Elite Political Party: The Egyptian Wafd*, Chicago: PhD dissertation, University of Chicago, 1966.
Cattaoui, Joseph Pacha, *Coup d'Oeil sur la Chronologie de la Nation Egyptienne*, Paris: Librairie Plon, 1931.
Chatterjee, Partha, *The Nation and its Fragments: Colonial and Postcolonial Histories*, Princeton: Princeton University Press, 1993.
Cole, Juan R.I., 'Feminism, Class and Islam in Turn-of-the-Century Egypt', *International Journal of Middle Eastern Studies*, 13, 1981.
Cromer, Earl of, *Abbas II*, London: Macmillan, 1915.
———, *Modern Egypt*, London: Macmillan, 1908.
Darwin, John, *Britain, Egypt and the Middle East: Imperial Policy in the Aftermath of War*, Oxford: Oxford University Press, 1982.
De Dijn, Annelien, *French Political Thought from Montesquieu to Tocqueville: Liberty in a Levelled Society?* New York: Cambridge University Press, 2008.
Deeb, Marius, *Party Politics in Egypt: The Wafd and Its Rivals*, London: Ithaca Press for the Middle East Centre, St. Anthony's College, Oxford, 1979.
Di-Capua, Yoav, *Gatekeepers of the Arab Past: Historians and History Writing in Twentieth-Century Egypt*, Berkeley: University of California Press, 2009.
———, '"Jabarti of the Twentieth Century": The National Epic of 'Abd al-Rahman al-Rafi'i and other Egyptian Histories', *International Journal of Middle East Studies*, 36 2004.
Douin, Georges, *Histoire du regne de Khedive Ismail*, 3 vols., Rome: Societé royale de geographie d'Egypte, Institute Poligrafico, 1935–1941.
Fahmi, Zaki, *Safwat al-'asr fi tarikh wa rusum mashahir rijal misr min 'ahd sakin al-jinan Muhammad 'Ali Pasha al-Kabir mutajan bi rasm sahib al-jilalat Fu'ad al-Awwal malik misr wa sudan*, Cairo: Matba'at al-I'timad, 1926.
Fahmy, Khaled M., *All the Pasa's Men: The Performance of the Egyptian Army During the Reign of Mehmed Ali Pasa*, Oxford: PhD dissertation St. Peter's College, 1993.
Gallagher, Nancy Elizabeth, ed., *Approaches to the History of the Middle East: Interviews with Leading Middle East Historians*, Reading: Ithaca Press, 1994.
Gasper, Michael Ezekiel, *The Power of Representation: Publics, Peasants, and Islam in Egypt*, Stanford: Stanford University Press, 2009.

Geertz, Clifford, *The Interpretation of Cultures: Selected Essays*, London: Fontana Press, 1993.
Gellner, Ernest and John Waterbury, *Patrons and Clients in Mediterranean Societies*, London: Duckworth, 1977.
Gerth, H.H. and C. Wright Mills, eds., *From Max Weber: Essays in Sociology*, London: Routledge, 1948.
Gershoni, Israel and James P. Jankowski, *Redefining the Egyptian Nation 1930–1945*, New York: Cambridge University Press, 1995.
———, *Egypt, Islam and the Arabs: The Search for Egyptian Nationhood, 1900–1930*, New York: Oxford University Press, 1986.
Gibb, H.A.R. and H. Bowen, *Islamic Society and the West*, London and New York: Oxford University Press, 1950.
Gilsenan, M., 'Nizam ma fi: Discourses of Order, Disorder and History in a Lebanese Context', *Problems of the Modern Middle East in Historical Perspective*, Reading: Ithaca Press, 1992.
Goldberg, Ellis, 'Peasants in Revolt - Egypt 1919', *International Journal of Middle East Studies*, 24, 1992.
Hanotaux, Gabriel, *Histoire de la nation égyptienne: L'Egypte de 1801–1802*, Cairo: Institute d'Egypte, 1931.
Hasan, Yusuf, *Al-Qasr wa dawrhu fi al-siyasa al-misriyya 1922–1952*, Cairo: Al-Ahram Center for Political and Strategic Studies, 1982.
Haykal, Muhammad Husayn, *Mudhakkirat fi al-siyasa al-misriyya*, Cairo: Dar al-Ma'arif, 1951–53.
Herf, Jeffrey, *Reactionary Modernism: Technology, Culture, and Politics in Weimar and the Third Reich*, Cambridge: Cambridge University Press, 1984.
Hobsbawm, E.J., *Primitive Rebels: Studies in Archaic Forms of Social Movements in the Nineteenth and Twentieth Centuries*, London: Norton, 1959.
Hourani, Albert, *A History of the Arab Peoples*, London: Faber and Faber, 1991.
———, *Arabic Thought in the Liberal Age 1798–1939*, Cambridge: Cambridge University Press, 2nd ed., 1983.
———, 'Ottoman Reform and the Politics of the Notables', *Beginnings of Modernization in the Middle East: The Nineteenth Century*, William R. Polk and Richard L. Chambers, eds., Chicago: University of Chicago Press, 1968.
Hunter, Robert F., *Egypt under the Khedives: From Household Government to Modern Bureaucracy*, Pittsburgh: University of Pittsburgh Press, 1984.
Husayn, Taha, *The Days*, Cairo: American University Press, 1997, originally published as *al-Ayyam* between 1929 and 1939.
———, *La Police judiciaire en Egypte*, Paris: Librairie de Jurisprudence Ancienne et Moderne, 1926.
Ibrahim, White, *La Nouvelle constitution de l'Egypte*, Paris: Librairie de jurisprudence ancienne et moderne, 1925.
Kamil, Mustafa, *Lettres Egyptienne-Francaises*, Cairo: Mustafa Kamil School, n.d..

Keddie, Nikki, 'Islamic Mirror for Princes', *Theory and Practice in Medieval Persian Government*, London: Variorum Reprints, 1980.
———, *Sayyid Jamal al-Din "al-Afghani"*, Berkeley and LA: University of California Press, 1972.
———, *An Islamic Response to Imperialism: Writings of Sayyid Jamal al-Din "al-Afghani"*, Berkeley and LA: University of California Press, 1968.
Kedourie, Elie, *Chatham House Version and Other Middle Eastern Studies*, London: Wiedenfeld and Nicholson, 1970.
Khoury, Philip S., *Urban Notables and Arab Nationalism: The Politics of Damascus 1860–1920*, London: Cambridge University Press, 1983.
Landau, Jacob M., *Parliaments and Parties in Egypt*, Tel Aviv: Israel Publishing House, 1953.
Lapidus, Ira M., 'The Golden Age: The Political Concepts of Islam', *The Annals of the American Academy of Political and Social Science*, 524/1, 1992.
Lewis, Bernard, and P.M. Holt, eds., *Historians of the Middle East*, London: Oxford University Press, 1962.
Lloyd, Baron George Ambrose, *Egypt Since Cromer*, London: Macmillan, 1933.
Lockman, Zachary, 'Imagining the Working Class: Culture, Nationalism and Class Formation in Egypt, 1899–1914', *Poetics Today*, 15, 1994.
MacIntyre, Alasdair, *After Virtue: A Study in Moral Theory*, London: Duckworth, 2nd ed., 1985.
Maghraoui, Abdesalam, *The Dilemma of Liberalism in the Middle East: A Reading of the Liberal Experiment in Egypt*, Ann Arbor: PhD dissertation University of Michigan, 1991.
Mahfouz, Naguib, *Fountain and Tomb*, Boulder: Lynne Rienner, 1998.
———, *Midaq Alley*, Cairo: American University Press, 1992.
———, *Sugar Street*, New York: Doubleday, 1992; originally published as *al-Sukkariyya* in 1957.
———, *Palace of Desire*, New York: Doubleday, 1992; originally published as *Qasr al-Shawq* in 1957.
———, *Palace Walk*, New York: Doubleday, 1990; originally published as *Bayn al-Qasrayn* in 1956.
Mannheim, Karl, *Essays on the Sociology of Knowledge*, London: Routledge, 1952.
———, *Ideology and Utopia: An Introduction to the Sociology of Knowledge*, London: Routledge, 1939.
Marx, Karl, *The Eighteenth Brumaire of Louis Bonaparte*, New York: International Publishers, 1898.
Merriam, Kathleen Howard, *The Role of Leadership in Nation-Building: Egypt 1922*, Bloomington: PhD dissertation University of Indiana, 1971.
Messiri, Sawsan El-, *Ibn al-Balad: A Concept of Egyptian Identity*, Leiden: E.J. Brill, 1978.
———, 'The Changing Role of the Futuwwa in the Social Structure of Cairo', in Ernest Gellner and John Waterbury, eds., *Patrons and Clients in Mediterranean Societies*, London: Duckworth, 1977.

Milner, Alfred, *England in Egypt*, London: Edward Arnold, 1898.
Mitchell, Timothy, *Colonising Egypt*, Cambridge: Cambridge University Press, 1988.
Moore, Barrington, *The Social Origins of Dictatorship and Democracy: Lord and Peasant in the Making of the Modern World*, Boston: Beacon Press, 1966.
Namier, Sir Lewis, *The Structure of Politics at the Accession of George III*, London: Macmillan, 1929.
Owen, Roger, *State, Power and Politics in the Making of the Modern Middle East*, London: Routledge, 1992.
———, 'Explaining Arab Politics', *Political Studies*, 26/4, 1976.
Rafi'i, 'Abd al-Rahman al-, *Fi a'qab al-thawra misriyya: Tarikh Misr al-qawm min Ibril sanat 1921 ila wafat Saad Zaghlul fi 23 Augustus 1927*, Cairo: Dar al-Sha'b, 1969.
———, *Thawra sana 1919: Tarikh misr al-qawm min sana 1914 ila sana 1921*, Cairo: Maktaba al-nahda al-misriyya, 1946.
———, *Mustafa Kamil ba'ith al-haraka al-wataniyya*, Cairo: Matba'at al-Sharq, 1939.
Reid, Malcolm, 'The Egyptian Geographical Society: From Foreign Laymen's Society to Indigenous Professional Association', *Poetics Today*, 13/3, 1993.
———, *Lawyers and Politics in the Arab World 1880–1960*, Chicago: Bibliothecha, 1981.
Roseman, Mark, ed., *Generations in Conflict: Youth Revolt and Generation Formation in Germany, 1770–1968*, Cambridge: Cambridge University Press, 1995.
Rude, George, *The Crowd in History: 1730–1848*, London: John Wiley and Sons, 1964.
Russell, Thomas, *Egyptian Service*, London: John Murray, 1949.
Sabry, Mohamed, *L'Empire égyptien sous Ismail et l'ingérence anglo-francais*, Paris: Paul Geuthner, 1933.
———, *La revolution égyptienne*, Paris: Librairie Vrin, 1919.
Safran, Nadav, *Egypt in Search of Political Community: An Analysis of the Intellectual and Political Evolution of Egypt*, Cambridge MA: Harvard University Press, 1961.
Saïd, Edward W., *Orientalism*, London: Routledge, 1978.
Saleh, Diaeddine, *Les Pouvoirs du roi dans la constitution Egyptienne*, Paris: Libraire Générale de droit et de jurisprudence, 1939.
Sammarco, Angelo and Zaki El Ibrachy Pasha, *Précis de l'histoire d'Egypte*, Cairo: Imprimerie de l'institute francais d'archaéologie orientale du Caire, 1935.
Sammarco, Angelo, *Le regne du Khedive Ismail de 1863–1882*, Paris: Association Linotypist, 1924.
Sayyid-Marsot, Afaf Lutfi al-, *Egypt's Liberal Experiment 1922–1936*, Berkeley: University of California Press, 1977.
Schulze, Reinhard, *Die Rebellion der Agyptischen Fallahin 1919 – A conflict between an agrarian-oriental society and a colonial state in Egypt 1820–1919*, Bonn: Ballbek Verlag, 1981.

Sha'rawi, Huda, *Mudhakkirati*, ed. and trans., Margot Badran, *Harem Years*, New York: Feminist Press CUNY, 1986.
Skinner, Quentin, *The Foundations of Modern Political Thought, Vol. 1: The Renaissance, Vol. 2: The Reformation*, Cambridge: Cambridge University Press, 1978.
Smith, Charles D., *Islam and the Search for Social Order in Modern Egypt*, Albany: SUNY Press, 1983.
———, 'The "Crisis of Orientation": The Shift of Egyptian Intellectuals to Islamic Subjects in the 1930s', *International Journal of Middle East Studies*, 4, 1973.
Springborg, Robert, *Family, Power and Politics in Egypt: Sayed Bey Marei - His Clan, Clients and Cohorts*, Philadelphia: University of Pennsylvania Press, 1982.
———, 'Patterns of Association in the Egyptian Political Elite', in *Political Elites in the Middle East*, ed. George Lenczowski, Washington DC: American Enterprise Institute, 1975.
———, *The Ties that Bind: Political Association and Policy Making in Egypt*, Ann Arbor: University of Michigan, 1974.
Stowasser, Barbara Freyer, *Religion and Political Development: Some Comparative Ideas on Ibn Khaldun and Machiavelli*, Georgetown: Center for Contemporary Arab Studies, Occasional Papers, 1983.
Terry, Janice J., *The Wafd, 1919–1952: Cornerstone of Egyptian Political Power*, London: Third World Centre for Research and Publication, 1982.
Thompson, Elizabeth, *Colonial Citizens: Republican Rights, Paternal Privilege, and Gender in French Syria and Lebanon*, New York: Columbia University Press, 2000.
Tidrick, Kathryn, *Empire and the English Character*, London: I.B. Tauris, 1992.
Tignor, Robert, "The Egyptian Revolution of 1919: New Directions in the Egyptian Economy", *Middle Eastern Studies*, 12 (1976).
———, *Modernization and British Colonial Rule in Egypt: 1882–1914*, Princeton: Princeton University Press, 1966.
Toledano, Ehud R., *State and Society in Mid-Nineteenth Century Egypt*, London: Cambridge University Press, 1990.
Tonnies, Ferdinand, *Community and Civil Society*, ed. Jose Harris, Cambridge: Cambridge University Press, 2001.
Tripp, Charles, *Ali Mahir Pasha and the Palace in Egyptian Politics 1936–1942: Seeking Mass Enthusiasm for Autocracy*, London: PhD dissertation University of London, 1984.
Vatikitotis, P.J., *The History of Egypt: From Muhammad Ali to Sadat*, London: Wiedenfeld and Nicolson, 2nd ed., 1980.
Warburg, Gabriel and Uri M. Kupfeschmidt, *Islam, Nationalism, and Radicalism in Egypt and the Sudan*, New York: Praeger, 1983.
Waterbury, John, *Commander of the Faithful: The Moroccan Political Elite: A Study in Segmented Politics*, New York: Columbia University Press, 1970.

Weber, Max, *Economy and Society: An Outline of Interpretive Sociology*, eds. Guenther Ross and Claus Wittich, New York: Bedminster Press, 1968.

Wendell, Charles, *The Evolution of the Egyptian National Image from its Origins to Ahmed Lutif al-Sayyid*, Berkeley: University of California Press, 1972.

Yapp, Malcolm, ed., *Politics and Diplomacy in Egypt: The Diaries of Sir Miles Lampson 1935–1937*, Oxford: Oxford University Press, 1997.

———, *The Near East since the First World War*, London: Longman, 1991.

Zubaida, Sami, *Islam, the People and the State: Essays on Political Ideas and Movements in the Middle East*, London: I.B. Tauris, 1989.

INDEX

A

Abaza, Ahmad, 81
Abaza, Ibrahim Dasuqi, 81
Abaza, Sulayman, 170
Abaza family, 85–6, 90–1
'Abbas, Khedive, 41
'Abbas II, Khedive, 14
'Abd al-Raziq, 'Ali, 26, 37, 142–5
'Abd al-Raziq, Hasan, 144, 147
'Abd al-Raziq family, 20
Abdin, 1
'Abduh, Muhammad, 37, 43, 151, 162, 190
al-Afghani, Jamal al-Din, 43, 44, 54
'Ali, Muhammad, 36
Allenby, Edmund, 7, 17, 19, 23, 24, 26–7, 72, 110–11, 113, 118–19, 121, 165–7, 172–3, 186
Amos, Maurice, 6, 7, 166–7, 192
'Anan, Salih Pasha, 161
anarchy, 18–20, 27, 37, 58, 60, 61, 78, 112, 121, 125, 129, 156, 173, 184
ancient regime, 38, 43, 188
anti-royalist plots, 20
aristocracy, 37, 52–63, 139, 164, 188–9
  see also notables

Article 48, 49–50
assembly of deputies, 43
autocracy, 38, 46, 48, 103, 143, 150–1, 173, 188
al-Azhar, 15, 116, 134, 140, 141, 145
Azhar Caliphate Committee, 142

B

Bakhit, Shaykh Muhammad, 134, 147–8
Bakr, Abu, 142–3
baksheesh, 42
Barakat, Fathallah, 163
Barakat, Muhammad Fathallah, 160
al-Barbari, Afifi Bey Husayn, 162
Baron, Beth, 134
Bentham, Jeremy, 42
Berque, Jacques, 103
bet-hedging, 101
Bey, Ahmad Muhammad Hasanayn, 174
Bey, Marqus Hanna, 84
Bey, Muhammad, 177
al-Biblawi, Sayyid Muhammad, 130
Binder, Leonard, 9, 74
al-Biyali, Abd al-Halim, 120
Black Hand, 24, 118

Boghos, Nubar, 13
British, 3
  judicial system and, 46
  negotiations with, 110–11, 114
  political culture, 60–1
  political divisions and, 102–3
  political ideology of, 68–9
  Protectorate, 13–32, 77, 153, 166, 167
  resistance to rule by, 14–20
  suppression of revolution of 1919 by, 16–17
British culture, 3
British Empire, 7, 30, 118, 166
British Foreign Office, 5
British High-Commission, 1, 27, 86, 117, 123
British policy, 23–4, 27, 30–1, 110–11, 118–19, 165–72, 186
British sources, 5–8
Brown, Nathan, 9, 67
bureaucratic cadre (effendiyya), 10, 11
bureaucracy, 15, 25, 40, 69, 80, 98, 112, 116, 121–2, 138–40, 154–5, 170, 186
Burke, Edmund, 4, 37, 39, 42, 49, 126
Butrus, Ghali, 13

C

caliphate, 142–8
Canal Zone, 31, 75
Cantori, Louis Joseph, 9, 94, 102
Capitulations, 31
Castro, Leon, 85, 114
centralization, 40
Chamberlain, Austen, 24, 118–19, 165
Chamberlain, Neville, 119
charismatic leader, 62–3, 66
Churchill, Winston, 7, 8, 18, 23–4, 118, 119, 165, 168, 173
citizenship, 3, 66

civil society, 9–10, 37, 69
class, 9, 101
clientelism, 162
colonialism, 5–6, 137–8, 167, 187–9, 192
colonial records, 5–8
colonial theory, 8
Communist Party, 32
community, 68, 74, 95–6, 97
Condominium, 21
conservatives/conservativism, 3, 5, 8, 11, 20, 113, 118–25, 126, 135, 187
constitution, 3, 22, 30–1, 38–9, 47–52, 59, 148, 149, 151–8
constitutional commission, 49–51, 59
constitutionalism, 43, 44, 45, 59–60
constitutional monarchy, 14, 17, 21–2, 44, 49, 55, 61, 133
constitutional process, 5
cooperatives, 67
coronation ceremony, 31
corporate unity, 180
corruption, 52–3, 83–4, 111, 112, 121
Council of Ministers, 1, 21, 49
coup d'état, 40
courts, 46
Cromer, Lord, 5–6, 13, 46, 52, 53, 118, 155–6, 167
Cromerism, 6, 8, 118
cultural change, 36
cultural development, 35
cultural divisions, 35, 67–8, 71, 95, 107–8, 131, 134, 140–1, 186
Curzon, Lord, 17, 19

D

decree of accession, 14
deference, 152
democracy, 4, 39, 42, 60, 139, 182
direct, 45

representative, 45
  threat of, 37–8
democratic nationalists, 3
democrats, 2
despotism, 22, 41, 143, 184, 196
al-Din, 'Ali Pasha Jamal, 79
al-Din, Shahin Sirah, 88
direct democracy, 45
dissentients, 19
Doss, Tawfiq, 86, 107, 147, 148, 170, 178
Douin, Georges, 53
Dufferin, Lord, 45, 46, 72
Dufferin Dispatch, 167
Durkheim, Emile, 192

E

Eden, Antony, 7, 31
Edward I, 60
effendiyya, 10, 11, 65–99, 116, 124, 167, 186
Egyptian culture, 3
Egyptian delegation, 14–15
Egyptian independence, 3, 17, 21
Egyptian model, 6–7, 8
Egyptian National Archives, 1
Egyptian sources, 1–5
elections, 68
  of 1923, 22–3, 74–84, 85–92
  of 1925, 25–6
  of 1926, 90, 178–9
  of 1938, 31–2
  tactics, 76–84
electoral committees, 81
electoral districts, 73–4
electoral laws, 71–6, 91, 136–7
electoral majority, 97
electoral reform, 23, 26, 29–30, 136–7
electoral rhetoric, 85–92
elites/elitism, 46–8, 58, 59, 103, 135–42, 151–64, 172–6, 180, 183–7, 191

El-Messiri, Sawsan, 93
Enlightenment theory, 39, 47
equality, 48
Erasmus, 57
European Debt Commission, 53
evolution, 33
evolutionary theory, 136, 137

F

factional conflict, 58
Fahmi, 'Abd al-'Aziz, 20, 22, 26, 50, 137, 145, 154, 171, 184
Fahmi, 'Abd al-Rahman, 112–13, 177
Fahmi, Qalini, 161
Fahmi, Zaki, 2, 35–8, 52–63, 125–7, 133, 151–64, 182, 191–2
Fakhri, Mahmud, 160–1
family connections, 84
al-Farabi, Abu Nasr, 58
Faruq, 31
fascism, 31
fellahin, 41, 66, 72, 77, 80, 113, 166
feminism, 108–10, 134–5
al-Fiqar, Ahmad dhu, 21–2, 160
al-Fiqar, Sa'id dhu, 161
First World War, 7, 77, 133
Foreign Office, 24, 25, 80–1, 111, 119, 160, 165, 166, 167
French culture, 55–6
French republicanism, 3
French Revolution, 34, 38, 60, 93, 125, 126
Fu'ad, Ahmad, 14, 15, 20, 25, 55–6
Fu'ad, al-Liwa Musa, 120
fundamentalism, 127
Furness, Robert, 81–2

G

generations, 34
gentleman's club, 169

Germany, 31
Gershoni, Israel, 134
Ghali, Wasif, 109
Gharabali, Najib, 121
Gorst, Sir Eldon, 13
grant, 47
guilds, 67

H

Hanna, Aida, 84
Hanna, Marqus, 160
Hasanayn, Ahmad Muhammad, 130, 161
Haykal, Muhammad Husayn, 22, 71, 89, 137–9, 184, 190
Henderson, Arthur, 29
Henderson, Neville, 123, 129, 144, 146, 168–72, 178–9
hierarchy, 40, 65–6, 69, 72, 74, 81, 152–3, 164
historical advancement, 34–5
historical context, 13–32
Hourani, Albert, 10, 35, 56, 57, 134, 148
Hunter, Robert, 160
Husayn, Ahmad Muhammad, 27
Husayn, Kamil, 81
Husayn, Taha, 35, 37, 125, 126, 142, 152, 154

I

Ibn Khaldun, 'Abd al-Rahman Muhammad, 37
Ibn Taymiyya, Taqi al-Din Ahmad, 58
Ibrahim, White, 2, 35, 38, 44–8, 51–2, 61
Ibrahim, Yahya, 21–3, 78–9, 81–2, 145–6, 159–60, 169
Ibrashi, Zaki Bey, 79

ideological conflicts, 2–3, 5, 8, 10, 26, 33–5, 103
Imperial Conference, 18
imperial policy, 6–7
inspector-general, 40
institutions, 40, 136
irrigation, 41–2
Islam, 134, 142–51
Islamic heritage, 37, 41
Islamic ideology, 4
Islamic law, 43, 57
Islamic political thought, 62–3
Islamic reformists, 54–5, 59, 97, 126, 150, 151, 152, 187
Isma'il, Khedive, 25, 42–4, 52, 53, 55, 72
Isma'il, Mahmud, 118
Italy, 31
Ittihad Party, 25, 26, 29, 30, 91, 119–25, 128–31, 135, 139–40, 142–51, 178, 189

J

Jankowski, James P., 134
jihad, 34, 62, 93–4, 97, 181
journals, 22
judicial system, 46

K

Kamal, Yusuf, 171–2
Kamil, Hasan, 87
Kamil, Mustafa, 34, 96, 97
Kamil, Prince Husayn, 14
Khaldun, Ibn, 3–4, 37, 58–9, 143, 152, 191–2
Khashaba, Ahmad Muhammad, 105, 107
al-Khayyat, Mustafa, 81
khedival regime, 39, 44–7, 49–50, 53–4, 153, 188

khedive, 13, 15, 25
khitat, 36
Khoury, Philip, 10
Kish Kish Bey, 83
Kitchener, Lord, 13, 45, 118, 167
Kleber, General, 40

L

Labour Party, 81, 113
labour unions, 16, 67, 112–13
Lampson, Sir Miles, 30, 31
Landau, Jacob, 72
land ownership, 41, 42, 140
legal codes, 46, 53, 70
Liberal-Constitutional Party, 19–21, 23–7, 29, 32, 49, 76, 85–6, 89, 90, 103, 119–23, 135–6, 139, 144, 146, 147, 174, 178, 184–6, 188–9, 191
liberal economy, 41–3
liberal era, 10
liberal nationalism, 133–6, 189–92
liberals/liberalism, 3, 4, 5, 8, 19–20, 22–3, 26–7, 31, 33, 50, 66, 68, 76, 77, 85–92, 102–3, 113, 133, 136, 138, 144, 149, 169, 170, 174–8, 185, 187, 191
liberty, 156
literary forms, 36, 56–7, 151
Lloyd, George Ambrose, 7, 17, 27, 168, 173–4, 179
Lorraine, Sir Percy, 30
Lower Egypt, 107
al-Lozi, Tahir, 115

M

MacDonald, Ramsay, 23, 110, 114
Machiavelli, 57
MacMahon, Sir Arthur Henry, 14
Mahfouz, Naguib, 62
Mahfuz, Rashwan, 121, 161
Mahir, Ahmad, 32
Mahir, 'Ali, 25, 27, 30, 31, 32, 119, 122
Mahmud, 'Abd al-Rahman, 82
Mahmud, Muhammad, 20, 26, 29, 32, 82, 89, 90, 112, 170, 171, 179
al-Makkabati, 'Abd al-Latif, 49, 50
Makram, William, 115, 116–17
Mannheim, Karl, 134
Mar'i family, 90
market economy, 41–2, 43
martial law, 118
Marx, Karl, 9–10, 66, 70
Michelet, Jules, 93
middle class, 67, 186
  see also effendiyya
military officers, 31
millets, 41
Milner, Lord Alfred, 7, 17, 165
Milner Report, 17, 18, 167
Ministry of Interior, 79–80, 112, 144, 170
'mirror for princes', 53, 56, 57, 59, 152
Misr al-Fatat (Young Egypt), 32
moderatism, 114
monarchists, 2, 4, 5, 11, 20–7, 31, 35–47, 55–6, 63, 66, 78, 91–2, 116, 133, 175, 188
  coup by, 118–25
  ideology of, 125–31
monarchy, 28, 37, 45, 103, 186, 188
  British and, 7–8
  constitutional, 14, 17, 21–2, 44, 49, 55, 61, 133
  creation of, 3, 20–1
  cultural policy of, 35
  legitimacy of, 39–40
  ministry and, 115–16
  patronage and, 9, 28, 31, 55, 119, 140

monarchy—(*Continued*)
  power of, 49–51
  role of, 151–8
Montesquieu, 3–4, 37, 38, 42, 47, 49, 54, 61, 126, 152
moral values, 126–7
moral virtue, 58–9
Mubarak, 'Ali, 36, 56
mudirs, 40, 46, 74, 80–1, 82, 85, 112, 121, 153, 158
Muhammad, Sa'id, 14
Muhammad, Shafiqa bint, 16
Muhammad 'Ali, 39–42, 46, 85, 151, 154–5
Murray, John, 25, 80–1, 118, 169
Musa, Nabawiya, 108
Muslim Brotherhood, 32, 140
Mustafa, Fahmi, 13
Mustafa, Riyad, 13

N

Nabarawi, Zeza, 108
al-Nahhas, Mustafa, Nahas Pasha, 28–9, 31, 181
Napoleon, 39–40
Napoleonic regime, 45–7
Nash'at, Hasan, 24–7, 84, 116–20, 122, 142, 149, 150–1, 173–4
Nasim, Tawfiq, 18–23, 30–1, 84, 105, 115, 172
al-Nasr, Mahmud Abu, 25, 27, 122, 148–9
National Archives, 5
national histories, 34, 55
national identity, 36–7, 66, 102, 191
nationalism, 3, 6, 7, 31, 33, 34, 44–5, 53, 60, 65, 95, 102, 133–5, 189–92
Nationalist Party, 33–4, 81
nation-states, 35, 45, 52, 68, 70, 99, 153, 186, 190
naturalism, 137–9
natural rights, 38, 39, 105

neo-colonialism, 6–8, 133, 165–82, 188–9
nepotism, 70, 78, 80, 82, 114–15, 122
new generation, 34–5
non-interference policy, 30
notables, 9–11, 30, 42, 52–63, 65–99, 101–2, 111, 123, 124, 127–8, 131, 164
Nubar Pasha, Boghos, 13, 43, 44, 45, 46, 53, 158, 161
al-Nuqrashi, Mahmud, 32, 79

O

obedience, 152
oligarchy, 60, 70
Orientalist perspective, 143, 144
Ottoman Empire, 13, 14, 37, 41, 43, 45, 153, 166, 167
Owen, Roger, 69, 70

P

pact, 47
Palestine, 31
parliament, 22, 25–31, 42, 50, 51, 55, 59–61, 77, 101–31, 136, 147, 155, 174, 176, 179
parliamentarianism, 3, 54
party ideology, 92–9
patriarchy, 102, 110, 135, 139, 141, 183
patriotism, 34, 96, 113, 127
patronage, 9, 28, 31, 55, 69, 71, 78, 80, 87, 91, 101, 119, 124, 133, 140, 153–4, 160, 164
Patterson, Reginald, 6, 7, 111–12
peasantry, 8–10, 42, 59
people's ministry, 104–18
People's Party, 30, 33
personal character, 97–8, 152, 164
Piccotto, Joseph, 83–4
police regime, 48

INDEX

political alliances, 101–2
political coalitions, 27–9, 32, 78–9, 82, 84, 120, 135, 139
political manifestos, 92–9
political mobilization, 68
political parties, 3, 33–4, 58, 68, 82, 92–9, 101–3, 125, 185
see also specific parties
political revolution, 9–10
politics, 69–70
politics of the notables, 101–2, 130
popular will, 47
postcolonial theory, 5
primordial groupings, 9
princes, 4, 15, 45, 51, 57–63, 134, 143, 164, 191
property rights, 41, 42, 47
Protectorate, 13–32, 77, 153, 166, 167
provinicial government, 40
public opinion, 28

Q

al-Qamis, Sum'an Bey Gabriel, 162
Qattawi, Yusef, 170

R

radical revolution, 9–10
radicals/radicalism, 5, 11, 19, 20–1, 28, 33, 90, 110–11, 133, 136, 139
al-Rafi'i, 'Abd al-Rahman, 2, 33, 34, 92–3, 97
al-Rafi'i, Amin, 105
Reid, Donald, 55, 56
religion, 39, 61, 126–7, 142–51, 176
religious elite, 41
religious law, 26
religious nationalism, 135–42, 150–1
representative democracy, 45
representative government, 42, 43, 49, 53, 60, 63, 148, 166–7
republicanism, 3, 25

revolution, 4, 33, 116–17, 149–50, 151
of 1919, 3, 4–5, 15–18
political, 9–10
radical, 9–10
Rida, Rashid, 134
royal absolutism, 29–30
royal patronage, 2, 31–2, 55, 91, 119, 140, 153–4, 160, 161, 163, 164
Rude, Georges, 93
rural notables, 67, 72, 73, 74, 187
rural population, 42, 59
Rushdi, Husayn, 14–17, 20, 50, 144, 147, 158–9, 170

S

Sa'adist Party, 32
Sabri, Ahmad Bey, 162
Sabri, Muhammad Bey, 162
Sadiq, Ahmad Bey, 162
Safran, Nadav, 189–90
Safwat al-'Asr (Fahmi), 2, 36, 56, 125, 133, 151–64
Sa'id, Muhammad, 18, 23, 160, 169, 172
Sa'id Pasha, 41
Saleh, Diaeddine, 2, 4, 8, 35, 38–42, 44–5, 48–53, 63, 66, 103, 126, 187–8
Sammarco, Angelo, 53
Savigny, Friedrich Carl von, 39
al-Sayyid, Ahmad Lutfi, 33, 153–4, 162
schools, 140–1
Schulze, Reinhard, 10, 62, 95
Scott, Ernest, 86
Scott, John, 46, 76
Secessionists, 143
secondary sources, 9–11
secularism, 3, 135
self-government, 6–7, 21, 166–7
self-interest, 89, 156
separation of powers, 38
Sha'b Party, 32, 189
Shakar, Shaykh Muhammad, 146
Shamsi, 'Ali, 90, 106, 115

Sha'rawi, Huda, 16, 108–10
sharecroppers, 42
shari'a law, 141, 147–8
al-Shawarbi, Hamid Pasha, 127, 161
al-Shawarbi, 'Umar Bey, 161
shaykh, 116
Sidqi, Isma'il, 14, 20, 25, 26, 29–30, 32, 90, 120–2, 169–71, 175, 178, 180
Smith, Adam, 42
Smith, Charles D., 137, 190
social contract, 39–40
social control, 68
social order, 48
social relations, 9, 65–99, 131, 164
sociological theory, 68
sources
  British, 5–8
  Egyptian, 1–5
  secondary, 9–11
sovereignty, 4, 34, 40, 45, 47, 49, 105, 110
Spencer, Herbert, 4
Springborg, Robert, 9, 69–70
Stack, Sir Lee, 23–5, 116–17, 172–3
state, 68, 70
status honours, 152–3
student committees, 112
student demonstrations, 30, 112, 113, 116, 117, 121
Sudan, 21, 105, 110, 116
Suez Canal, 7, 166
Sulayman, Hajj Muhammad, 128
Sulayman, Yusef, 160
Sultan, 'Umar, 161
sultanate, 153
summary justice, 46
Syria, 10

T

tabaqat, 36, 56
al-Tahtawi, Rifa'a, 3
Tawfiq, Khedive, 44
tazkiyya, 97
territorial nationalism, 137

Tharwat, 'Abd al-Khaliq, 14, 17, 19–23, 26–9, 71, 77, 79–80, 133, 136, 169–70, 178
traditionalism, 37–8, 133–64, 181, 191–2
treaty negotiations, 4, 7, 18, 21, 23, 29, 31, 104, 107, 109–11, 165, 167–8, 172, 173
treaty of 1936, 7, 31
Tusun, 'Umar, 156–7, 171–2
tyranny, 60

U

'Ubayd, William Makram, 84
ulama, 140–1, 145
umma, 37, 54–5, 57, 60, 70, 95, 126, 143–4, 148, 149, 151, 159, 191
Umma Party, 30, 33, 143–4
Union Party, 24, 119
United Front, 31
universal suffrage, 73, 103–4
Upper Egypt, 107, 123
'Urabi, Ahmad, 54
urban social groups, 67, 73–4

V

Vatikiotis, P. J., 103
Veiled Protectorate, 13
Versailles Peace Conference, 14–15
voting market, 82–3
voting rights, 48, 73, 103–4

W

Wafd Party, 4–5, 7, 10, 11, 15, 17–32, 44, 49, 68, 71, 76–9, 82–92, 94–6, 98–9, 102, 103, 104, 108, 111–16, 121–2, 131, 135, 138–40, 150, 157, 162, 172–4, 178, 180–1, 185, 190–1
wage labour, 42
Wasif, Husayn Pasha, 161–2

Watani (Nationalist) Party, 33–4, 81, 105
Waterbury, John, 101
Weber, Max, 67, 68, 70, 126, 183–4
Westernization, 43
Wingate, Sir Reginald, 14, 138, 167
wizara al-sha'biyya, 104–18
women's rights, 23, 48, 102–4, 108–10, 139, 141
working class, 113

Y

Yahya, 'Abd al-Fattah, 30
Yakan, 'Adli, 14, 17–23, 27–9, 72, 89–90, 133, 144, 158, 169, 170, 171, 174, 175, 179, 180
Yapp, Malcolm, 66, 184
Yassin, Hasan, 116, 141, 177
youth, 34

Z

Zaghlul, Fathi, 145
Zaghlul, Sa'd, 13–19, 23–8, 62, 65–6, 85, 87, 89–90, 94, 98, 104–18, 120, 123, 129, 133, 136, 155–6, 168–9, 172–82, 184, 185, 190–1
Zaynab, Sayyida, 95
Ziwar, Ahmad, 24, 119, 136, 145, 171, 175, 188
zu'ama', 176–82, 184, 185–6
Zubaida, Sami, 70
Zulficar, Ahmad, 49

King Ahmad Fu'ad.

From the popular journal *Kashkul*, the cartoon represents the uneasy alliance between effendi politicians and the notables during the election campaign of 1923.

Sa'd Pasha Zaghlul reading the speech from the throne before the king and the national deputies, 1924.

This cartoon from *Kashkul* depicted the cultural and political schisms in the parliament, exploited by the Watani Party deputy, Amin al-Rafi'i, during the first sitting of parliament in 1924.

As Egyptian Prime Minister in 1924 Zaghlul was also attacked by Huda Sha'rawi, who was frustrated that the Wafd Party failed to revise constitutional and electoral laws to meet feminist demands.

After the fall of the Wafd government in late 1924, Muhammad Pasha al-Shawarbi was one of the first of the great landed notables to support the monarchist Ittihad Party: his interest in politics was largely to gain access to state patronage.

The Imam Shaykh Muhammad Bakhit abandoned the Liberal-Constitutional Party for the Ittihad Party in September 1925 because of the controversy occasioned by 'Ali 'Abd al-Raziq's *Islam and the Bases of Government*. Bakhit's opinion was that Islamic law had to be the fundamental basis of any constitutional law in Egypt.

Sa'd Pasha Zaghlul (centre) and his rivals, 'Abd al-Khaliq Tharwat (left) and 'Adli Yakan Pasha (right). The photograph was taken in 1926 when the Liberal-Constitutional Party and the Wafd Party formed a coalition to defeat the monarchists.

www.ingramcontent.com/pod-product-compliance
Lightning Source LLC
Chambersburg PA
CBHW072144290426
44111CB00012B/1967